Philosophy of Mind

A Beginner's Guide

Philosophy of Mind

A Beginner's Guide

Ian Ravenscroft

OXFORD
UNIVERSITY PRESS

OXFORD
UNIVERSITY PRESS

Great Clarendon Street, Oxford OX2 6DP

Oxford University Press is a department of the University of Oxford.
It furthers the University's objective of excellence in research, scholarship,
and education by publishing worldwide in

Oxford New York

Auckland Cape Town Dar es Salaam Hong Kong Karachi
Kuala Lumpur Madrid Melbourne Mexico City Nairobi
New Delhi Shanghai Taipei Toronto

With offices in

Argentina Austria Brazil Chile Czech Republic France Greece
Guatemala Hungary Italy Japan South Korea Poland Portugal
Singapore Switzerland Thailand Turkey Ukraine Vietnam

Published in the United States
by Oxford University Press Inc., New York

First published 2005

British Library Cataloguing in Publication Data
Data available

Library of Congress Cataloging in Publication Data
Data available

ISBN 978-0-19-925254-1

10 9 8 7 6 5 4

Typeset by Newgen Imaging Systems (P) Ltd., Chennai, India
Printed in Great Britain
on acid-free paper by
Ashford Colour Press, Gosport, Hants

For Tamara, Max, and Willard

Contents

Acknowledgements

Many people helped me write this book, and I am very glad to have this opportunity to acknowledge my debts and express my thanks. Frank Jackson read much of the book in draft, and made many helpful suggestions. Anyone lucky enough to be familiar with Frank's work will see how much I have learned from him. His confidence in the book greatly boosted my own. Greg O'Hair read an early version of the first three chapters and picked up an embarrassing error; Gerard O'Brien and Tamara Zutlevics read the connectionism chapter and provided very useful feedback; and Andy Young answered a desperate email and set me straight on face recognition. My thanks to you all.

I owe a very special debt to Ruth Anderson of Oxford University Press. Ruth made a great many useful suggestions, said nice things at the right moments, and demonstrated extraordinary patience. Douglas Adams once remarked that he likes deadlines—he likes the noise they make as they whizz past. I loathe deadlines and I cringe as they whizz past. Unfortunately for Ruth, this book's deadlines have gone past at a terrifying rate. I would also like to take this opportunity to thank my copy-editor, Susan Faircloth, for spotting a number of mistakes and making some very helpful suggestions.

I also owe a special debt to my friends and colleagues in the Philosophy Department at Flinders University for their friendship, support, and good humor during what has been a very trying period in Australian higher education. In addition, I owe a very great deal to my friends and former colleagues in the Philosophy Department at King's College London. I learned much from their example and benefited much from their kindness. In a similar way, Martin Davies, Michael Smith, Kim Sterelny, and Steve Stich taught me a great deal about how to write philosophy and what's worth writing about.

My greatest debts are to my wife Tamara and our sons Max and Willard. Tamara's advice and encouragement were crucial, and she selflessly took time away from her own research to read and comment on my manuscript. Max observed that he thinks with his brain, and offered to help on numerous occasions. Willard arrived mid-way through Part 1 and has provided much happy distraction. This book is dedicated to them.

Introduction

This book is an introduction to the philosophy of mind. It is primarily intended for undergraduates, but it may also be of value to graduate students seeking a quick overview of the key issues.

Philosophers of mind ask very general questions about the mind. Examples include: What are mental states? Are they states of the physical brain or of a nonphysical 'soul'? What is consciousness? How can states of mind be about (or 'represent') things outside the mind?

Psychologists also study the mind. Very often they perform experiments on human and animal subjects, and build substantial theories about the mind on the basis of experimental results. Philosophers of mind do not, as a rule, do experiments. Rather, many philosophers engage with issues which are sometimes described as 'conceptual'. For example, they seek to clarify what terms like 'consciousness' mean; they look for logical flaws in arguments about the nature of the mind; and they consider the ways in which claims about the mind fit—or fail to fit—with other claims we are inclined to accept as true. A number of examples of conceptual issues in the philosophy of mind are discussed in this book.

Many philosophers have, however, refused to limit themselves to these sorts of conceptual questions. The great French philosopher René Descartes (1596–1650), for example, advanced substantial claims about the mind. (We will examine some of Descartes' claims in Chapter 1.) Increasingly, contemporary philosophers are advancing substantial claims about the mind based in part on experiments undertaken by psychologists. In fact, it's sometimes a bit hard these days to tell where the philosophy stops and the psychology begins. So don't be surprised by the occasional mention of topics which traditionally would have been discussed by scientists rather than philosophers.

The first Part of this book addresses the question, 'What are mental states?' The mental states include *perceptions* like seeing, smelling, and hearing; *sensations* like hunger, thirst, and pain; *emotions* like anger, love, and grief; and what we might broadly call *thoughts* like beliefs, desires, and decisions. So Part 1 examines various attempts to explain what sorts of states perceptions, sensations, emotions, and thoughts *are*. Are they states of a nonphysical 'soul'? Are they states of the brain? Do they exist at all?

Before we begin to address the question, 'What are mental states?', it will be useful to have before us a list of the most significant features of mental states. Such a list will help us assess theories of mental states by determining the extent to which a theory explains the existence of these features. In general, a theory of mental states which makes sense of these features is to be preferred to a theory which does not.

Here's my list of general features of mental states.

1. *Some mental states are caused by states of the world.* For example, Bloggs's pain (mental state) is caused by a pin sticking in his foot (state of the world). Again, Bloggs's belief that there is a cup of coffee in front of him (mental state) is caused by there being a cup of coffee in front of him (state of the world).
2. *Some mental states cause actions.* For example, Bloggs's desire for a coffee (mental state) together with his belief that there is coffee in the kitchen (mental state), caused him to go into the kitchen (action). Again, Bloggs's fear of the dentist (mental state) caused him to run away (action).
3. *Some mental states cause other mental states.* For example, the pain Bloggs experienced when he last had a filling (mental state) caused him to be afraid of dentists (mental state). Another example: Bloggs's belief that today is Friday (mental state), together with his belief that Friday is payday (mental state), caused him to believe that today is payday (mental state).

   The second example illustrates a very important feature of causation between mental states. Notice that Bloggs's belief that today is Friday, together with his belief that Friday is payday, give him *good reason* to believe that today is payday. The causal relations between some mental states respect the *logical* or *evidential* relations between them. Another way to make this point is to say that very often our thought process is *rational.* We will return to the rationality of our thought processes in Part 2.
4. *Some mental states are conscious.* Exactly what it means for a mental state to be conscious is an issue we will take up in Part 4. For the moment we can simply note that some mental states have a subjective 'feel' or 'quality'. Perhaps the easiest way to grasp the idea that some mental states have a subjective feel or quality is to contrast the mental life of a person with normal color vision with that of a person who is colorblind. When they stand together looking at a sunset, the visual experiences of the person with normal color vision are quite different from those of the colorblind person. The former's experiences have a feel or quality which the latter's lack.
5. *Some mental states are about things in the world.* That is, they *represent* the world as being a certain way. For example, Bloggs's belief that Mt Everest is 8,848 meters tall is *about* Mt Everest and *represents* it as being 8,848 meters tall. Philosophers sometimes say that the *content* of Bloggs's belief is 'Mt Everest

is 8,848 meters tall'. Theories of content attempt to explain how thoughts have the content they have. (We take a look at some theories of content in Chapter 9.)

6. *Some kinds of mental states are systematically correlated with certain kinds of brain states.* With advances in neuroscience, it's becoming increasingly clear that there are correlations between mental states and brain states. For example, in the 1950s Wilder Penfield showed that by stimulating parts of the brain with a tiny electrical current, it was possible to elicit certain memories in the subject. When the electrode was shifted slightly to a different area of the brain, a different memory was elicited. There is thus a correlation between particular memories and particular parts of the brain. (For a description of these experiments see Penfield and Rasmussen 1968.)

The list of general features of mental states just given is important because it facilitates the assessment of theories of mental states. Other things being equal, a theory which explains lots of these features is better than a theory which explains few of them. But we should admit that mental states might turn out to be somewhat different from how we commonly conceive them to be. In particular, we have to accept that mental states might lack some of the listed features. In that case, our list of general features would have to be revised.

This kind of revision is not uncommon. Here's an example. A few hundred years ago it was widely assumed that whales were fish. That is, one of the general features ascribed to whales was that they are fish. Subsequent investigations revealed that whales aren't fish at all—they're mammals. In fact, whales have a lot more in common with cows than with cod. Consequently, no list of general features of whales drawn up today would say that they are fish. Similarly, it was once widely accepted that all mental states are conscious. More recent investigations suggest that this is not true: you might, for example, have an unconscious desire or even an unconscious belief. If these more recent investigations are on the right track, it isn't true that all mental states share the feature of being conscious. (Notice that feature 4 on the list given above claims only that *some* mental states are conscious.)

I have suggested that the list of features of mental states I have given might have to be revised. What value, then, does the list have? Simply this: the elements of the list are plausible claims about the nature of mental states. In any investigation we can only begin with what, given our current evidence, are plausible claims about the subject matter. (Where else should we begin our investigation? With *implausible* claims?) Subsequent research may reveal that some (or even all) of our initial claims about the mind are false, and at that point rationality requires that we revise our ideas.

Part 1 is the longest part of this book. It sets the stage for subsequent chapters in two ways. First, it introduces concepts, arguments, and terminology which play a role in the later parts. Second, it presents us with many issues which are taken up in subsequent parts. Thus Part 2 addresses the idea that thinking is, in important respects, a kind of computation; Part 3 addresses issues about physicalism, mental content, and mental causation; and Part 4 takes up the vexed issue of consciousness.

One of my aims in writing this book is to make the vast literature on the philosophy of mind somewhat more accessible to undergraduate philosophy students. At the end of every chapter is a list of reading materials you should find useful in furthering your understanding of the issues discussed in the chapter. The reading lists are 'annotated'; that is, I very briefly describe the contents, approach, and strengths (or weaknesses) of each item on the list. There is also, towards the end of the book, a list of resources (including online resources) which you may find helpful when studying the philosophy of mind. Sometimes I refer in the main body of the text to a book or paper which is an especially important source for the idea being discussed. I have adopted the author/date reference system. For example, when discussing some aspects of the problem of consciousness, I refer in the text to 'Jackson 1982'. In the References list at the back of the book you will find the entry:

Jackson, F. (1982). 'Epiphenomenal qualia'. *Philosophical Quarterly* 32: 127–36. Reprinted in Lycan 1990.

The entry tells you the title of Jackson's paper ('Epiphenomenal qualia'); the title of the journal in which it's published (*Philosophical Quarterly*); the volume number of the journal (32); and the page numbers (127–36). The date after the author's name indicates the year of publication. Jackson's article has been conveniently reprinted in Lycan 1990, which has its own entry in the References list.

The References list is arranged alphabetically by the author's surname. If an author has more than one entry, the entries are arranged by date (earliest first). Very occasionally I refer to two or more publications by the same author in the same year. In that case I distinguish the publications by adding a letter to the date. Thus the References list includes both Lewis 1983*a* and Lewis 1983*b*.

A few more pointers. First, at the end of each chapter you will find a list of 'tutorial questions' which you can use to deepen your understanding of the issues. Trying to explain a philosophical issue to someone else is one of the best ways to enhance your own understanding of it. If you're an undergraduate philosophy student, why not form your own discussion group with other members of your class?.

Second, at the back of the book you will find a glossary which explains a variety of philosophical terminology. If a term is in the glossary it's printed in **bold** the first time it's used in the text (occasionally terms are printed in bold more than once).

Third, I have included a few brief tips on writing a philosophy paper (or 'essay'). They are not intended to be a complete guide to writing a philosophy paper, nor are they intended to challenge your philosophy instructor's advice. Rather, they're a few pointers based on my having read and assessed over a thousand undergraduate philosophy papers. (In the Resources section you will find references to a couple of guides to writing a philosophy paper which are much more comprehensive than my brief notes on the subject.)

Finally, I have included both an index and a fair amount of cross-referencing. My aim throughout has been to make the book as 'user friendly' as possible.

I hope you enjoy the book.

Part One
What are mental states?

1

Dualism

You gotta have soul.

—Billy Joel

According to an ancient tradition, the mind is a nonphysical object. This doctrine is called **substance dualism**, and is the focus of the first half of this chapter (Sections 1.1 and 1.2). According to substance dualism, the mind is an entirely different sort of thing to the body. The body is a physical object—it's located in space; it's made from the atoms familiar to chemistry; it has a certain weight and height; and it can be seen and touched. The mind, on the other hand, is a nonphysical object. It's not located in space; it's not made from the atoms familiar to chemistry; it has neither weight nor height; and it can't be seen or touched. (In Chapter 8 we will refine our understanding of the difference between the physical and the nonphysical. For the moment we'll proceed on an intuitive understanding of the distinction.)

We've seen that, according to substance dualism, mind and body are different sorts of things or **substances**. (If it helps, read 'substance' as 'stuff'.) We can now see where the label 'substance dualism' comes from. According to substance dualism there are two distinct kinds of substances in the world: mental substances and physical substances. In other words, there is a *duality* of substances. Later in this chapter we will consider another form of dualism—**property dualism**. Whereas *substance* dualism claims that there are two fundamentally different kinds of *substances* in the world, *property* dualism claims that there are two fundamentally different kinds of *properties* in the world. (When philosophers use the word **property** they mean, roughly, 'feature'.) I'll say more about the distinction between properties and substances in Section 1.4.

Before getting started one brief terminological point is in order. Sometimes substance dualists call the nonphysical mind they postulate the 'soul'. However, when discussing substance dualism I'll tend to avoid the term 'soul' because of its associations with religious doctrines that are not part of substance dualism. For example, according to common usage the soul is an entity which survives the death of the body. However, the philosophical doctrine of substance dualism takes no stand on the afterlife one way or the other.

1.1 Substance dualism

Imagine that, whilst on safari, Bloggs sees a lion a short distance away and runs back to his car. A few quick strides and he's safe inside. Here's how the substance dualist accounts for this series of events. First, light waves from the lion hit Bloggs's retina, stimulating it in a particular way. Bloggs's brain then extracts sensory information from the activation pattern on his retina, and passes that information on to his nonphysical mind. His mind interprets the sensory information it has received from the brain and recognizes that there is a lion present. It then decides that the best thing to do is to run quickly back to the vehicle. A message (RUN!) is sent from Bloggs's mind back to his brain. His brain sends the relevant signals to his leg muscles and he runs quickly back to the car.

According to substance dualism, mind and body, whilst quite distinct, interact with one another. Sensory information about the state of the world is sent from brain to mind, and decisions about how to react are sent from mind to brain. Your body is like a probe, sent by NASA to explore a distant planet. The probe sends pictures back to mission control, where scientists decide what the probe should do next. Instructions are then sent back to the probe which responds accordingly. The probe itself is entirely unintelligent. Similarly, information about the world is communicated by the body to the mind; the mind decides on a course of action and communicates the decision back to the body. The body itself makes no decisions.

It's important to note that the relations between the mind and the body are *causal relations*. The sensory information sent by the brain to the mind *causes* the mind to register the presence of the lion. And the mind's decision to run *causes* the brain to activate the relevant muscles. In other words, there are two-way causal interactions between the mind and the brain.

It's worth briefly considering two more examples.

1. Say that Bloggs burns his hand on the stove and, accordingly, feels a painful sensation. According to substance dualism, the damage to Bloggs's hand causes a message to be sent to his brain, which in turn sends a message to his nonphysical mind. The mind is then brought into a state which Bloggs recognizes as a painful sensation. According to substance dualism, experiences of pain are states of the nonphysical mind; the brain itself has no conscious experiences.

2. Say that Bloggs knows the following two things. (1) If it's Friday then it's payday. (2) It's Friday. From (1) and (2) he works out something else: (3) It's payday. According to substance dualism, all of these knowledge states are states of Bloggs's nonphysical mind. Moreover, his nonphysical mind's being in states (1) and (2) *caused* it to be in state (3). On this view, all rational inference occurs in the nonphysical mind; the brain is just plain dumb.

1.2 Arguments in favor of substance dualism

In this section we will consider four arguments in favor of substance dualism. The first three arguments all have the following structure:

1. Minds can ______.

2. No physical object can ______.

Therefore,

3. Minds are not physical objects.

Different arguments are obtained by filling in the empty slots in different ways.

1. *Could a physical object use language?* We obtain the first argument for substance dualism by filling in the empty slots with 'use language':

1a. Minds can use language.

2a. No physical object can use language.

Therefore,

3. Minds are not physical objects.

This argument was articulated by the seventeenth-century French philosopher, scientist, and mathematician, René Descartes (1596–1650). It seemed to him impossible that a physical object could generate and understand the rich variety of sentences which humans so effortlessly handle. Consequently, it seemed impossible to Descartes that the human mind could be a physical object.

Since Descartes' day, a great deal has been learned about language. In particular, we have come to appreciate that languages are regulated by a series of rules that specify which sequences of words count as grammatical sentences. These rules are called the **syntax** of the language. The syntax of English, for example, specifies that 'The boy ate the ice cream' is a grammatical sentence whereas 'Ate boy ice cream the the' is not. Syntax is *mechanical* in the sense that, in principle, a computer could be programmed to determine of any sequence of English words whether or not it's grammatical. I say 'in principle' because our understanding of syntax remains incomplete. Nevertheless, we have good reason to accept that a certain kind of physical object—a suitably programmed computer—could process the rules of language. Consequently, it seems that Descartes was wrong to at least this extent: a physical object could handle the syntax of language.

However, there is more to language than syntax. In particular, words and sentences have *meaning*. The ways in which meanings are assigned to the words and sentences of a language is called the **semantics** of that language. Recently, linguists and philosophers have began to unravel the mysteries of semantics. It's fair to say that, at present, we don't have a fully worked out theory of semantics. But it's also fair to say that, at present, there seems to be little reason to doubt that a physical object could use language meaningfully. Descartes' argument from the claim that minds use language to the claim that the mind is a nonphysical object therefore seems mistaken.

2. *Could a physical object reason?* The second argument for substance dualism we will consider is very much like the first. Descartes not only doubted that a physical object could use language; he also doubted whether such an object could reason:

1b. Minds can engage in reasoning.

2b. No physical object can engage in reasoning.

Therefore,

3. Minds are not physical objects.

Descartes begins his defense of the crucial second premise by noting that reasoning is universal in this sense: there are many circumstances about which we can reason. He admits that there could be a mechanism for responding to any one circumstance (e.g. responding to dogs); however, he claims that there could not be a mechanism which responded to a multiplicity of circumstances (say, dogs, breakfast, and algebra). Consequently, a machine which could respond universally would require a vast number of mechanisms—one for each circumstance. But, he says, that's impossible: the number of mechanisms involved would be too great.

I'm unconvinced by Descartes' argument for the second premise. However, rather than directly discussing the second premise, I propose to briefly consider one kind of reasoning which modern machines can, at least to some extent, achieve—mathematical reasoning. (As a significant mathematician, Descartes would have been intrigued by the mechanization of mathematical reasoning.)

Just what do we mean by the expression 'mathematical reasoning'? If by 'mathematical reasoning' we mean something like 'the ability to correctly apply mathematical rules' then it's clear that physical objects *can* do mathematical reasoning. After all, the cheapest pocket calculator can apply the rules of addition, subtraction, multiplication, and so forth to a range of numbers.

'Mathematical reasoning' might, though, mean something else. It might refer to the ability to discover new mathematical truths and methods. Newton and Leibniz, for example, invented calculus—an entirely new way of solving certain mathematical problems. Could a computer be programmed to do mathematical reasoning in this sense? Could a computer discover calculus? This is a hard question, and one which we cannot address very fully here. What can be said is that *certain kinds* of mathematical discoveries can now be made by computers. These discoveries involve deriving new mathematical truths ('theorems') from established mathematical claims ('axioms'). There are limits to how effective computers can be at making these sorts of discoveries. Nevertheless, it seems that at least some sorts of mathematical reasoning can be achieved by physical objects, and it is likely that future research will expand the range of mathematical problems which computers can solve.

3. *Could a physical object be conscious?* The third argument for substance dualism is as follows:

1c. Minds can be conscious.

2c. No physical object can be conscious.

Therefore,

3. Minds are not physical objects.

I suspect that considerations of consciousness weigh heavily with many dualists. Sometimes these considerations amount to little more than the bald intuition that no physical object could be conscious; sometimes they consist of sophisticated arguments. For the moment I propose to simply set aside the issue of consciousness. That issue is so important—and so difficult—that Part 4 of this book is devoted to discussing it. We will consider there whether the existence of consciousness provides good reason to endorse some form of dualism.

Before moving on to the final argument in favor of substance dualism, it is worth mentioning that each of the three arguments just discussed relies on Leibniz's *principle of the indiscernibility of identicals*. The German philosopher and mathematician Gottfried Leibniz (1646–1716) pointed out that if X and Y are identical then they have exactly the same properties. So, if there are properties of the mind which no physical object could have then, by the principle of the indiscernibility of identicals, the mind cannot be a physical object. And this is exactly the strategy adopted by the three arguments we have been considering.

4. *Doubt and existence*. The last argument for substance dualism which we will consider is also due to Descartes. In the *Meditations*, Descartes noticed that he could doubt the existence of his body. He begins by observing that sometimes when we dream we mistake our dreams for reality. For example, I might dream that I'm falling off a cliff, and whilst dreaming it seems to me entirely real that I'm falling off a cliff. Nevertheless, I'm actually asleep in bed. It follows that at least many of my present beliefs might be false. For example, it seems to me that at this moment I'm wide awake, sitting in front of my laptop. But it must be admitted that I could be asleep, dreaming that I'm sitting in front of my laptop. Consequently, my present belief that I'm sitting in front of my laptop can be called into doubt. Similarly, my

present belief that I have a body can be called into doubt. Perhaps I have no body but am presently dreaming that I do.

Descartes strengthened this line of thought by introducing a new thought experiment. It seems that I must admit that there might be an incredibly powerful alien determined to mislead me in all possible ways. This creature controls my thoughts, making me believe all sorts of things which are not true. But once I admit that such a creature is possible, it seems that I must admit that my present belief that I have a body could be mistaken. Perhaps I am a disembodied spirit who has been deceived by the powerful alien into believing that I have a body.

Considerations like these led Descartes to the first premise of his argument:

(A) I can doubt that I have a body.

Next, Descartes took his thought experiments a little further. We have admitted that I might be dreaming that I'm sitting in front of my laptop. However, even if I'm dreaming, one thing remains certain: that I exist. My belief that I exist must be true, because even if I'm dreaming, I must exist in order to dream. Similarly, the alien might deceive me in all sorts of ways. Nevertheless, it remains certain that I exist. My belief that I exist must be true because, even if the alien is controlling my thoughts, I must exist in order to be controlled.

Considerations like these led Descartes to his second premise:

(B) I cannot doubt that I exist.

From (A) and (B) it seems to follow that:

(C) I am not my body.

We will return to the inference from (A) and (B) to (C) shortly. For the moment, notice that if we accept that I am my mind, then (C) entails the claim that:

(D) My mind is not my body.

Now (D) is not quite the same as substance dualism; nevertheless, establishing (D) would go a long way towards establishing substance dualism.

Let's now think about the inference from (A) and (B) to (C). At first glance, the inference from (A) and (B) to (C) would appear to have the same structure as this argument:

(A1) My car is red.

(B1) The car in front of me is not red.

Therefore,

(C1) The car in front of me is not mine.

The argument from (A1) and (B1) to (C1) is a good one. By the principle of the indiscernibility of identicals, if the car in front of me is my car it must have exactly the same properties as my car. Consequently, if my car is a different color to the one in front of me, then the car in front of me is not mine.

Now the argument from (A) and (B) to (C) also seems to rely on the principle of the indiscernibilty of identicals. For it points out that I have one property—the property of it not being doubted that I exist—and my body has another property—the property of it being doubted that it exists. Since I and my body have different properties, it seems to follow that I am not my body.

But there's a catch. Consider the following argument.

(A2) I think my car is red.

(B2) I think the car in front of me is not red.

Therefore,

(C2) The car in front of me is not mine.

At first glance, this argument appears to rely on the principle of the indiscernibility of identicals. For it says that whilst my car has the property of being thought to be red, the car in front of me does not, and so the car in front of me is not mine. But it's clear that this argument does not work. Say that I have just won a blue car in a lottery, but mistakenly believe that I have won a red car. I go to pick up my new car and the lottery organizers show me a blue car. It really is my car, but I don't think that it is because I expect a red car. In that case premises (A2) and (B2) are both true: I think my car is red and I think the car in front of me is not red. Nevertheless, the conclusion (C2) is false: the car in front of me *is* mine.

More generally, the principle of the indiscernibility of identicals does not work when the properties in question involve psychological states like believing and thinking. Now this is crucial for the evaluation of Descartes' argument. For premises (A) and (B) both involve properties which involve the psychological state of *doubting*. Another example will make it quite clear that Descartes' argument doesn't work:

(A3) I can doubt I am the author of this book.

(B3) I cannot doubt that I exist.

Therefore,

(C3) I am not the author of this book.

Descartes has shown how I can doubt that I am the author of this book: I might have merely dreamed that I wrote it or my thoughts might be under the control of a powerful alien. And he has shown us how I cannot doubt that I exist. But it certainly does not follow that I am not the author of this book. Similarly, whilst I can doubt that I have a body and not doubt that I exist, it does not follow that I am not my body.

1.3 Arguments against substance dualism

In the previous section we considered four arguments in favor of substance dualism. None of these arguments was very convincing. In this section I will present three arguments *against* substance dualism.

1. *Princess Elizabeth's argument.* The substance dualist makes two claims about the mind. (1) Mind and body are radically different kinds of substances. (2) Mind and body causally interact. These two claims are in tension. If mind and body are supposed to be radically different, how can they causally interact? This objection was first put to Descartes by his contemporary, Princess Elizabeth of Bohemia (1618–80). Descartes' replies were highly evasive!

Princess Elizabeth's argument has a certain amount of force. Nevertheless, the argument can be overplayed. Notice that there are causal interactions between very different kinds of *physical* substances. For example, sunshine can heat metal, and yet sunshine and metal are quite different kinds of substance. The former is a kind of electromagnetic radiation; the latter an assembly of atoms. If quite different kinds of physical substances can interact, why can't physical and nonphysical substances interact? The crucial point, it seems to me, is not that mind and brain are (according to substance dualism) radically different kinds of stuff; rather, the crucial point is that the substance dualist has said absolutely nothing about the details of the interaction. Physics can tell us in considerable detail about the ways light affects matter, but the substance dualist can provide no details at all about the way the soul and brain affect each other.

2. *The explanatory completeness of physiology.* If you ask a physiologist to describe what happens when Bloggs runs away from a lion, they will say something like this. Running occurs when certain muscle groups—especially the muscles in the thigh—contract powerfully. The thigh muscles contract because they are stimulated by certain nerves. Those nerves arise in the spine, and are in turn stimulated by special spinal nerves. The spinal nerves in their turn are stimulated by the motor cortex—the part of the brain devoted to the initiation and control of movement. At this point the physiologist's account gets very complicated, but this much is clear. The motor cortex is stimulated by those parts of the brain responsible for decision making, which in turn receive input from the visual cortex—the part of the brain responsible for vision. (Remember that Bloggs ran away because he *saw* the lion.) And the activity in the visual cortex came about because Bloggs's retina was stimulated by the lion.

I have, of course, left out a great deal of detail. The sum total of what physiology has discovered about the causal background of even a simple movement would fill a dozen books. Nevertheless, it's clear that the theory offered by the physiologist is a *physical* one. There has been no mention whatsoever of nonphysical substances. But if we can account for people's actions without appealing to nonphysical substances, then substance dualism is mistaken to at least this extent: the nonphysical mind does not cause people to behave as they do. Of course, the substance dualist could concede this point but still insist that the nonphysical mind is responsible for other aspects of our mental life. For example, it might be argued that, whilst not causally responsible for our actions, the nonphysical mind is nevertheless the seat of consciousness. We return to the issue of consciousness in Part 4. For the moment we can say this much: there is no need to believe in a nonphysical mind in order to explain action.

3. *The explanatory weakness of substance dualism.* In the Introduction we noted six general features of mental life which a good theory of mental states should be able to explain (or explain away):

1. Some mental states are caused by states of the world.
2. Some mental states cause actions.
3. Some mental states cause other mental states.
4. Some mental states are conscious.
5. Some mental states are about things in the world.
6. Some kinds of mental states are systematically correlated with certain kinds of brain states.

What is striking about substance dualism is the extent to which it fails to illuminate the items on this list. We have already seen that substance dualism has trouble explaining the first two items on the list. Moreover, it is completely silent about the third item: it says nothing at all about how one mental state causes another. How do states of nonphysical stuff bring about other states of nonphysical stuff? In particular, how is it that some of the causal relations between nonphysical states respect the canons of rationality? No answers are forthcoming.

Turning to the fourth item we can observe that substance dualists do not offer a *theory* of consciousness. They assert that nonphysical mental stuff is conscious; they do not tell us what it is about nonphysical stuff that facilitates consciousness. This problem is especially telling if we allow that some mental states are *unconscious*. What is the difference between conscious, nonphysical mental states and unconscious, nonphysical mental states?

Item (5) on the list of general features of mental states notes that at least some mental states are about things in the world: my belief that Mt Everest is 8,848 meters high is about Mt Everest. Theories of the 'aboutness' of mental states are called 'theories of **content**', and we discuss theories of content in Chapter 9. It is not entirely out of the question that nonphysical states could be about things in the world; nevertheless, we don't at present have a dualist theory of content.

Finally, let's consider item (6). Why should states of a nonphysical mind be correlated with states of the physical brain? According to substance dualism, the brain plays a crucial role in mediating between the world and the nonphysical mind. Perceptual information about the world is conveyed to the mind via the brain, and instructions to move in certain ways are conveyed from the mind to the body via the brain. Consequently, the existence of correlations between mental states and brain states is not entirely unexpected. However, we know that damage to certain parts of the brain causes deficits of reasoning. In other words, we know that there are correlations between reasoning processes and certain brain states. According to substance dualism, though, reasoning occurs entirely in the soul. The correlations between reasoning processes and brain states are thus an embarrassment to substance dualism.

So far I have argued that substance dualism has little to say about the six items on our list. Moreover, there is little reason to expect that the explanatory situation will change. There simply are no obvious ways of developing nonphysicalist theories of perception, thought, action, or consciousness. In contrast, we shall see in later chapters that there are at least the beginnings of physicalist theories of most of the items on the list. Moreover, there are reasons to think that those physicalist theories might be developed in coming years.

The relative lack of explanatory power of substance dualism is, in my view, the most decisive reason available for discarding substance dualism. We should endorse the theory of mental states which most helps us understand the place of minds in the world, and substance dualism does very little to advance that understanding.

1.4 Property dualism

So far in this chapter we have largely been concerned with substance dualism. In this section I will briefly discuss an alternative kind of dualism—property dualism.

We haven't said very much yet about the distinction between substances and properties. For our purposes, a substance is something which could be the only thing in the universe. My body is therefore a substance, for we can easily imagine a universe which contains only my body. On the other hand, having a mass (roughly, weight) of 80 kg is not a substance, for we cannot imagine a universe which contains 80 kg *and nothing else*: there would have to be something else in the universe which had that mass. (This way of defining 'substance' is due to David Armstrong (1968: 7). I'm not entirely happy with it, but it will do for present purposes.)

We have seen that my body is a substance whereas having a mass of 80 kg is not. Having a mass of 80 kg is a *property*. Say that my body weighs 80 kg. Then one of my body's properties is having a mass of 80 kg. More generally: substances have properties.

Here are a few more examples. My car is a substance: we can imagine a universe which contains nothing but my car. One of my car's properties is being white. Another is having four tires. And a third is having the license plate 'UZR 155'. The Australian one-dollar coin in my pocket is a substance. It has various properties including being gold colored; being minted in 1998; and being in my pocket.

With the distinction between substance and property in place, we can now turn to the doctrine of property dualism. According to property dualism, mental states are nonphysical properties of the brain. The brain is a physical substance with various physical properties. For example, the typical human brain weighs about one kilogram; contains billions of neurons; has a blood supply; and so forth. That much is common ground. What's radical about property dualism is that it claims that, besides all of these physical properties, the brain has some *nonphysical* properties. These include being conscious; being in pain; believing that it is Monday; and wishing that it were Friday. In short, mental states are nonphysical properties of the brain.

There are various kinds of property dualism, but here we will focus on one especially important sort: *epiphenomenal* property dualism. Since 'epiphenomenal property dualism' is a bit of a mouthful, I will just say 'epiphenomenalism'. According to **epiphenomenalism**, physical properties of the brain cause nonphysical properties of the brain, but not vice versa. Consider again the example of seeing a lion (Section 1.1). According to epiphenomenalism, light waves from the lion stimulate Bloggs's retina in a certain way, and that in turn causes his brain to be activated in a certain way. In other words, his brain is caused to have a particular physical property—the property of being activated in a certain way. Bloggs's brain's having the physical property of being activated in that way causes it to have the nonphysical property of thinking 'LION!'

So far we have seen that, according to epiphenomenalism, mental states are nonphysical properties of the brain which are brought about by physical properties of the brain. The distinctive feature of epiphenomenalism is that the nonphysical properties of the brain do not, in turn, bring about physical states of the brain. Bloggs's 'LION!' thought has no causal powers—it doesn't *do* anything. But if his 'LION!' thought doesn't do anything, it does not cause him to run away. What, then, makes Bloggs run away when he sees a lion? According to epiphenomenalism, it is physical states of his brain alone which cause him to run away. So the full story according to epiphenomenalism is this. Light waves strike Bloggs's retina and cause his brain to be activated in a certain way. Call the physical property of having

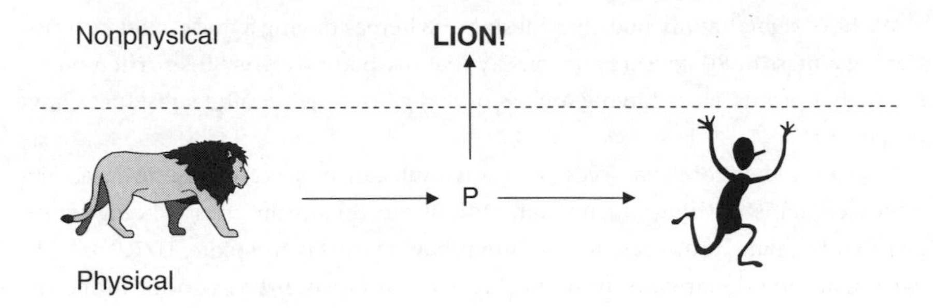

Figure 1.1 A diagrammatic representation of epiphenomenalism. The arrows represent the causal relation, with the arrowhead located at the effect

the brain activated in a certain way 'P'. P has two effects. First, it causes Bloggs's brain to have the nonphysical property of thinking 'LION!'. Second, it causes his legs to move so that he runs away. Figure 1.1 illustrates epiphenomenal property dualism.

It's important to stress that, according to epiphenomenalism, mental states are causally inert. My thought 'LION!' does nothing. What causes me to run away is a state of my brain.

1.5 Assessing epiphenomenalism

We saw in Section 1.3 that substance dualism faces three major difficulties: (i) Princess Elizabeth's problem; (ii) the **explanatory completeness of physiology**; and (iii) the explanatory weakness of substance dualism. Each of these problems also arises—in some form or other—for epiphenomenalism. Because the problems faced by epiphenomenalism overlap to a large extent the problems faced by substance dualism, my discussion of the former will be relatively brief. For more details, refer back to Section 1.3.

1. *Princess Elizabeth's problem*. Princess Elizabeth pointed out that there is a tension at the very heart of substance dualism: if mind and brain are radically different kinds of substance, how can they interact? A similar problem arises for epiphenomenalism: how can physical properties of the brain give rise to nonphysical properties of the brain? It must be admitted that this argument has a certain amount of force; however, since we allow causal interactions between quite different kinds of physical properties, why can't we allow causal interactions between physical and nonphysical properties? (For details, see Section 1.3.)

2. *The explanatory completeness of physiology*. When discussing substance dualism, we took note of the following difficulty. It's plausible that human actions like running away from a lion can be fully explained in terms of physical events like

muscle contractions and neuron discharges. But if every human action can be fully explained in terms of physical events, then it cannot be the case that nonphysical states play a crucial role in bringing about human actions.

Notice, though, that this difficulty does not arise for epiphenomenalism. According to epiphenomenalism, Bloggs's thought that there is a lion present is causally inert, and his running away from the lion is entirely due to activity in his brain. That is, epiphenomenalism is entirely compatible with the claim that physiology is explanatorily complete.

Epiphenomenalism, however, pays a high price for avoiding the objection from the explanatory completeness of physiology. For if mental properties are causally inert, we have to give up two of the general features of mental states which we noted in the Introduction:

(2) Some mental states cause actions.

(3) Some mental states cause other mental states.

(These were the second and third items in the list of general features of mental states given in the Introduction, hence the labels '(2)' and '(3)'.)

As the lion example makes clear, mental states do not, according to epiphenomenalism, cause actions. Consequently, accepting epiphenomenalism involves abandoning feature (2). Moreover, if mental states are causally inert, one mental state cannot cause another. Intuitively, we might think that Bloggs's LION! thought caused him to experience fear. However, according to epiphenomenalism, Bloggs's experience of fear was not caused by his LION! thought; rather it was caused by a physical property of his brain. Call the physical property of Bloggs's brain which caused the LION! thought 'P'. Then, according to epiphenomenalism, P also caused a further physical property of Bloggs's brain—call it 'R'—which in turn caused the nonphysical property of being afraid. (Figure 1.2 represents one way in which the details of this story might be filled in.) Consequently, accepting epiphenomenalism involves abandoning feature (3).

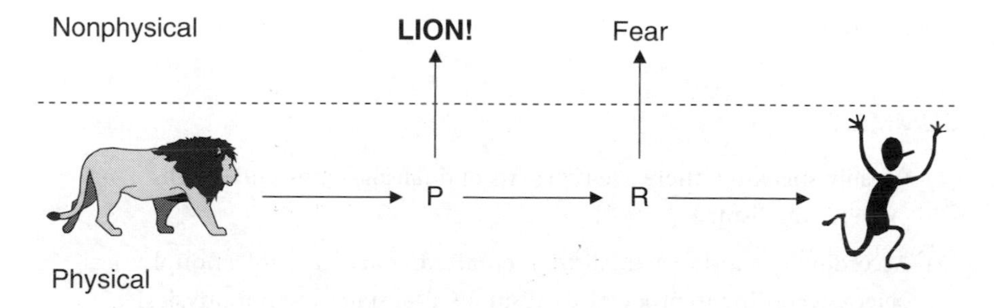

Figure 1.2 Epiphenomenalism. Note that the LION! thought doesn't cause the state of fear. Again, the arrows represent the causal relation, with the arrowhead located at the effect

Now it may be that our ordinary understanding of mental states is pretty much completely wrong and that we have to give up features (2) and (3). However, we would have to have very powerful arguments in favor of epiphenomenalism before it would be wise to give up so much of our ordinary understanding of mental states.

3. *The explanatory weakness of property dualism*. We saw in Section 1.3 that substance dualism explains very little about the mind. Moreover, it's not at all clear how substance dualism could be developed so that it began to illuminate the general features of the mind listed in the Introduction. Similar remarks apply to epiphenomenalism. Epiphenomenalism simply takes it for granted that physical properties of the brain can cause nonphysical properties of the brain, that mental states can be conscious, and that mental states can be about the world. Moreover, as we have just seen, epiphenomenalism *denies* that mental states cause action and that mental states cause other mental states.

I will bring this section to a close with a brief remark about consciousness and epiphenomenalism. We saw in Section 1.3 that substance dualism *takes it for granted* that some mental states are conscious; it does not *explain* how mental states could be conscious. There exists, however, a very powerful argument for the conclusion that consciousness is epiphenomenal. On this view, physical states of the brain give rise to nonphysical conscious properties which do not, in turn, cause anything. The argument, due to Frank Jackson, is discussed in Chapter 12.

1.6 Conclusion

In this chapter we have explored the idea that the mind is not physical. We have discovered that whilst the various arguments in favor of dualism are not especially convincing, the arguments against dualism are pretty powerful. In the next chapter we will consider one of the earliest physicalist theories of mental states—behaviorism.

SUMMARY

(1) Broadly speaking, there are two sorts of dualism—substance dualism and property dualism.

(2) According to substance dualism, mental states are states of a nonphysical object; according to property dualism, mental states are nonphysical properties of the (physical) brain.

(3) One way to defend substance dualism is to argue that there are things which the mind can do but which no physical object could do. We considered three examples of this style of argument. Two examples were unconvincing; assessment of the third, which concerned consciousness, was postponed until Chapter 12.

(4) Descartes offered an argument in support of substance dualism that was based on what can and cannot be doubted. However, his argument contains a serious error.

(5) One important version of property dualism is epiphenomenalism. According to epiphenomenalism, physical properties of the brain cause nonphysical mental properties, but not vice versa.

(6) Epiphenomenalism denies that mental states cause actions, and that one mental state can cause another mental state.

(7) The most significant difficulty for dualism in its various forms is its lack of explanatory power.

FURTHER READING

Churchland 1988: 7–22 provides a very elementary introduction to dualism. More advanced discussions are found in Armstrong 1968: Chs 2–4; Campbell 1984: Ch. 3; and Braddon-Mitchell and Jackson 1996: 3–13.

Descartes' concerns about language and reasoning are found in his *Discourse on the Method*, Part 5 (Descartes 1970: 41–2); for his argument based on doubt see his *Discourse on the Method*, Part 4 (Descartes 1970: 31–2). Princess Elizabeth's objection can be found in one of her letters to Descartes, dated 6–16 May 1643 (Descartes 1970: 274–5). (Note: Several good translations of Descartes' philosophical writings are available. Don't feel obliged to use the one to which I refer.) A good discussion of Descartes on substance dualism is Smith and Jones 1986: Ch. 3.

In Section 1.2 I mentioned contemporary theories of language. Pinker 1994 is a highly readable introduction to this fascinating area. In Section 1.3 I mentioned the possibility of providing a complete physical account of human movement. A nice introduction to the neuroscience of movement is Kosslyn and Koenig 1992: Ch. 7.

TUTORIAL QUESTIONS

(1) Describe substance dualism. (Use a picture if it helps.)

(2) What is Leibniz's principle of the indiscernibility of identicals?

(3) In your view, are there things which minds can do but physical objects could not achieve?

(4) What does it mean to say that physiology is explanatorily complete? How does the explanatory completeness of physiology pose a threat to substance dualism?

(5) How did Descartes establish that he can doubt the existence of his body?

(6) Describe property dualism.

(7) Describe epiphenomenalism.

(8) Give an argument against epiphenomenalism.

2

Behaviorism

Behave yourself.

—My mother

This chapter begins our exploration of physicalist theories of mental states by examining behaviorism. Two sorts of behaviorism will be discussed—**philosophical behaviorism** and **methodological behaviorism**. These two doctrines are closely related, although there is an important difference of focus. Philosophical behaviorism (also called 'logical' or 'analytic' behaviorism) offers a physicalist answer to the question, 'What are mental states?' In contrast, methodological behaviorism offers an account of how psychologists should go about their research. That is, methodological behaviorism proposes a *methodology* for doing psychological research. Despite these differences, both types of behaviorism emphasize the behavior people are disposed to produce under certain circumstances.

2.1 Philosophical behaviorism

According to philosophical behaviorism, mental states are **dispositions** (or 'tendencies') to behave in certain ways under certain circumstances. Pain, for example, is the tendency to cry or wince or . . . when you have broken your leg or burned your hand or . . . The first set of dots is intended to indicate that the behaviors associated with pain are not exhausted by crying and wincing—there are lots of things people do when they are in pain. Similarly, the second set of dots is intended to indicate that the circumstances associated with pain are not exhausted by broken legs and burnt hands—there are lots of painful **stimuli**.

According to philosophical behaviorism, to be in pain is to be disposed to do certain things when certain things happen to you. Here are a few more examples of philosophical behaviorist analyses of mental states. To believe that a lion is nearby is to run quickly to safety, or reach for your gun, or . . . when you see a lion, or hear a lion, or . . . Again the dots indicate that the lists of characteristic behaviors and circumstances may be very long indeed. Another example: to be afraid of the dark is to scream or tremble or . . . when the light bulb fails or the candle blows out or . . .

It's important not to confuse philosophical behaviorism with two quite different claims. First, philosophical behaviorism does not claim that mental states are *the causes of* our dispositions to behave in certain ways under certain circumstances. According to philosophical behaviorism pain is the disposition to behave in certain ways when certain things happen to our bodies; it is not the cause of our disposition to behave in certain ways when certain things happen to our bodies.

Second, philosophical behaviorism must be distinguished from the claim that we *know about* the mental states of others by observing the way they react to the circumstances they are in. I might work out that Bloggs is afraid of the dark by noticing that he tends to scream or tremble or . . . when the light bulb fails or the candle blows out or . . . But claiming that that is how I work out what mental state Bloggs is in is quite different from claiming that his fear of the dark *is* his tendency to scream or tremble or . . . when the light bulb fails or the candle blows out or . . . (Compare: I might work out that there's a wildfire in the hills when I smell smoke, but that doesn't show that the wildfire *is* the smoke.)

When philosophical behaviorists use the term 'behavior', they are referring to physical events. Crying, wincing, running, reaching, screaming, trembling—these are all physical responses of the physical body. Similarly, behaviorists are only interested in the physical circumstances that trigger behavior. Breaking your leg, burning your hand, and seeing or hearing a lion are all physical events, as are the failure of a light bulb and the blowing out of a candle. It follows that philosophical behaviorism offers a physicalist account of mental states. According to philosophical behaviorism, mental states are dispositions to behave in certain ways under certain circumstances, and both the behavior and the circumstances that trigger it are understood to be physical events.

2.2 Arguments in favor of philosophical behaviorism

In the Introduction I gave a list of six features of mental states which a good theory of mental states should be able to explain. (I emphasized at the time that we may end up discarding one or more of the features on this list, but we would require good reasons for doing so.) One way to argue in favor of a theory of mental states is by showing that it is able to explain a number of these features. How well does philosophical behaviorism perform in this respect?

Philosophical behaviorism goes some way towards explaining three of the six features, and might—just might—have something to say about a fourth feature.

However, the two remaining features present a serious challenge to philosophical behaviorism. After briefly discussing the four features philosophical behaviorism can—or might—begin to explain, we will look in detail at two important arguments for philosophical behaviorism. (The two features philosophical behaviorism cannot explain will be discussed in the next section.)

The features of mental states which philosophical behaviorism goes some way towards illuminating are as follows. (I have retained the numbering used in the Introduction.)

1. *Some mental states are caused by states of the world.* Standing on a tack, for example, causes pain. Now, according to philosophical behaviorism, mental states are dispositions to behave in certain ways under certain circumstances. So, if philosophical behaviorism is to respect the first feature of mental states, it must be plausible that standing on a tack can make me disposed to say 'ouch', rub the sore spot, cry, and so forth. And surely that *is* plausible: when I stand on a tack I am disposed to do just those sorts of things.
2. *Some mental states cause actions.* Let's stick to the pain example. If philosophical behaviorism is to respect the second feature of mental states, it must be the case that my being disposed to say 'ouch', rub the sore spot, cry, and so on causes me to (for example) cry. And that's plausible. Consider a glass which is fragile. Something is fragile if it is disposed to break when dropped. If I drop the glass, one aspect of the cause of its breaking is its fragility. ('The antique glass broke when I dropped it *because* it was very fragile.') Similarly, part of the cause of my crying is that I was disposed to say 'ouch', rub the sore spot, cry, and so on. In other words if, as the philosophical behaviorist claims, pain is a disposition to cry (etc.), then one aspect of the cause of my crying is my being in pain.
5. *Some mental states are about things in the world.* Consider my belief that Mt Everest is 8,848 meters tall. That belief is about Mt Everest and represents Mt Everest as being 8,848 meters tall. In Chapter 9 we will look in detail at the issue of content. It is not entirely out of the question that a theory of content could be worked out within the framework of philosophical behaviorism. However, no one has yet provided the details of such a theory.
6. *Some kinds of mental states are systematically correlated with certain kinds of brain states.* Philosophical behaviorism respects the sixth feature of mental states. In the glass example, we said that the glass was disposed to break when it was dropped. Underpinning this disposition is a certain molecular structure. It's because the glass has that molecular structure that it broke when dropped. (The features of an object which underpin its dispositional properties are called the *categorical properties* of the object.) Now, plausibly, the features of the human body which underpin our behavioral dispositions are certain brain states. So

philosophical behaviorism is entirely consistent with the claim that mental states are systematically correlated with certain brain states.

I now turn to two important arguments in favor of philosophical behaviorism.

First argument. When someone wants a coffee they exhibit a certain behavioral disposition: they tend to drink coffee. And if someone often says that they want a coffee but never accepts one when it's offered, we're inclined to think that they don't really want a coffee. These observations illustrate an important point about mental states: there is a strong connection between mental states and dispositions to behave in ways characteristic of those mental states. Indeed, the connection is so strong that a person's persistent failure to exhibit the characteristic behavioral disposition of some mental state M is good evidence that they're not in mental state M.

How can the connection between mental states and behavioral dispositions be explained? If, as the philosophical behaviorist claims, to want a coffee is to be disposed to drink coffee, then it is no surprise that someone who wants a coffee tends to drink one. The connection between mental states and behavioral dispositions follows immediately from the philosophical behaviorist's analysis of mental states.

We can now sum up the first argument for philosophical behaviorism. There is a strong connection between mental states and behavior. Philosophical behaviorism can readily explain that connection since, according to philosophical behaviorism, mental states are behavioral dispositions. So the connection between mental states and behavior supports the claim that philosophical behaviorism is true.

There are, however, other theories of mental states which can explain the strong connection between mental states and behavioral dispositions. (We will look at one such theory in Chapter 4.) Consequently, the fact that philosophical behaviorism can explain the connection between mental states and behavioral dispositions isn't enough to establish that philosophical behaviorism is true. One of the *other* theories that can explain the connection may be true instead.

Second argument. In the 1920s and 1930s, a group of philosophers called the 'Vienna Circle' developed a new account of the meaning of a statement. A statement is a sentence which claims that the world is a certain way. 'The Eiffel tower is in Paris' and 'The moon is made of cheese' are both statements. The first makes a (true) claim about the location of a famous landmark; the second makes a (false) claim about the constitution of the moon. The theory of the meaning of statements advocated by the Vienna Circle is called **verificationism**. On this view, the meaning of any statement is its method of verification. Let me explain.

To verify a statement is to show that it is true (if it is true). Members of the Vienna Circle insisted that the only way to show that a statement is true is by making *sensory* observations (that is, by looking, hearing, feeling, etc.). Let's take as our example the statement, 'The cat is on the mat'. That statement can be verified by *looking* for the cat; or *feeling* for the cat; or (I guess) *listening* for the cat. According to verificationism, then, 'The cat is on the mat' means 'If a normal observer looks in the right way they will have a cat-on-mat visual experience *and* if a normal observer feels in the right way they will have a cat-on-mat tactile experience *and* if a normal observer listens in the right way they will have a cat-on-mat auditory experience'.

To grasp the force of the verificationist theory of meaning, think about this. If I tell you that the cat is on the mat, what have I conveyed to you? Surely this: if you look in the right place you'll see that the cat is on the mat; and that if you touch in the right way you'll feel that the cat is on the mat; and if you listen in the right way you'll hear that the cat is on the mat; and so on. These considerations suggest that the meaning of a statement is its method of verification.

Statements which cannot be verified are, according to the Vienna Circle, meaningless. They thought that some statements made by earlier philosophers were meaningless because they could not be verified. For example, they rejected Descartes' statement that our minds are nonphysical objects because, since nonphysical objects cannot be seen, touched, smelled, heard or tasted, there is no way to verify Descartes' statement.

Now let's return to philosophical behaviorism. According to verificationism, the meaning of a statement is its method of verification. How would we verify a statement like 'Bloggs is in pain'? Well, we would note that Bloggs is crying or wincing or . . . after certain sorts of things have happened to his body. So according to verficationism, the meaning of 'Bloggs is in pain' is 'If a normal observer listens in the right way after certain things have happened to Bloggs's body they will have a Bloggs-is-crying auditory experience *or* if a normal observer looks in the right way after certain things have happened to Bloggs's body they will have a Bloggs-is-wincing visual experience *or* . . .'. But if that's what 'Bloggs is in pain' means, then pain must be the behavioral disposition to cry or wince or . . . when certain things have happened to our bodies. (Compare: if 'triangle' *means* 'three-sided figure' then a triangle *is* a three-sided figure.) So the verificationist theory of the meaning of statements leads quite quickly to philosophical behaviorism.

Most contemporary philosophers of language, however, no longer think that the meaning of a statement is its method of verification. The great American philosopher W. V. O. Quine (1908–2000), for example, thought that individual statements could not be verified; rather, entire theories comprising many individual statements are verified or rejected. Consequently, for Quine it is *whole theories* that have meaning; individual statements get their meaning only in virtue of being embedded in a much broader framework.

Important though Quine's ideas are, this is not the place to investigate them. For our purposes it is enough to say that the second argument for philosophical behaviorism rests on the verificationist theory of meaning, and that theory is almost universally rejected by contemporary philosophers.

2.3 Arguments against philosophical behaviorism

I remarked at the beginning of the previous section that there are two general features of mental states which present a very serious challenge to philosophical behaviorism. Those features are consciousness and causal relationships between mental states (again I retain the numbering from the Introduction):

3. *Some mental states cause other mental states*. For example, say that Bloggs has the following two beliefs:

   A. He believes that today is Friday.

   B. He believes that Friday is payday.

   These beliefs are likely to cause him to hold a further belief:

   C. He believes that today is payday.

   Notice that, besides the causal relationship between the first two beliefs and the last one, there is also an *evidential* relation between the first two beliefs and the last one. That is, the first two beliefs make it *reasonable* to believe the third. This is an example of the way in which our thought processes are often *rational*. Can philosophical behaviorism account for the rationality of our thought processes?

   In Chapter 6 we will look at one account of the rationality of thought—an account which takes the idea that the mind is a computer entirely literally. It is controversial whether the computational theory of the rationality of thought is the right theory. Nevertheless, two things are clear: (1) the computational theory of the rationality of thought is the only well-developed theory of rational thought we currently possess; (2) the computational theory is quite incompatible with philosophical behaviorism. Consequently, the fact that thought is often rational provides a major challenge to philosophical behaviorism: at present no behaviorist theory of the rationality of thought is available, nor is it clear how one could be developed.

4. *Some mental states are conscious*. In Part 4 we will examine the issue of consciousness in some detail. For the moment let us just note that philosophical behaviorism has nothing to say about consciousness. Say that I step on a tack and am immediately aware of a sharp pain in my foot. Now, according to philosophical behaviorism,

my pain is a disposition to behave in certain ways—to scream, wince, and so on. But it is utterly mysterious how my disposition to scream, wince, and so on could *hurt*. Why does my being disposed to act in certain ways feel like something? Isn't it possible that I could be disposed to scream and wince without actually *feeling* pain? Couldn't someone build a robot which has sensors to detect when it has stood on a tack, and which automatically makes a screaming noise whenever that occurs, but which has no feeling of pain?

I turn now to a pair of closely related arguments against philosophical behaviorism.

First argument. Imagine that Bloggs has decided to be the ultimate tough guy. When he stubs his toe he doesn't wince or cry or rub the sore spot; he just carries on as though nothing has happened. Even if he broke his leg he wouldn't scream or cry—he'd just calmly hobble to the nearest hospital. Of course, Bloggs still *feels* pain—it still hurts when he stubs his toe or breaks his leg—but he is no longer disposed to cry, wince, and so on.

Now imagine an entire community of people who, like Bloggs, have decided to become super-tough. In that community people still stub their toes and break their legs, and those members of the community who are unfortunate enough to stub their toe or break their leg still experience pain. Nevertheless, no one in that community is ever disposed to produce pain behavior—no one is ever disposed to cry or wince or scream.

This example shows that you can be in pain without being disposed to produce the kind of behavior typically associated with pain. Moreover, since no one in the community just described is inclined to produce pain behavior, the example shows that it can be perfectly *normal* for those in pain not to be disposed to produce pain behavior. (Indeed, anyone who did produce pain behavior would be considered very weird.) In other words, the example shows that being disposed to produce pain behavior is not **necessary** for being in pain. This point was first made by the contemporary American philosopher Hilary Putnam who coined the term 'superstoics' for people like our tough friend Bloggs. (See Putnam 1965.)

The superstoic example shows that being disposed to produce pain behavior is not necessary for being in pain. A similar example shows that being disposed to produce pain behavior is not **sufficient** for pain. Imagine someone who never felt pain. When they stub their toe it doesn't hurt; even if they broke their leg they wouldn't be in pain. For convenience we will call this person 'Smith'. As it happens, Smith is rather embarrassed about her condition, so she learns how to pretend to be in pain. When she stubs her toe she remembers to say 'ouch' and rub the sore spot. When she breaks her leg she screams and winces. Eventually, after a lot of practice, she learns to produce pain behavior indistinguishable from that of a normal person. Nevertheless, she never feels pain.

Smith is an example of a 'perfect pretender'. That we can coherently imagine a perfect pretender shows that a person can be disposed to produce pain behavior without actually being in pain. That is, it shows that being disposed to produce pain behavior is insufficient for being in pain.

Taken together, the superstoic and perfect pretender examples show that being disposed to produce pain behavior is neither necessary nor sufficient for pain. You can be in pain but not be disposed to produce pain behavior, and you can be disposed to produce pain behavior without being in pain. It follows that pain is not a disposition to behave in certain ways under certain conditions.

Second argument. Philosophical behaviorism assumes that for every mental state there is a corresponding set of behaviors. If you are in pain then you will do one or more of the following: cry, wince, scream, rub the sore spot . . . If you believe that there is a lion nearby you will do one or more of the following: run back to the vehicle, reach for your gun, call for help . . .

The superstoic example shows that this isn't true. When a superstoic is in pain he does not cry or wince or scream or rub the sore spot. He doesn't do those things because he wants to appear not to be in pain. Similarly, imagine that there is a lion nearby, and that you think that the best way to avoid being attacked by the lion is to stand perfectly still. In that case you wouldn't run back to the vehicle or reach for your gun—you'd stand very still.

These examples illustrate the point that how we react to our circumstances depends on our beliefs and desires. The superstoic's reaction to pain depends not just on the pain but also on his *desire* to appear not to be in pain. Similarly, how you react to a nearby lion will depend on your *beliefs* about lions. If you believe that the best way to avoid a lion is by standing very still, then you stand very still.

It's worth thinking a bit more about the lion example. Say that I believe that the best way to avoid a lion is to stand very still, but that I'm fed up with life and want to die. In that case I won't stand perfectly still because I believe that I won't get eaten if I stand still, and I desire to get eaten because I'm suicidal.

This example illustrates the complex relationships between mental states and behavior. It is rare that your behavior is determined by a single mental state; rather, how you behave is typically determined by a complex of mental states. Consequently, philosophical behaviorism is doomed. There is no set of behaviors which are characteristic of pain; what you do when you are in pain depends on what you believe and desire. And the same applies to every other mental state: what you do when you are in love, or want an ice cream, or believe in Santa Claus, depends on what else you feel, want, and believe. This fact about the relationship between mental states and behavior is a very important one. We will return to it in Chapter 4.

One final observation. Remember that whenever we gave an example of a philosophical behaviorist analysis of a mental state, we relied on a series of dots to show that the associated list of behaviors was incomplete. For example, we said that pain is the tendency to cry or wince or . . . under certain circumstances. We can now see that the list of behaviors is inevitably incomplete. How someone reacts to pain depends, as we have noted, not just on the pain itself but also on their other mental states. There are a great many mental states capable of influencing the way a person responds to pain, and different mental states will typically influence the pain response in different ways. Consequently, there are a very large number of possible pain responses. If I believe that the best way to relieve my pain is to jump in the air, I will (other things being equal) jump in the air; if I believe that the best way to relieve my pain is to walk backwards, I will (other things being equal) walk backwards; and so on (and on and on).

Our discussion of philosophical behaviorism is now complete. In the next three sections of this chapter we will examine methodological behaviorism.

2.4 What is methodological behaviorism?

The methodological behaviorist proposes that psychology restricts itself to seeking laws which link stimuli to behavior. 'Stimuli' includes both the sensory inputs which the organism is currently receiving and any relevant sensory inputs the organism has received in the past. Let's briefly look at an example.

A rat is placed in a cage which also contains a lever and a light. A pellet of food is released into the cage if, and only if, the bar is pressed when the light is on. As the rat wanders around the cage, it accidentally presses the lever when the light is on and receives a pellet of food. Quite quickly the rat's behavior is modified so that it persistently presses the lever when (and only when) the light is on. Ordinarily we would say that the rat has learned to get food by pressing the lever when the light is on. We will see shortly, though, that the methodological behaviorist will be disinclined to use everyday psychological terms like 'learn'.

By the end of the experiment, there's a correlation between the light going on (the 'stimulus') and the rat's pressing the bar (the 'operant'): the rat presses the bar when (and only when) the light is on. The correlation comes about because the experimental set-up links getting a food pellet (the 'reinforcer') with pressing the bar when the light is on. This is an example of what is called the *law of effect:* if an organism receives a reinforcer shortly after producing the operant in response to the stimulus, its tendency to produce the operant in response to the stimulus will increase. The law of effect is an example—indeed, it's the core example—of the sort of law the methodological behaviorist is after: it describes a relationship between stimuli and behavior.

Notice that the law of effect makes no mention of the internal states of the organism. It does not say that the rat *learns* that it can get food by pressing the bar when the light is on, nor does it say that the rat *wants* food and *believes* that it can get it by pressing the bar. The methodological behaviorist insists that there is nothing to be gained by talking about the inner or psychological states of organisms. The best way to get on with psychology is to forget about what's in the mind and look for correlations between the inputs (stimuli) and outputs (behavior) of the mind.

In summary, methodological behaviorism instructs the psychologist to ignore the internal states of the mind and concentrate on seeing how organisms react to various stimuli. The aim is to find laws which relate stimuli to behavior. The laws will be of the form: if the organism receives stimuli S1, S2, S3, . . . then it will tend to respond with behavior B.

2.5 Arguments for methodological behaviorism

Methodological behaviorism advises the psychologist to avoid talking about mental states and concentrate on locating laws which link stimuli to behavior. A variety of arguments have been advanced in favor of this view. Here we will consider two.

First argument. The American methodological behaviorist B. F. Skinner (1904–90) insisted that it is bad science to theorize about unobservable states and properties. His concern was that, since such states and properties cannot be observed, we have no way of checking if our claims about them are true. Since science is only concerned with truths which can be established by good evidence, it should ignore claims about unobservable states and properties. (See Skinner 1980: 37–40.)

Now mental states cannot be directly observed. I cannot see your pains, nor can I see your belief that it's Thursday. Skinner concludes, therefore, that it's bad science to theorize about mental states. Consequently, he insists that psychologists should give up all talk about mental states.

The trouble with this line of argument is that pretty much all the best science deals with unobservables. The physicist can't see electrons; the paleontologist can't see dinosaurs (at best they can see the fossilized *remains* of dinosaurs); the geologist can't see the Earth's core. Nevertheless, our best theories in physics, paleontology, and geology talk about (respectively) electrons, dinosaurs, and the Earth's core.

One of Skinner's own examples is quite telling. He objected to the way in which early chemists tried to explain combustion by saying that a substance called 'phlogiston' is given off by burning objects. His worry was that phlogiston was not supposed to be observable. We now know that the phlogiston theory of combustion is wrong. The great French chemist Antoine Lavoisier showed that combustion involves the interaction of oxygen with a flammable material. Lavoissier's theory is now universally accepted. But notice that oxygen is no more observable than phlogiston! The phlogiston theory wasn't rejected because it trafficked in unobservables; it was rejected because it was inconsistent with the experimental findings of Lavoissier and others.

Scientists routinely develop theories which posit unobservable states and properties. The theories are assessed by comparing the events that the theory predicts will occur with the events that actually occur. If a theory gets lots of predictions right—and doesn't get any predictions glaringly wrong—then we have grounds for thinking that the unobservables it posits actually exist. We will see shortly that an argument of this sort can be given in favor of the existence of mental states.

One final point. It might be argued that Skinner is wrong when he claims that mental states cannot be observed since we can all look inside ourselves and 'see' our own mental states. Skinner is aware of this move and rightly rejects it. A truly scientific psychology must rely on evidence which can be carefully checked. My reports about my own mental life cannot be carefully checked because no one else has that kind of access to my mental life. For all you know I might be lying when I say that I believe that it is Thursday, or I might suffer from a speech disorder which leads me to say words I don't mean.

Second argument. Previously we noted that if a theory gets lots of predictions right, and doesn't get any predictions glaringly wrong, then we have grounds for thinking that it is true. From the 1920s to the 1950s, methodological behaviorists were very successful at predicting a range of behaviors in a number of experimental animals (rats and pigeons were Skinner's favorites). Consequently, up until the 1950s, there were grounds for accepting methodological behaviorism. However, from the end of the 1950s onwards, it became increasingly clear that methodological behaviorism was of little value in human psychology. (We return to this point in the next section.) By the 1960s, the so-called 'cognitive revolution' was under way, with psychologists no longer wary of theorizing about mental states. Much of the best work currently being done in psychology makes unabashed reference to mental states.

2.6 Arguments against methodological behaviorism

We have already noted a powerful objection to methodological behaviorism: many of our best theories of human behavior make reference to mental states. In this section I will briefly note two further objections to methodological behaviorism.

First objection. In the example of the rat discussed above, the light going on was the stimulus and the pressing of the bar was the response. In a case like this we have no difficulty identifying the stimulus and the response. But when we turn to real-life human behavior it is typically much harder to identify the stimulus and the response. Consider the following situation, based on an example by the linguist Noam Chomsky.

You go to the art gallery with a friend and look at a painting by the Dutch master, Rembrandt. Your friend might say any of the following: 'Dutch'; 'Wow!'; 'It's a Rembrandt'; 'This old stuff really bores me'; 'Let's steal it'; 'Can you believe the City paid 32 million dollars for *that*?' The range of responses your friend might make to the Rembrandt is both very large and very diverse; consequently, there will be no law linking the stimulus (i.e. the Rembrandt) with a single response (or even with an easily identified set of responses). (See Chomsky 1959.)

In reply to this problem, Skinner is likely to claim that the Rembrandt is not a single stimulus. Rather, the Rembrandt is a large collection of stimuli, each of which elicits a different response. For example, it may be the way the paint is applied that prompts the response, 'It's a Rembrandt', whereas the amazing use of perspective prompts the response, 'Wow!' However, as Chomsky points out, the behaviorist has no way of predicting what the subject will say, nor of identifying in advance which aspect of the painting triggers which utterance (Chomsky 1959). When applied to cases like this, methodological behaviorism is empty. It amounts to nothing more than an unsupported assertion that every response is in fact under the control of some stimulus.

Second objection. Methodological behaviorism assumes without argument that the way we respond to every situation is entirely determined by our experiences. That assumption underpins the claim that we can predict how an organism will respond if we know what stimulation it is currently receiving and has received in the past. However, there is evidence that some aspects of our verbal responses are partly determined by innate knowledge—that is, by knowledge with which we are born. Many contemporary linguists (including Chomsky) think that we are born with knowledge of a 'deep' grammar common to all human languages. This is an extraordinary claim, and this is not the place to pursue it (see below under Further Reading for useful references). Note, though, that if we are in fact born with knowledge of some aspects of our world, our responses to the world are *not* entirely determined by our history of stimulation. Consequently, methodological behaviorism could be very wide of the mark indeed.

SUMMARY

(1) Broadly speaking there are two sorts of behaviorism—philosophical behaviorism and methodological behaviorism.

(2) Philosophical behaviorism answers the question, 'What are mental states?' According to philosophical behaviorism, mental states are dispositions to behave in certain ways under certain circumstances.

(3) Methodological behaviorism is a methodological stricture. According to methodological behaviorism, psychologists should restrict themselves to seeking laws which link stimuli to behavior.

(4) Historically, the most important argument for philosophical behaviorism is that based on the verificationist theory of meaning. However, the verificationist theory of meaning has largely been abandoned by philosophers of language.

(5) Taken together, Putnam's superstoic example and the related perfect pretender example show that pain behavior is neither necessary nor sufficient for pain.

(6) Methodological behaviorism was largely motivated by the mistaken idea that science should not traffic in unobservables.

(7) The existence of innate knowledge would seriously undermine methodological behaviorism.

(8) Chomsky pointed out that, in many cases of human behavior, there is no principled way of identifying the stimulus.

FURTHER READING

One of the most important presentations of philosophical behaviorism is Carl Hempel's 'The Logical Analysis of Psychology' (Hempel 1949). Hempel was strongly influenced by Rudolf Carnap's work in this area (see for example Carnap 1959). Gilbert Ryle's *The Concept of Mind* (Ryle 1949) is another important source. Hilary Putnam presents a devastating attack on philosophical behaviorism in his 'Brains and Behavior' (Putnam 1965). His superstoic example appears in that paper.

For good discussions of philosophical behaviorism see Campbell 1984: Ch. 4; Braddon-Mitchell and Jackson 1996: 29–38; and Kim 1996: Ch. 2.

The most important proponent of methodological behaviorism is B. F. Skinner. The most relevant of his copious works are *Science and Human Behavior* (Skinner 1953) and *Verbal Behavior* (Skinner 1957). Block 1980: Ch. 3 consists of key selections from *Science and Human Behavior*.

Famously, Noam Chomsky launched a devastating attack on methodological behaviorism in a review of Skinner's *Verbal Behavior* (Chomsky 1959). Chomsky's paper is rightly regarded as one of the most important publications in twentieth-century literature on the mind. An extract is reprinted in Block 1980 (Ch. 4). For a clear description of Chomsky's attack on Skinner see Bolton and Hill 1996: 7–10.

For a highly accessible account of the claim that some linguistic knowledge is innate see Pinker 1994. For a critique of that idea see Cowie 1999. (Unfortunately Cowie's book is rather hard.)

TUTORIAL QUESTIONS

(1) Describe philosophical behaviorism.

(2) Describe methodological behaviorism.

(3) What is the verificationist theory of meaning, and how can it be used to support philosophical behaviorism?

(4) Describe (i) the superstoic example and (ii) the perfect pretender example. Explain how these examples challenge philosophical behaviorism.

(5) Should science avoid postulating unobservable entities?

(6) What's wrong with saying that there must be *something* about the picture (or the picture plus the viewer's prior experiences) which disposed her to say 'Wow!'?

(7) How would the existence of innate knowledge challenge methodological behaviorism?

3

The identity theory

If you gave him a brain cell it'd be lonely.

—Old Australian insult

Very roughly, the **identity theory** asserts that the mind is the brain. More precisely, it claims that mental states are physical states of the brain. The qualification 'physical' is important. After all, property dualism asserts that mental states are properties of the brain (see Section 1.4). However, according to property dualism, mental states are *nonphysical* properties of the brain. Consequently, if the identity theory is to be distinct from property dualism, it must assert that mental states are *physical* states of the brain. For ease of expression, in this chapter I will simply say 'brain states' rather than 'physical states of the brain'. It is important to remember, though, that it is physical brain states that are being discussed.

The identity theory gets its name because it *identifies*—claims an identity between—mental states and certain brain states. I say 'certain' brain states because whilst the identity theory claims that every mental state is a brain state, it is not committed to the converse. In fact, it's certainly not the case that every brain state is a mental state. For example, in addition to billions of neurons, the human brain contains a large number of *glial* cells which play a supportive and protective role. It's unlikely that any mental state is identical with a state of one or more glial cells.

3.1 More about the identity theory

The idea that mental states are brain states is not new. The English philosopher Thomas Hobbes (1588–1679) and his French contemporary Pierre Gassendi (1592–1655) both made the claim more than three hundred years ago. However, the idea wasn't carefully expressed and defended until the 1950s when a group of Australian philosophers including J. J. C. Smart explored the idea.

These days the idea of mind-brain identity is commonplace. Indeed, it has crept into ordinary language with expressions like 'He's brainy' and 'I can't get my head around it'. However, when the idea was proposed back in the 1950s, it was ridiculed. One English philosopher went so far as to suggest that Smart must have spent too much time in the hot Australian sun! (I owe this story to David Armstrong.)

When Smart articulated the identity theory he used a couple of analogies to convey his claim that mental states are brain states. According to Smart, mental states are brain states in the same way that water is H_2O and lightning is an atmospheric electrical discharge. These analogies are important for two reasons.

First, Smart's analogies are cases in which it took considerable scientific investigation to make the identifications. That water is H_2O cannot be established by casual observation, nor by thinking about the meanings of the terms 'water' and 'H_2O'. Similarly, the claim that mental states are brain states is not supposed to be an obvious truth which can be established by simple observation or by reflecting on the meanings of expressions like 'belief' and 'cortex'. (The cortex is a part of the human brain.) Rather, the claim that mental states are brain states is plausible in part because of advances in our understanding of the human brain.

In order to grasp the second reason why Smart's analogies are significant we need to understand the important distinction between **tokens** and **types**. Let's begin with an example.

Dingoes are a kind of wild dog found in many parts of the Australian outback. Say that we are camping in the outback and see four dingoes prowling around our campfire. In that case we have four tokens of the type *dingo*. The tokens are the individual animals; the type is the kind or class to which the individuals belong.

Notice that the four dingo tokens belong to a great many other types besides the type *dingo*. For example, they are tokens of the types *mammal, animal, material object,* and *scary thing which prowls around the campfire*.

Here's another example of the type/token distinction. On my bookshelf are two copies of Newton-Smith's nice book about the philosophy of science. One I bought for myself; the other was given to me by a friend. So on my shelf I have two tokens of the type *Newton-Smith's nice book about the philosophy of science*.

Now that we have in place the distinction between tokens and types, we can make a further distinction between **token identity** and **type identity**. Some examples will be useful. Posh Spice used to be a member of the British pop band *The Spice Girls*. After she left the band she married English soccer star David Beckham and now calls herself 'Victoria Beckham'. If you are invited to a party by Posh Spice you have simultaneously been invited to a party by Victoria Beckham. Posh Spice and Victoria Beckham are one and the same person. They are token identical. Similarly, the current President of the United States is George W. Bush. If you are invited to the White House by the current President you have simultaneously been invited to the White House by George W. Bush. George W. Bush and the current President of the United States are one and the same person. They are token identical.

In contrast, the identities between water and H_2O, and between lightning and atmospheric electrical discharge, are *type identities*. Every token of the type *water* is a token of the type *H_2O*, and every token of the type *lightning* is a token of the type *atmospheric electrical discharge*. Science has discovered that the type *water* and the type *H_2O* are identical, as are the types *lightning* and *atmospheric electrical discharge*.

We are now in a position to clarify the kind of identity which identity theorists want to assert between brain states and mental states. According to the identity theory, there is a type identity between mental states and brain states. For example, every token of the type *pain* is a token of the type *c-fiber firing*. Consequently, there is a type identity between pain and c-fiber firing. (I will often use the example 'pain is c-fiber firing' to illustrate the identity theory. This is a common practice in the philosophy of mind, but is not intended to be taken very seriously. There *are* nerve fibers called 'c-fibers' and they have something to do with painful sensations. However, it is unlikely that pain is identical to that particular type of neurological state. Moreover, whilst I will sometimes describe c-fiber firings as 'brain states', c-fibers are in fact peripheral nerves.)

Summing up, the identity theory asserts that every type of mental state is identical to a type of brain state. (It is not committed, though, to the converse.) The brain states in question are physical states of the brain. Moreover, the identities are not supposed to be discoverable by either simple observation or examining the meanings of the terms involved. Rather, they are analogous to scientific identities like 'water is H_2O'.

3.2 Arguments in favor of the identity theory

How well does the identity theory explain the six features of mental states noted in the Introduction? It's fair to say that the identity theory offers convincing explanations of three of the six features, and that it may turn out to be compatible with sophisticated attempts to explain two of the remaining features. However, one feature of mental states—consciousness—presents a serious challenge to the identity theory. In this section we will discuss those features of mental states which the identity theory, or a theory compatible with it, can explain. In the next section we will touch on, amongst other things, the issue of consciousness. A fuller discussion of consciousness will have to wait until Part 4. In what follows I have retained the numbering used in the Introduction.

1. *Some mental states are caused by states of the world.* Example: Bloggs's belief that there is a cup of coffee in front of him (mental state) is caused by there being a cup of coffee in front of him (state of the world).

If, as the identity theory claims, mental states are brain states, then the first feature amounts to the claim that some brain states (the ones held by the identity theory to be identical with certain mental states) are caused by states of the world. Research in neuroscience gives us grounds for thinking that this is true. For example, the causal impact of seeing a cup of coffee can be traced deep into the brain. Light from the cup stimulates the light-sensitive cells at the back of the eye (the retina), and information about the pattern of stimulation on the retina is carried into the brain by the optic nerve. (Intriguingly, the pattern of activation on the retina is reproduced many times in the visual centers of the brain.)

2. *Some mental states cause actions*. Example: Bloggs's desire for another coffee (mental state) together with his belief that there is more coffee in the kitchen (mental state), caused him to go into the kitchen (action).

If the identity theory is to explain the second feature of mental states, it must be the case that certain brain states cause actions like going to the kitchen for a coffee. Research in neuroscience makes it overwhelmingly likely that this is the case. We have very good evidence that actions are caused by activity in a part of the brain called the *motor cortex*.

3. *Some mental states cause other mental states*. Example: Bloggs's belief that it's Friday (mental state), together with his belief that Friday is payday (mental state), caused him to believe that it's payday (mental state).

If, as the identity theory insists, mental states are brain states, then the claim that some mental states cause other mental states is supported by the fact that some brain states cause other brain states. However, as we noted in the Introduction, there is something special about the way mental states interact with each other. Notice that my belief that it was Friday, together with my belief that Friday is payday, give me *good reason* to believe that it's payday. To put this point another way: the causal relations between mental states often respect the *rational* relations between them. In Chapter 6 we will look in a little detail at one theory of the rationality of thought. That theory is a **physicalist** one, and to that extent is compatible with the identity theory. However, it is controversial whether that account of the rationality of thought can be squared with the claim that mental states are brain states.

5. *Some mental states are about things in the world*. That is, they *represent* the world as being a certain way. For example, Bloggs's belief that Mt Everest is 8,848 meters tall is *about* Mt Everest and *represents* Mt Everest as being 8,848 meters tall. In Chapter 9 we will look at a range of theories of mental representation which are broadly compatible with the identity theory.

6. *Some kinds of mental states are systematically correlated with certain kinds of brain states*. According to the identity theory, mental states literally are brain states. Consequently, the identity theory smoothly explains the systematic correlation of mental states with brain states.

In the next section I briefly describe a historical case which strikingly illustrates the existence of mind-brain correlations.

3.3 Evidence from deficit studies

Deficit studies provide particularly striking evidence of mind-brain correlations. In a deficit study neuroscientists attempt to determine the function of a part of the brain by examining subjects who, due to brain damage, have lost a particular mental function. A great many mind-brain correlations have been explored in this way. In what follows I will sketch just one example to give the flavor of this research.

The 1840s was a period of great expansion of the American railway system. In those days construction teams relied on gunpowder to help clear away rock. A hole was drilled into the rock and a fuse inserted. The hole was then packed with gunpowder and the fuse lit. Everybody ran as fast and as far as possible before the gunpowder exploded. Finally, the rubble was cleared away by hand and the whole process repeated.

Phineas Gage was a highly responsible leader of a railway construction team. It was his job to carefully pack down the gunpowder before lighting the fuse—a process called 'tamping'. Gage had his own iron 'tamping rod' made. Now in a museum, it was just over a meter long and weighed around 6 kg. One end—the end inserted into the hole—was flat; the other pointed.

One day there was a terrible accident. It seems that Gage's tamping rod struck a spark from the wall of the hole, setting off the gunpowder prematurely. The rod, pointed end first, passed through Gage's left cheek and the front part of his brain (crucially, the prefrontal cortices), before exiting through the top of his skull. It was subsequently found some distance away. Incredibly, Gage survived. His personality was, however, drastically altered. Prior to the accident he was described as 'efficient and capable' (Damasio 1994: 4); after the accident he was careless and irresponsible. 'Gage', his friends observed, 'was no longer Gage' (Damasio 1994: 8). He could no longer hold down his job as team leader and began to drink heavily. He died in San Francisco at the age of thirty-eight.

The tragic case of Phineas Gage provides striking evidence of a correlation between a mental process—impulse control—and a part of the brain—the prefrontal cortices. Whilst Smart and his fellow identity theorists didn't know enough about the brain to predict the details of that particular correlation, cases like Gage's provide important support for their view.

3.4 Arguments against the identity theory

There are two important ways of arguing against the identity theory. The first way appeals to Leibniz's principle of the indiscernibility of identicals; the second involves the distinction between type identity and token identity. As we might expect, consciousness is a difficult problem for the identity theory; it will be discussed in the context of Leibniz's principle of the indiscernibility of identicals.

1. *Arguments based on Leibniz's principle*. As we saw in Section 1.2, Leibniz's principle of the indiscernibility of identicals says that if X and Y are identical, then they have all their properties in common. Example: say that Sally is the tallest person in the room. In that case, if Sally has an IQ of 175, so does the tallest person in the room; and if the tallest person in the room rides a Harley Davidson, so does Sally.

The example just given involves a case of token identity: Sally and the tallest person in the room are one and the same *individual*. However, Leibniz's principle also applies to types. For example, the type *water* is identical to the type H_2O. So if water boils at 100 degrees Celsius, so does H_2O; and if H_2O conducts electricity, so does water. Similarly if, as the identity theorist claims, pain is c-fiber firing, then any property of pain is a property of c-fiber firing, and vice versa. Consequently, if we can locate a property of pain which is not a property of c-fiber firing, or a property of c-fiber firing which is not a property of pain, then we will have proven the identity theory false.

Various suggestions have been made of properties which pain has but c-fiber firing does not, or vice versa. For example, my pain has the property of being located in my foot, whereas my c-fiber firing does not; my pain is sharp but c-fiber firings are neither sharp nor dull; and my c-fiber firing has a frequency (say 20 firings per second) whereas my pain has no frequency. Since my pain and my c-fiber firings have different properties, they cannot be identical. Consequently, the identity theory is false.

Let's take each of these examples in turn.

(i) *My pain is in my foot but my c-fiber firing is not*. In reply, the identity theorist can insist that, strictly speaking, my pain is not in my foot. The brain state which is identical to my pain is in my head. Rather than talk about a pain in my foot we should talk about having a pain of the in-the-foot kind. One state of my brain—call it 'B1'—is identical to my having a pain of the in-the-foot kind; another state of my brain—call it 'B2'—is identical to my having a pain of the in-the-hand kind; and so on.

The identity theorist's reply gains in plausibility when we reflect on the phenomenon of phantom pains. Some unfortunate folk who have lost a body part continue to feel pain which they say is in the missing part. For example, it is not uncommon for people who have had a foot amputated to experience what they call a pain in their foot. These pains can be excruciating, and are very difficult to treat. Now it's clear that there is no pain located in their foot for the simple reason that they have no foot. Rather, they have a brain state of the kind we earlier called 'B1'—a brain state identical to having a pain of the in-the-foot kind.

(ii) *My pain is sharp but nothing in my brain is sharp.* This argument takes too literally the expression 'sharp' in 'sharp pain'. Clearly, the expression is metaphorical. To have a sharp pain is to have a pain which feels a certain way—it is not to have a knife-like pain. The identity theorist can say that pains of the sharp kind are identical to a certain kind of brain state, whereas pains of the throbbing kind are identical to a different kind of brain state.

(iii) *My c-fiber firings have a frequency but my pains do not.* In reply to this objection the identity theorist will simply assert that we have discovered (somewhat surprisingly) that pains have a frequency. Remember that the identity theorist offers scientific identities like 'lightning is an atmospheric electrical discharge' as examples of the kind of identity she has in mind. Now if the identity between lightning and atmospheric electrical discharge is correct, lightning has a *voltage*. I guess that to the modern mind that may not sound too surprising, but two hundred years ago someone would have been puzzled by that claim. Similarly, given the current state of understanding of psychology and neuroscience, it will strike many people as a bit odd to say that pain has a frequency. Nevertheless, science has discovered that it does.

There is one more application of Leibniz's principle which we should briefly consider. There is something that it is like to be in pain—*it hurts*. On the other hand, it is very hard to conceive how electrical activity in a nerve cell could hurt. As Colin McGinn put it, how could technicolor consciousness arise from gray brain matter (McGinn 1991: 1)? So, it seems that pains have a property—hurting—which no brain state could ever have. Consequently, pains cannot be identical to c-fiber firing.

It must be admitted that consciousness raises very serious difficulties for the identity theory. However, further discussion of consciousness will be deferred until Part 4.

2. *Type identity and token identity revisited.* We saw in Section 3.1 that the identity theory identifies mental state types with brain state types. The emphasis on type identity has, however, been challenged. There is a general consensus amongst contemporary philosophers of mind that the type identities proposed by the identity theory have to be either restricted or replaced with token identities. To get

a grip on the concern about the type identities proposed by the identity theory, we will consider a few examples.

Let's agree that, for the sake of argument, in humans pain is c-fiber firing. Now we can easily imagine animals with nervous systems quite different from our own; more specifically, we can imagine animals which don't have c-fibers. Let's agree, again for the sake of argument, that squid have nervous systems quite different from our own and lack c-fibers. (This isn't at all implausible. The squid brain *is* very different from our own. From an evolutionary perspective, humans and squid are only very distantly related. You have to go back a very long way to find a creature which was an ancestor of both ourselves and the squid.)

So far we have assumed only that squid don't have c-fibers. It seems quite likely, though, that they experience pain (or at least we have no very good reasons to doubt that they can be in pain). Consequently, the identity theory is in trouble: if squid can lack c-fibers but feel pain, then it cannot be the case that pain is identical to c-fiber firing. Another example will help reinforce the point.

Imagine a group of aliens whose brains (if you can call them that) are made up of silicon chips. They certainly don't have anything even remotely like c-fibers. Nevertheless, we can imagine that they feel pain when, for example, they stub their toe on the way into the teletransporter, or get a sore throat from repeatedly shouting, 'Exterminate all Earthlings'.

The examples we have just considered support the idea that pain is identical to different physical states in different kinds of creatures. Pain is said to be **multiply realized**: in different creatures pain is 'realized' in different ways. One way to respond to the multiple realizability of pain is to restrict the type identities to species:

Pain-in-humans is type identical to c-fiber firings.

Pain-in-squid is type identical to d-fiber firings.

Pain-in-aliens is type identical to activity in silicon chip E.

This list of type identities could, in principle, be extended indefinitely. I will call the resulting theory of mental states the *restricted type identity theory* to indicate that the type identities proposed are restricted to a given species.

However, it's quite likely that there are relevant differences *within a single species*. For example, I believe that the Eiffel Tower is in Paris. Chances are you do too. So we both have a token of the type *belief that the Eiffel Tower is in Paris* 'stored' in our heads. However, it's likely that the exact way in which my token of that belief is stored in my head differs slightly from the way in which your token of that belief is stored in your head. Whilst there's good reason to think that the coarse anatomy of your brain is very similar to mine, and that the mechanisms whereby information is stored in the brain are similar in both cases, it's unlikely that information about the location of the Eiffel Tower is stored in precisely the same 'place' in both brains. Exactly how a piece of information is stored seems to depend on the other information your brain has already soaked up, and your brain has no doubt soaked up different information from mine.

By way of analogy, think about the way information is stored on the hard drive of a computer. The exact pattern of storage on a hard drive depends on the information already stored on it. New information often ends up scattered around on unused portions of the drive. Consequently, even if copies of the same document are stored on computers of the same model, it's unlikely that the document will be stored in exactly the same way in both machines.

So once again we have an example of multiple realization: the way your belief about the Eiffel Tower is realized will probably differ slightly from the way my belief is realized. However, unlike the pain case discussed earlier, these multiple realizations occur within a single species. (I am assuming here that you're a human being!) These considerations have led some philosophers of mind to abandon even the restricted type identity theory. On their view, the most we can say is that each mental state *token* is identical to some brain state token. In other words, these philosophers endorse only the token identity of mental states with brain states. I will sometimes refer to this view as the 'token identity theory'.

I will not try to settle the dispute between those who advocate the restricted type identity theory and those who only advocate the token identity of mental states and brain states. (If you want to explore that issue, see Further reading, below.) It's enough for our purposes to note that the identity theory, *as originally stated*, is mistaken: there are no simple type identities between mental states and brain states.

3.5 Reductive and nonreductive physicalism

The term 'reduction' is used in a great many ways, and for some people is a term of abuse. Even in the philosophy of mind the term is used in at least two ways.

1. *Intertheoretic reduction*. Sometimes it is possible to show that one theory (the 'reduced' theory) can be derived from another (the 'reducing' theory). In that case an **intertheoretic reduction** has been achieved. Notice that the emphasis here is on *theories*—'intertheoretic' means 'between theories'. The example of intertheoretic reduction standardly given is the derivation of classical thermodynamics from the kinetic theory of gases. The former theory describes the behavior of gases in terms of their temperature, pressure, and volume; the latter describes the behavior of gases in terms of the kinetic energy and impacts of gas molecules. The derivation is achieved with the help of 'bridge laws' which identify the terms of one theory with those of another. For example, the pressure of a gas is identified with the mean (or 'average') kinetic energy of its gas molecules.

2. *Ontological reduction*. Sometimes it's possible to show that what appear to be two distinct kinds of phenomena are in fact the same kind of phenomena; that is, sometimes we can establish type identities (see Section 3.2). In that case we can say that one phenomenon has been **ontologically reduced** to another. The classic example is water and H_2O. Water is type identical to H_2O, and the discovery that water is H_2O facilitated the (ontological) reduction of water to H_2O. (Why has water been reduced to H_2O rather than vice versa? The general idea is that chemistry has the resources to deal with a much wider range of phenomena than does a science that is restricted to studying water. Consequently, chemistry is held to be the more 'basic' or 'fundamental' science.)

We have seen that Smart's version of the identity theory proposes type identities between mental states and brain states. That is, it asserts a series of ontological reductions between the kinds found in psychology and those found in brain science: the former are to be (ontologically) reduced to the latter. Moreover, the identity theorist asserts that, if we can locate the appropriate bridge laws, psychology will be intertheoretically reduced to neuroscience. Smart's kind of physicalism is therefore often called *reductive* physicalism.

In contrast, the position which I have called the 'token identity theory' is a kind of *nonreductive* physicalism. It denies that there are type identities between mental states and brain states, and so is opposed to ontological reduction. Moreover, it denies that there is any meaningful sense in which intertheoretic reduction could be achieved. Since mental states are, according to the token identity theory, multiply realized, there can be no simple bridge laws linking mental states with brain states.

You might like to keep the expressions 'reductive physicalism' and 'nonreductive reductive physicalism' in mind as you read around the topic: you're very likely to come across them.

3.6 Conclusion

The identity theory has a great many advantages but also some striking disadvantages. Is it possible to avoid what is problematic about the identity theory without losing what is valuable? In the next chapter we will examine **functionalism** which neatly sidesteps the issues raised by multiple realization whilst retaining many of the attractive features of the identity theory.

SUMMARY

(1) According to the identity theory, mental states are brain states.

(2) According to the identity theory, the identities between mental states and brain states are analogous to scientific identities (e.g. water = H_2O).

(3) Types are kinds of things; tokens are individual members of types. Example: Lassie is a token of the type *dog*.

(4) According to the identity theory, the identities between mental states and brain states are type identities.

(5) The identity theory accounts for a number of the features of mental states discussed in the Introduction. In particular, it predicts the existence of mind-brain correlations.

(6) The multiple realization of mental states creates a major difficulty for the identity theory. The restricted identity theory and the token identity theory were developed in response to multiple realization.

(7) The identity theory is a kind of reductive physicalism; the restricted identity theory and the token identity theory are kinds of nonreductive physicalism.

FURTHER READING

The most important contemporary source for the identity theory is Smart's 'Sensations and Brain Processes' (1959); see also Place 1956. Good discussions of the identity theory can be found in Armstrong 1968: Ch. 6, Sections I–IV; Churchland 1988: 26–35; Braddon-Mitchell and Jackson 1996: Ch. 6; and Kim 1996: Ch. 3. The papers in Part 2 of Block 1980 are both relevant and of outstanding quality; they are, however, all rather hard. For an excellent discussion of the issue of token identity versus restricted type identity see Braddon-Mitchell and Jackson 1996: 96–101.

For a good discussion of intertheoretic reduction see Churchland 1986: Section 7.2. For more on reductive and nonreductive physicalism see Kim 1996: Ch. 9.

For a fascinating account of Phineas Gage's case see Damasio (1994: Chs 1 and 2).

TUTORIAL QUESTIONS

(1) Explain the type/token distinction.

(2) Give examples of (i) token identities and (ii) type identities.

(3) Does the identity theory assert type or token identities between mental states and brain states?

(4) Which of the features of mental states given in the Introduction can the identity theory easily account for? Which does it struggle to account for?

(5) The Phineas Gage case is an example of a deficit study. Can you find another example of a deficit study which reveals a mind-brain correlation?

(6) What does it mean to say that mental states are multiply realized?

(7) How does multiple realization challenge the identity theory?

(8) Describe (i) intertheoretic reduction and (ii) ontological reduction.

4

Functionalism

> . . . one of the major theoretical developments of twentieth-century analytic philosophy.
>
> —Ned Block

Philosophy is a hard subject, and even amongst professional philosophers there are major disagreements. The philosophy of mind is no exception, and as yet there is no consensus about the nature of mental states. (This is not to say that there has been no *progress* on the issue: we are now much clearer on which answers are the *wrong ones*, and we have a keener sense of what problems need to be solved.) Whilst there isn't complete agreement about the nature of mental states, it's fair to say that functionalism plays a central role in contemporary philosophy of mind. Even those philosophers who reject functionalism agree that they need to explain in detail what's wrong with it.

4.1 Introducing functionalism

In the previous chapter we noticed that mental states can be multiply realized. In humans the state which realizes pain is (say) c-fiber firing; in squid it's (say) d-fiber firing. Multiple realization raises a puzzle: what do old Eight-legs and I have in common when we are both in pain? It can't be c-fiber firing because Eight-legs has no c-fibers (or so I will assume). And it can't be d-fiber firing because I have no d-fibers (or so I will assume). In virtue of what, then, is it true that Eight-legs and I are both in pain?

Functionalism provides an answer to this puzzle. According to functionalism, c-fiber firing *does the same job* in me as d-fiber firing does in Flipper. On this view, to be in pain is to have an internal state which does a certain job. Which job is that? Very roughly, an internal state does the 'pain job' if it is caused by bodily damage and causes us to say 'ouch' and rub the sore spot. So, according to functionalism, to be in pain is to have an internal state which is activated by bodily damage and which causes us to say 'ouch' and rub the sore spot. More generally, according to functionalism, to be in (or have) mental state M is to have an internal state which does the 'M-job'.

Confused? Not to worry. Let's work through some analogies and a couple of examples. After that, I'm pretty sure you'll get the idea.

First analogy. Practically all cars have carburetors. A carburetor is a device which combines petrol with air and delivers the resulting mixture to the engine. In my car the carburetor is mainly made out of brass. (I drive an old Ford.) In more modern cars the carburetor is made out of a more sophisticated alloy. In the future, car manufacturers may make carburetors out of high-tech plastic. It doesn't matter what a carburetor is made out of as long as it can combine petrol with air and deliver the resulting mixture to the engine. That is, something is a carburetor because it does a certain job—mixing petrol with air and delivering the resulting mixture to the engine—not because it is made out of some particular material.

In summary, carburetors are multiply realized. What my carburetor has in common with yours is that they both perform the same job: they both combine petrol and air and deliver the resulting mixture to the engine. It is irrelevant that my carburetor is brass and yours some high-tech plastic. All that matters is that they get the job done.

Second analogy. An antibiotic is a substance which does a certain job: it kills disease-causing bacteria without doing serious harm to the patient. Penicillin kills disease-forming bacteria without doing undue harm to the patient; consequently it's an antibiotic. Erythromycin also kills disease-causing bacteria without doing serious harm to the patient; consequently it too is an antibiotic. However, penicillin and erythromycin have quite different chemical structures.

In summary, antibiotics are multiply realized. What penicillin and erythromycin have in common is that they both do the same job: they kill disease-causing bacteria without doing serious harm to the patient. It is irrelevant to their being antibiotics that penicillin and erythromycin have different chemical structures. All that matters is that they get the job done.

According to functionalism, mental states are in important ways like carburetors and antibiotics. What makes a carburetor a carburetor is that it does the 'carburetor job'; what makes an antibiotic an antibiotic is that it does the 'antibiotic job'. Similarly, what makes a mental state the particular state it is, is that it does the job associated with that mental state. Here are a few examples.

First example. Let's return to the case of pain. The doctrine of multiple realization says that pain can be realized in a variety of different ways. Functionalism explains the multiple realization of pain as follows. According to functionalism an organism

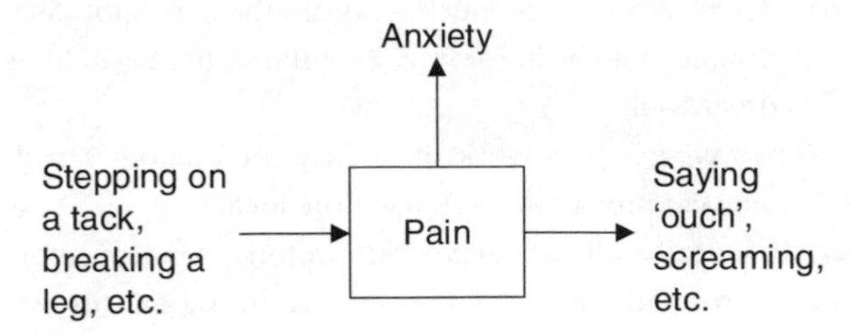

Figure 4.1 A highly simplified account of the pain role. The arrows represent the causal relation, with the arrowhead located at the effect

is in pain if it has a state inside it which does the pain job—or, as philosophers of mind prefer to say, if it has a state inside it which *occupies the pain role*. I'll say more about the pain role shortly—for the moment just think of it as the job pain does. Now in principle lots of different sorts of things could occupy the pain role, just as lots of different sorts of things can occupy the carburetor role or the antibiotic role. Consequently, pain is multiply realizable.

So what is the pain role? The pain role is defined in terms of *inputs, outputs,* and *internal connections*. The inputs are the circumstances which cause pain; they include stepping on a tack, breaking a leg, and burning your hand. The outputs are the behaviors which pain causes, including saying 'ouch', screaming, and rubbing the sore spot. The internal connections are the causal links between pain and other mental states. They include, for example, the causal link between pain and anxiety: pains (especially severe ones) often cause anxiety. (Figure 4.1 summarizes the pain role.) Putting all of this together, we can say that pain is a state which is caused by stepping on a tack (etc.), often makes us anxious, and causes us to say 'ouch' (etc.).

Second example. Consider my belief that a lion is near. (Let's assume that it's a wild lion.) On the input side my belief is caused by hearing a lion, or seeing a lion, or being told by a reliable witness that a lion is near. My belief has internal connections to, for example, fear: believing a lion is near very often causes fear. Things get more complex when we consider the output side. Typically, when we believe that there is a lion near we run away. That's because the belief that there is a lion near, together with the desire to live and the belief that the best way to escape is to run, causes running away. However, in combination with other beliefs and/or desires, my belief that there is a lion near may not cause me to run away. For example, imagine that Bloggs (foolishly) believes that the best way to escape from a lion is to stand perfectly still. In that case, his belief that there is a lion nearby, together with his desire to live, will cause him to stand perfectly still rather than run away. Again, imagine that Bloggs believes that there is a lion nearby and believes that the best way to escape is to run away, but does not desire to live. In that case he may do nothing at all.

4.2 Functionalism and brain states

So far we've noted that, according to functionalism, mental states are the occupants of characteristic causal roles. In addition we've noted that, since in principle the roles characteristic of the various mental states could be occupied by a variety of different states, functionalism explains the multiple realizability of mental states. We turn now to the relationship between functionalism and (i) type identity theory; (ii) restricted type identity theory; and (iii) token identity theory. (For an explanation of the various kinds of identity theory see Section 3.4.)

Descartes had been dead for a couple of hundred years before functionalism was invented, so it's very hard to know what he would have thought of functionalism. But let's imagine that Descartes had not only thought of functionalism, but decided to accept it as an accurate account of the nature of mental states. Would he have had to give up substance dualism?

It is in fact possible to be a functionalist *and* a substance dualist. Consider pain. According to functionalism, an organism is in pain in virtue of having a state which occupies the pain role. Now it's conceivable that the pain role could be occupied by a state of a nonphysical substance. Consequently, it's conceivable that *functionalist* substance dualism is true.

Contemporary functionalists are, however, physicalists. They take it to be overwhelmingly likely that the characteristic causal roles of the various mental states are occupied by physical states of the brain. In other words, if functionalism is true then it is very likely that *some version* of the identity theory is true.

The contemporary Australian philosopher David Armstrong and the American philosopher David Lewis (1941–2001) independently struck on a very neat way of expressing these ideas. I will call the Armstrong/Lewis argument the *Transitivity Argument* because it relies on the logical principle of the **transitivity of identity**. Let's start with that principle.

Say that the tallest person in the room is identical to Sally, and that Sally is identical to the smartest person in the room. Then by the transitivity of identity we can conclude that the tallest person in the room is identical to the smartest person in the room. Using ' = ' for 'is identical to', we can express the principle of the transitivity of identity like this:

1. A = B.
2. B = C.

Therefore,

3. A = C.

Let's return to functionalism and take pain as our example. According to functionalism, pain is identical to the occupant of the pain role. Let's call the occupant of the pain role 'R'. Thus we arrive at our first premise:

1. Pain = R.

Now let's assume for the moment that R—the occupant of the pain role—is identical to c-fiber firing. Thus we have our second premise:

2. R = c-fiber firing.

By the principle of the transitivity of identity we can now obtain:

3. Pain = c-fiber firing.

In other words, if we assume that the occupant of the pain role is c-fiber firing, we can derive the type identity theory of mental states from functionalism.

However, as we saw in Chapter 3, pain is very likely to be multiply realized; for example it may be the case that whilst in humans pain is identical to c-fiber firing, in squid it is identical to d-fiber firing. Consequently, the assumption that R is identical to c-fiber firing is very probably mistaken. Far more plausible is the claim that *in humans* R is identical to c-fiber firing. Reconstructing our argument we get:

1. Pain = R.

2′. In humans, R = c-fiber firing.

Therefore,

3′. In humans, pain = c-fiber firing.

The conclusion expresses what in Chapter 3 we called the 'restricted identity theory'.

Finally, it may turn out that even the restricted identity theory is false. Perhaps the most that we can say is that in Bloggs R is identical to some brain state B. In that case we can derive the token identity theory from functionalism:

1. Pain = R.

2″. In Bloggs, R = B.

Therefore,

3″. In Bloggs, pain = B.

We have seen that from functionalism we can derive three versions of the identity theory: the type identity theory, the restricted type identity theory, and the token identity theory. The three derivations differ in that each relies on a different second premise. In each case the second premise is an empirical claim—a claim that can only be established by observation and experiment. In the case of pain it's plausible that neuroscience will establish that the same type of brain state plays the pain role in all humans. However, it is likely that some mental states (for example, the belief that the Eiffel Tower is in Paris) are realized by subtly different brain states in different people.

4.3 Functionalism and the six features of mental states

In the previous section we saw that functionalism easily yields various versions of the identity theory. Consequently, functionalism's capacity to explain the six features of mental states identified in the Introduction closely parallels that of the identity theory.

1. *Some mental states are caused by states of the world.* We have seen that it is very likely that the states which occupy the functional roles characteristic of the various mental states are states of the brain. Consequently, for the functionalist the claim that some mental states are caused by states of the world is true only if some brain states are caused by states of the world. And, as we saw in Section 3.2, some brain states are indeed caused by states of the world.
2. *Some mental states cause actions.* Again recall that it is very likely that the states which occupy the functional roles characteristic of mental states are states of the brain. Consequently, for the functionalist the claim that some mental states cause actions is true only if some brain states cause actions. And, again as we saw in Section 3.2, some brain states do indeed cause actions.
3. *Some mental states cause other mental states.* If mental states are brain states, then the claim that some mental states cause other mental states amounts to the claim that some brain states cause other brain states. And that is certainly true. However, as we have noted in previous chapters, it's not merely the case that some mental states cause other mental states; in addition the causal relations between mental states sometimes mirror the rational relations between them. I'm getting a bit tired of the old examples, so here's a new one.

Say that Bloggs has a terrible hangover and that, whilst he can remember it's the weekend, he doesn't know which day of the weekend it is:

1. Bloggs believes that either it's Saturday or it's Sunday.

He then notices that he can't hear church bells, and realizes that it's not Sunday:

2. Bloggs believes that it's not Sunday.

Together, these two beliefs cause Bloggs to have a third belief:

3. Bloggs believes that it's Saturday.

Notice that in addition to the causal relation between Bloggs's beliefs, there is also a rational relation between them. (Strictly speaking there is a rational relation between the *contents* of Bloggs's beliefs.) The following is a valid argument:

1. Either it's Saturday or it's Sunday.

2′. It's not Sunday.

Therefore,

3′. It's Saturday.

So far we've just seen an example of the way in which the causal processes between mental states sometimes mirror the rational relations between them. Can functionalism explain that feature of mental states? The only detailed theory of this phenomenon we presently have—the computational theory—is in some important respects similar to functionalism. However, the computational theory insists that mental states are something more than the occupants of characteristic functional roles. In particular, it insists that they have a particular kind of *structure*. (We will develop this idea in Chapter 6.) If the computational theory is right, functionalism cannot be the whole story about mental states.

4. *Some mental states are conscious*. As usual, consciousness is a major headache. It seems that we can imagine a robot whose central computer has states which occupy the functional role characteristic of pain but which does not *feel* pain. If that's right, consciousness presents functionalism with a very serious problem.
5. *Some mental states are about things in the world*. In Chapter 9 we will see that there are, broadly speaking, two theoretical approaches to this issue. One of them—functional role semantics—sits very comfortably with functionalism. However the other approach, which includes the causal theory of content, requires at the very least additions to the basic functionalist framework.
6. *Some kinds of mental states are systematically correlated with certain kinds of brain states*. As we have noted, it's overwhelmingly plausible that the functional roles characteristic of the various mental states are occupied by brain states. Consequently, functionalism is compatible with the claim that there are systematic correlations between mental states and certain brain states.

Overall, the result is a mixed bag. Functionalism straightforwardly explains some of the six features; may succeed at explaining others; and struggles with the remainder.

We turn now to a pair of well-known antifunctionalist arguments.

4.4 Two famous arguments against functionalism

According to functionalism, mental states are the occupants of characteristic causal roles. This suggests two strategies for devising objections to functionalism. Consider some mental state M. If functionalism is true, any organism which is in M has a state which occupies the M-role, and any organism which has a state which occupies the M-role is in M. So, if we could find an organism that is in M but does not have a state which occupies the M-role, we would have shown functionalism to be false. Alternatively, if we could find an organism that has a state which occupies the M-role but which is not in M, we would have shown functionalism to be false.

The antifunctionalist arguments we will consider here all take the latter form: they all purport to describe a situation which, intuitively, involves no mental states but which is such that the relevant functional roles are occupied.

1. *The China Brain.* As we have seen, functionalists accept that, at least in principle, mental states could be realized by a wide range of physical—or even nonphysical—states. In the human case, mental states are most plausibly realized by brain states. We can, however, imagine them being realized by something quite different. For example, imagine that the entire population of China is enlisted to realize the mental states of a typical person—say Bloggs. The realization is achieved as follows. Each person in China is given a mobile phone and a set of instructions. The instructions tell them which numbers to ring when they have been rung by certain numbers.

For example, Jiang's instructions might be:

- If rung by 724 1144 then ring 722 9768 and 667 1849.
- If rung by 532 8181 and 95 5949 then ring 291 4245.

What Jiang is in fact doing is simulating the function of one of Bloggs's neurons—and this goes for every other person in China as well. Taken together, the population of China is simulating, neuron by neuron, Bloggs's brain. Consequently, whatever functional roles are occupied in Bloggs's brain are also occupied by the population of China. For example, if Bloggs believes that it is raining, the population of China believes that too. But that's absurd: a bunch of people ringing each other on mobile phones doesn't believe anything.

It's important to stress that when I say that according to functionalism the population of China believes that it is raining, I'm not referring to the beliefs of individual citizens. Rather, I'm referring to the entire population taken as a single unit. The point can be put this way. Say that there are a billion people in China, all of whom take part in the China Brain experiment. In that case, according to functionalism there will be a billion *and one* minds in China. There will be a billion minds each of which belongs to exactly one Chinese citizen, and there will be, in addition, the mind realized by the entire population during the phone link-up.

There would, of course, be very many *practical* difficulties in actually setting up the China Brain experiment. For one thing, there are far more neurons in the human brain than there are people in China. In addition, we don't know anywhere near enough about the human brain to write out the instruction sheets for the participants. Nevertheless, functionalism is committed to the view that *if* such an experiment were undertaken, the population of China really would realize a mind.

The China Brain is supposed to be a case in which all the relevant functional roles are occupied but the corresponding mental states don't exist. For some people, the intuition that the China Brain has no mental states is very strong. But should we accept that intuition? Two factors would appear to drive the intuition. In my view, careful consideration of those factors reveals that the intuition based on those factors isn't worth much.

First factor: consciousness. My guess is that many people will doubt whether what it's like for the China Brain to believe that it's raining is the same as what it's like for Bloggs to so believe. Indeed, I suspect that most people will think that there is *nothing* that it is like for the China Brain to believe this or fear that. But we have already admitted that consciousness is a big problem for functionalism; the question is whether the China Brain presents a *further* problem to functionalism. We can put the issue this way: would the China Brain have a mind identical in all *nonconscious* aspects to Bloggs's mind? Will it process the same stimuli in the same way to yield the same output? Will its thoughts follow the same patterns? I suspect that for most people the answer will be 'yes'. In other words, what was driving their initial claim that the China Brain would not have a mind was a worry about consciousness, and we have already acknowledged that functionalism has a problem with consciousness.

Second factor: chauvinism. Chauvinism is a bias in favor of the familiar. Racism is a kind of chauvinism because it's a bias in favor of the race most familiar to the racist—his or her own. Now the mind realized by the China Brain would be a very different sort of mind to those with which we are presently most familiar. The minds with which we are presently most familiar are human minds, and human minds are found inside skulls and are realized by billions of brain cells which communicate with each other using special chemicals called 'neurotransmitters'. In contrast, the China Brain is not found in any single skull. It is distributed throughout a billion skulls which are widely located over a vast country. Moreover, the China Brain's 'neurons' (i.e. the individual Chinese citizens) communicate with each other by mobile phones rather than by neurotransmitters. Consequently, there is a risk of chauvinism here—a risk of a bias in favor of minds realized in the way ours are realized.

Chauvinism about minds is nothing new. Europeans used to think that non-Europeans didn't have sophisticated minds. Such attitudes are now quite properly denounced as chauvinist. Similarly, some people have expressed chauvinism about animal minds, declaring that chimpanzees, for example, don't 'really' feel pain. But how do these cases differ from the China Brain? Isn't our rejection of the China Brain as mindless merely a chauvinistic refusal to accept that there might be minds realized in different ways to our own minds? Without an *argument* to show that the differences which exist between our minds and the China Brain's mind are significant, refusal to countenance the China Brain is just chauvinism.

In sum, the China Brain presents no *new* problems to functionalism. There is little reason to doubt that the China Brain's mind is identical in all nonconscious aspects to Bloggs's mind. Beyond that, it merely shows that, with a little bit of effort, we can create some pretty wild examples of multiple realization.

2. *Blockhead*. We are presented with choices every moment of our lives. Do I get up or stay in bed? Do I take a shower or a bath? Do I walk or take the bus? Usually we respond to a choice situation by *behaving* in some way: we stay in bed, or take a shower, or walk into town.

Now imagine that a scientist wants to build a robot which responds to every choice situation just as a typical human would respond. She begins by writing down all the circumstances the robot might find itself in: the alarm clock is ringing; in a café; in a burning building; on the Clapham bus; confronted by an enraged lion; and so on and on. (The list will be a very long one.) For each item on the list, the scientist thinks of a sensible response. So one small fragment of the list might look like this:

Circumstance	*Response*
The alarm clock is ringing.	Get up.
In a café at breakfast time.	Order breakfast.
In a burning building.	Find the fire escape.
On the Clapham bus.	Read a book.
Confronted by an enraged lion.	Run away.

The scientist now builds a robot which works as follows. First, the robot identifies the circumstances it is in. For example, it notes that it's in a burning building. It then searches through its list of possible circumstances until it finds the entry,

'In a burning building'. Next, the robot reads off the corresponding response, 'Find the fire escape'. Finally, it acts on that response—it looks for the fire escape. Since looking for the fire escape is exactly the sort of thing a typical human would do if they were in a burning building, the robot's behavior is just like that of a typical person.

The account of the robot I have just given is a bit rough. For one thing, descriptions like 'The alarm clock is ringing' and 'Order breakfast' are insufficiently precise. How a person responds to an alarm clock ringing depends on a number of factors including whether they are in bed or at an important meeting; the time of day the ringing takes place; and which day of the week it is. So the single entry, 'The alarm clock is ringing' needs to be replaced with a great many more specific entries with corresponding responses. (For example: The alarm clock rings on the morning of your exam → Get up.) Similarly, exactly how you order breakfast, and what you order, varies from place to place—there's probably not much point ordering kippers in central Mongolia. Consequently, the circumstance, 'In a café at breakfast time' needs to be refined, with each refinement matched to a refined response. (For example: In a café at breakfast time in central Mongolia → Order a glass of mare's milk.)

Second, the list of circumstances and responses needs to be carefully constructed so that the robot's responses are fairly consistent over time. People usually exhibit a degree of consistency in the responses they make to their circumstances: if a person has fried eggs, bacon, and sausages (with extra cholesterol) for breakfast, they're not likely to have a carrot sandwich (hold the butter) for lunch. Consequently, if the robot is to behave like a typical person, the list of circumstances and responses must exhibit an appropriate level of consistency.

The robot we have been discussing was first described by Ned Block (1981), and has since been called 'Blockhead' in his honor. In fact, Block's robot is a little different from the one just described as Block arranges the table of circumstances and responses into a branching structure called a 'look-up tree'. This technicality need not detain us; the robot as I have described it is enough to make Block's point. Let us turn now to the antifunctionalist argument Block makes with his Blockhead example.

Most people have the strong intuition that Blockhead has no mental states. That intuition is supported by the observation that Blockhead just blindly follows the instructions provided by the scientist. There is nothing going on inside Blockhead that looks remotely like deliberation. Blockhead no more has mental states than does a door bell which rings when you press a button. (Block himself remarked that Blockhead is no more intelligent than a toaster.) Block argues, however that functionalism is committed to the claim that Blockhead has mental states. If Block's right, functionalism is in big trouble.

Why might Block think that, according to functionalism, Blockhead has mental states? Consider what happens when Blockhead finds itself in a burning building. Seeing the flames causes Blockhead to search the list of circumstances for the entry, 'In a burning building'. Corresponding to that entry is the response, 'Find the fire escape', so Blockhead hurries around looking for the fire escape. Now, putting it crudely, functionalism says that Blockhead believes that it is in a burning building if it has an internal state caused by seeing flames and causing fire-escape-seeking behavior. And Blockhead does have such a state. As we have seen, the entry in the table of circumstances, 'In a burning building' is activated by seeing flames and causes fire-escape-seeking behavior. So, according to functionalism, Blockhead believes that it is in a burning building. But we have already seen that Blockhead has no mental states. So functionalism is false.

The trouble with Block's argument is that it misrepresents functionalism. When I sketched Block's argument I said that *putting it crudely* functionalism says that Blockhead believes that it is in a burning building if it has an internal state caused by seeing flames and causing fire-escape-seeking behavior. But that is to describe functionalism *far too crudely*. It's more accurate to say that, according to functionalism, the belief that the building is burning is a state which occupies a certain functional role. That role has inputs which include, but are not exhausted by, seeing flames; has outputs which include, but are not exhausted by, looking for the fire escape; and has internal connections to other mental states (for example to the belief that the situation is life threatening). Moreover, the outputs of the belief that the building is burning in part depend on the presence of other beliefs and desires. For example, the belief that the building is burning will only lead to fire-escape-seeking behavior in conjunction with the belief that the fire escape is the best way out of the building.

Once we articulate in a little bit of detail the functional role of the belief that the building is burning, it's clear that Blockhead has no such belief. Let's call the state in Blockhead which is caused by seeing flames and causes fire escape seeking the 'B-state'. The B-state would not cause fire extinguisher operating, nor would it cause 999 dialing, nor any of the other things people typically do when they believe the building is burning. Moreover, the B-state would not be caused by hearing the fire alarm or by being told by a reliable witness that the building's on fire. In addition, the B-state would not cause the belief that the situation is life-threatening, nor exhibit any of the other internal connections which the belief that the building is burning exhibits. And finally, the B-state's links to behavior do not involve any other mental states. In other words, the B-state does not occupy the functional role characteristic of believing that the building is burning, and so functionalism does not regard Blockhead as believing that the building is burning.

In sum, whilst the intuition that Blockhead has no mental states is very strong, that intuition is compatible with functionalism. Indeed, functionalism explains *why* Blockhead has no mental states.

4.5 Conclusion

Functionalism has made a very important contribution to our understanding of mental states. In particular it gives a beautiful account of multiple realization and allows us to understand much more clearly the relationship between mental states and brain states. Functionalism struggles to account for consciousness but—as we have seen—so does every other theory of mental states.

The real difficulty for functionalism lies, in my view, in explaining the rationality of thought. That's a theme to which we will return in Part 2.

SUMMARY

(1) According to functionalism, mental states are the occupants of characteristic causal roles.

(2) The causal roles of mental states are defined in terms of inputs, outputs, and connections to other mental states.

(3) Typically, a mental state causes behavior only in conjunction with other mental states.

(4) The Transitivity Argument has the following form:

(1) Mental state M = the occupant of causal role R.

(2) R = some brain state B.

Therefore,

(3) M = B.

Different versions of the identity theory are obtained by placing restrictions on the second premise.

(5) Functionalism readily accounts for some of the general features of mental states described in the Introduction. Whether functionalism can account for the remaining features remains an open question.

(6) Two standard objections to functionalism—the China Brain and the Blockhead—are not very convincing.

FURTHER READING

The classic early presentations of functionalism are Lewis 1966, Putnam 1967, and Armstrong 1968. Whilst these can all be recommended as marvelous examples of contemporary philosophical writing, Putnam's is probably the best place to start.

Excellent textbook presentations of functionalism can be found in Braddon-Mitchell and Jackson 1996, Chs 3 and 7, and Kim 1996, Ch. 5. Both books are quite a bit harder than this one.

What I have called the 'Transitivity Argument' was independently articulated by David Armstrong (1968) and David Lewis (1966, 1972, 1994). A more accessible discussion of the relationship between functionalism and the identity theory can be found in Braddon-Mitchell and Jackson 1996: Ch. 6.

Ned Block described both the China Brain and the Blockhead example in his important paper 'Troubles with Functionalism' (Block 1978). In that paper he also made significant distinctions between different types of functionalism, and discussed concerns about functionalism and consciousness.

TUTORIAL QUESTIONS

(1) Describe functionalism.

(2) In your view, which of the six features of mental states can functionalism handle?

(3) Sketch the Transitivity Argument, and show how functionalism is compatible with (i) the identity theory; (ii) the restricted identity theory; and (iii) the token identity theory.

(4) Describe the China Brain. Does it present a serious challenge to functionalism?

(5) Describe the Blockhead. Does it present a serious challenge to functionalism?

5

Eliminativism and fictionalism

I ain't got no use for what you loosely call the truth.

—Tina Turner

So far we've taken it for granted that mental states exist—that they're real. But what if mental states don't exist? What if they aren't real? Most of us are pretty confident that mental states are real, but it must be conceded that in the past people have been mistaken about the existence of all sorts of things. A thousand years ago there was widespread belief in the existence of dragons; now we know that dragons don't exist. A century ago it was believed that even 'empty' space was filled with a super-fine fluid called 'ether'. Now, thanks to Einstein, we know that ether doesn't exist. Couldn't a similar thing happen to our acceptance of mental states? Couldn't we come to reject mental states just as we have rejected dragons and ether?

Some philosophers think that we already have grounds for rejecting mental states. They think that mental states don't exist. Curiously, these philosophers are divided in their attitudes towards mental states. *Eliminativists* think that there are no mental states and it would be a good idea if we stopped kidding ourselves that there are. In contrast, *fictionalists* think that whilst there are no mental states, it's very useful to pretend that there are. We will return to this point towards the end of the chapter.

In order to understand **eliminativism** it's necessary to have a general grasp of the way in which theories give us access to reality. That's the topic of the next section.

5.1 From theory to reality

Why do we believe in atoms? After all, we can't *see* atoms in the way we can see bricks and books. In fact, even armed with the world's most powerful light microscope we can't see atoms. (Whilst images of atoms can be generated by electron microscopes, scientists were firmly convinced of the existence of atoms long before electron microscopes were invented.) Our belief in atoms cannot, therefore, be based on direct sensory evidence. Rather, we believe in atoms because our best theory of matter—atomic theory—says that there are atoms in the world.

The atomic theory of matter says that material objects like tables, air, water, and planets are made up of atoms. Over one hundred different sorts of atoms (or *elements*) have been identified. Each element has different properties, and the properties of the elements determine the ways in which the atoms interact. (There are a few elements—the so-called 'noble gases'—which barely interact at all.) Scientists have been able to explain a great many of the properties of matter in terms of the interactions between atoms, and this information has allowed them to develop new, high-tech, materials.

Atomic theory has been extremely effective at predicting and explaining the properties of matter. Consequently, we have reason to think that it's *true*—or at least that it is a close approximation to the truth. If there really are atoms with the properties described by atomic theory, then matter will behave as atomic theory says it does. Since matter behaves as atomic theory says it does, we have good reason for thinking that there really are atoms with the properties described by atomic theory. Of course, we can't be *absolutely sure* that there are atoms; it could be a fluke that atomic theory accurately describes the behavior of matter. Nevertheless, the likelihood of such a fluke occurring is exceedingly low.

Time for a little jargon. A theory **quantifies over** something when it says that that thing exists. Atomic theory quantifies over atoms; Einstein's theory of special relativity quantifies over space-time but—as we saw earlier—it doesn't quantify over ether.

We can now sum up this section. The success of a theory gives us reason to believe in the existence of the things over which the theory quantifies. In particular, our best theory of some phenomenon provides us with good reason to believe in the existence of the things over which that theory quantifies. Good theories give us access to the way the world actually is.

5.2 Introducing eliminativism

In the previous section we noted how our best theories give us good reason to accept as real the things over which they quantify. The flip-side of this doctrine is that bad theories don't give us good reason to believe in the things they quantify over. Accordingly, if some theory T is the only grounds we have for believing in some entity E, and T turns out to be a bad theory, then we no longer have grounds for believing in E. When this happens we say that E has *been eliminated:* we used to think that E existed, but it turned out that we were wrong and now we think that E doesn't exist. (Notice that eliminativism is *not* the doctrine that E used to exist but now it doesn't. Paleontologists are not eliminativists about dinosaurs; they merely think that dinosaurs are extinct.)

There are a couple of standard examples which are used to illustrate eliminativism. Let's quickly run through them before turning to eliminativism about mental states.

First example. 'Combustion' is the name given to the process of burning. An important eighteenth-century theory of combustion was the phlogiston theory. According to the phlogiston theory, burnable things (or 'fuel') contain phlogiston, and burning is the process whereby phlogiston is released from fuel. Things that aren't flammable—for example, bricks—contain no phlogiston.

The phlogiston theory has quite a bit of explanatory power. For example, with the addition of a further hypothesis it explains why sustained combustion requires a supply of fresh air. The additional hypothesis is that there is a limit to how much phlogiston a given volume of air can absorb. Once that limit is reached, no more phlogiston can be given off by the fuel, and so combustion ceases. A supply of fresh air sustains combustion by absorbing more and more phlogiston.

The phlogiston theory of combustion quantifies over phlogiston. For much of the eighteenth century, the phlogiston theory was the best theory available. Consequently, eighteenth-century scientists had good reason to believe in the existence of phlogiston. However, the brilliant French chemist Antoine Lavoisier proposed an alternative account of combustion: the oxygen theory. According to the oxygen theory, combustion is an interaction of oxygen and fuel. On this view, a supply of fresh air is needed to sustain combustion because the amount of oxygen in any given volume of air is limited. Once the available oxygen is used up, combustion ceases. A supply of fresh air sustains combustion by providing more and more oxygen.

Lavoisier's oxygen theory triumphed over the phlogiston theory because there was a striking fact about combustion which the oxygen theory could explain but the phlogiston theory could not. Somewhat surprisingly, the residue left over after combustion is complete *weighs more* than the original fuel. (Careful experiments are required to establish this result since the weight of any smoke released must be taken into account.) The increase in weight is very hard to explain on the phlogiston theory since, according to that theory, something is *given off* during combustion. On the other hand, the increase in weight is to be expected on the oxygen theory since, according to that theory, something is *absorbed* during combustion.

Scientists now universally accept that the phlogiston theory is false and that there is no such thing as phlogiston. In other words, phlogiston has been eliminated. We used to think that there was such a thing as phlogiston; now we realize that there is not.

Second example. Human populations are subject to epidemics in which a disease sweeps through a community, often with fatal results. The great plagues which swept Europe in the Middle Ages are well-known examples of epidemics. People living at that time theorized about the origin of the plague. One very popular idea was that the plague was caused by witches—women who had thrown their lot in with the devil. Let's call this idea the 'witch theory of epidemics'. The witch theory quantifies over witches, and it supported the widespread belief that witches existed.

Very few people in the Western world would subscribe to the witch theory of epidemics today. Due to Joseph Lister, Ignaz Semmelweis, and others, the germ theory of epidemics is now universally endorsed in the West. According to the germ theory, epidemics are caused by the rapid transmission of microscopic organisms from one person to the next. In other words, germ theory quantifies over germs. (I'm using the expression 'germs' here to cover the whole range of microscopic pathogens, including viruses.)

The rise of the germ theory and consequent demise of the witch theory has led to the elimination of witches. We used to think that there were such things as witches; now we believe in germs instead.

5.3 Eliminativism about mental states

According to eliminativism, there are no such things as mental states. What motivates this extraordinary conclusion? To understand the eliminativist's argument, we must first understand the idea of **folk psychology**.

Practically everyone will tell you that agony is a kind of pain; that pains are unpleasant; that people who stand in front of a tree in good light will see the tree; that seeing generally leads to believing; and that love is very different from hate. They will tell you that people can remember some things about their past but not others; that if Sally wants to buy a book and believes that the bookshop is open, she will go to the bookshop; and that if Sally believes that it's Friday she will almost certainly believe that tomorrow is Saturday.

These are just a small sample of the very many obvious claims about the mind that are accepted by just about everyone. Such claims are sometimes called 'platitudes' about the mind. Taken together, the platitudes paint a highly detailed picture of the mental states and their interactions with each other and the environment; in other words, taken together the platitudes constitute an informal theory about the mind. That theory is called 'folk psychology' (sometimes 'commonsense psychology'). Folk psychology quantifies over a range of entities—beliefs, desires, pains, emotions, perceptions, and so on—and attributes various properties to those states. For example, it claims pains are unpleasant and that wanting to buy a book (together with other beliefs and desires) causes bookshop-going behavior.

This is where we return to eliminativism. According to eliminativism, folk psychology is 'radically false'; consequently, the states it posits—the mental states—don't exist. Just as the failure of the phlogiston theory gave us reason to turn eliminativist about phlogiston, and the failure of the witch theory of epidemics gave us reason to turn eliminativist about witches, the failure of folk psychology gives us reason to turn eliminativist about mental states.

Why, though, do the eliminativists think that folk psychology is a radically false theory? We will briefly explore three arguments offered by eliminativists against folk psychology. (These arguments are all from Churchland 1981: Section II.)

1. *Folk psychology is a 'stagnant research program'*. Scientific theories sometimes give rise to what are called 'scientific research programs'. A scientific research program consists of a number of scientists who share a common conception of what scientific problems need to be addressed, and how to address them. Newton's theories, for example, gave rise to a scientific research program which flourished for about two hundred years. It consisted of a number of scientists who applied Newton's theories to a large range of scientific problems. Research programs are said to be *progressive* when the scientists involved make a lot of progress; and they are said to be *stagnant* when the scientists fail to make significant progress. Stagnant programs are generally abandoned in favor of progressive ones, and are eventually forgotten by everyone except historians of science. (See Lakatos and Zahar 1978.)

Eliminativist Paul Churchland suggests that folk psychology is analogous to a scientific research program—a research program in which we are all engaged. And he suggests that it's a stagnant research program because it has made no progress—indeed, it has hardly changed—for centuries. Since folk psychology is a stagnant research program it's likely to be replaced by a more progressive one. In other words, folk psychology is likely to go the way of the witch theory of epidemics and the phlogiston theory of combustion. (In Churchland's opinion, neuroscience is likely to be the progressive research program which supplants folk psychology.)

Reply. It must be admitted that, in general, stagnation is evidence against a research program. So the crucial question is this: is folk psychology a stagnant research program? Churchland has urged that it is, but the issue is more complex than he makes out. To see why, we need to distinguish between folk psychology and theories in scientific psychology which, whilst closely related to folk psychology, are nevertheless advances on folk psychology. Let me explain.

We have seen that folk psychology quantifies over a range of mental states including perceptions, sensations, emotions, and—importantly—propositional attitudes like beliefs and desires. Churchland's claim is that, since folk psychology is a stagnant research program, it's unlikely that these states exist. However, many theories in scientific psychology quantify over a similar range of states. Indeed, it's reasonable to suggest that scientific psychology has made important discoveries about the mental states originally posited by folk psychology. Here's an analogy. The ancient Greeks had ingenious arguments which showed that matter consisted of very tiny particles which they called 'atoms'. According to the Greeks, atoms were indivisible. However, we now know that atoms are *not* indivisible. In other words, modern physics has made important discoveries about the entities which the Greeks called 'atoms'. Similarly, modern psychology has made important discoveries about the entities originally posited by folk psychology. It has discovered, for example, that beliefs are not necessarily conscious. Consequently, whilst folk psychology itself may be a stagnant research program, it does not follow that the entities over which it quantifies don't exist since the very same entities are extensively discussed by highly progressive research programs in scientific psychology.

It will be helpful to have a label for those scientific psychological theories which quantify over states originally posited by folk psychology. For want of a better term I will, for the remainder of this chapter, use the term 'scientific folk psychology' for any such theory.

2. *Folk psychology fails to illuminate many important features of our mental lives.* Churchland draws attention to a wide range of topics about which folk psychology is largely silent. His list includes mental illness, creativity, sleep, vision, memory, and learning. These are important aspects of our cognitive lives, and any psychological theory which fails to contribute to our understanding of them is decidedly unattractive.

Reply. This argument is very similar to the previous one. In part folk psychology strikes us as stagnant because it fails to address the sorts of issues Churchland mentions. In replying to the previous argument we noted that whilst folk psychology itself may not have changed much for centuries, scientific folk psychology has made brisk progress. In particular, these sorts of theories have important things to say about many of the items on Churchland's list. I will briefly mention three examples.

First example: mental illness. According to an influential theory of depression, depressed people hold erroneous beliefs about themselves; in particular, they believe that they are much less capable of dealing with life's difficulties than they really are. This has led to a form of therapy in which the therapist helps the patient identify and correct their erroneous self-beliefs. Interestingly, these forms of therapy are approximately as efficacious as drug therapies. For our purposes what is important is that this theory of depression quantifies over states which are quite recognizably folk psychological—beliefs about oneself.

Second example: vision. According to many contemporary theories of vision, seeing involves processing information. Some of this information is present in the retinal image; some of it is provided by the visual mechanisms themselves. The information-bearing states postulated by these theories are similar in important ways to the beliefs postulated by folk psychology. For example, both have content and both are involved in rational inferences.

Third example: memory. Folk psychology recognizes that we can store and retrieve information from memory. Scientific psychology also recognizes that fact, although it has gone much further than folk psychology in exploring both the varieties and limitations of human memory. For example, scientific psychology recognizes both *short-* and *long-term* memory, and has explored the relationship between them. Moreover, scientific psychology has discovered that there are quite distinct forms of memory involved in the storage and recall of different sorts of linguistic information. Interestingly, these different sorts of linguistic memory are stored in subtly different areas of the brain. Whilst scientific psychology has made many important discoveries about memory, it's clear that these are discoveries about a process originally identified by folk psychology.

3. *Folk psychology lacks extensive evidential links with the sciences.* One of the striking facts about science is the way scientific theories support each other. Here's my favorite example of this phenomenon. Darwin's theory of natural selection is supported by evidence from a vast range of other scientific endeavors. The theory of continental drift plays an important role in understanding the distribution of species; geology more generally has provided crucial evidence about the age of the Earth. Genetics plays an essential role in explaining how the fittest organisms pass on their genes, and biochemistry has played an essential role in understanding the chemical basis of genetics. Comparative anatomy has helped construct plausible hypotheses about the interrelationships of species, and the physics of isotopes has played a crucial role in dating the ancient remains of animals and plants. The list goes on and on. In each case the theory of natural selection gains support—sometimes a lot; sometimes just a little—from other scientific research.

Any theory which lacks these sorts of connections to other well-established theories is likely to be largely unsupported. According to Churchland, folk psychology is just such a theory, lacking almost entirely significant connections with other well-established theories. We have therefore further grounds for thinking that folk psychology may indeed be radically false.

Reply. It's hardly surprising that folk psychology lacks a rich network of connections to scientific theories. After all, folk psychology is not a scientific theory. Rather, folk psychology is a collection of platitudes which ordinary people are inclined to accept, and ordinary people are not likely to be sufficiently knowledgeable about science to explore in detail the connections between folk psychology and, say, neurobiology. Moreover, there *are* connections between scientific folk psychology and various other sciences. For example, there is currently a great deal of interest in connecting theories in scientific folk psychology to research in the theory of evolution.

5.4 Anti-eliminativist arguments

So far we have considered three arguments which seek to support eliminativism by debunking folk psychology. In this section I will briefly discuss two anti-eliminativist arguments.

1. *The predictive success of folk psychology*. Eliminativists often draw attention to folk psychology's failings. However, we must not overlook folk psychology's *successes*. A number of theorists—especially the contemporary American philosopher Jerry Fodor—have emphasized how impressive folk psychology is as a predictive tool. Here's an example of a successful folk psychological prediction. My students can predict with considerable reliability where I will be at 10 a.m. next Monday morning: they know that I will be in Lecture Theater North 1. They can do this because they have attributed to me certain folk psychological states. For example, they know that I *believe* that my philosophy of mind lecture starts at 10 a.m. every Monday and is located in Lecture Theater North 1, and they know that I always *like* to get to class on time.

So commonplace are predictions of this kind that we tend to forget how remarkable they are. Notice that predicting where I will be at 10 a.m. next Monday morning is completely beyond the powers of contemporary neurosciences. Even if my brain was subjected to the most rigorous testing currently available, neuroscientists could not predict the movements I will make in five days' time. Nevertheless, my undergraduate students can easily and accurately predict where I will be in five days' time. So when it comes to predicting the movements of human beings, folk psychology completely trumps neuroscience.

A theory which is so predictively successful deserves our respect. Of course, predictive success does not *guarantee* truth. Newton's theories, for example, were staggeringly predictively successful but turned out to be wrong. However, in general predictive success is evidence in favor of a theory, and folk psychology has predictive success in spades.

2. *The success of scientific folk psychology*. In the previous section we noted that much scientific psychology quantifies over states originally posited by folk psychology. For want of a better term, I called such theories 'scientific folk psychology'. We saw that scientific folk psychology is highly successful at explaining a range of features of our cognitive lives. As we discussed in Section 5.1, the success of a theory gives us good reason to accept the existence of the states over which it quantifies. Since scientific folk psychology is successful, and since it quantifies over folk psychological states, we have good reason to think that those states actually exist.

5.5 Fictionalism

Fictionalism in the philosophy of mind is the doctrine that, whilst strictly speaking there are no mental states, it's extremely useful to pretend that there are. (Fictionalism is also known as 'instrumentalism' since it views the attribution of mental states as having instrumental value—and nothing more.) In this section I'm going to take Daniel Dennett's position as my example of fictionalism. Dennett sometimes objects to being labeled a 'fictionalist'; however, at least some of his writings strongly give the impression that he is one. My apologies to Professor Dennett if I've misrepresented him.

Let's begin by acknowledging just how useful is the ascription of mental states. Following Dennett, we can recognize three 'stances' from which we can predict the behavior of a complex system like a chess-playing computer or a human being: the *physical* stance; the *design* stance; and the *intentional* stance.

1. *The physical stance*. Both chess-playing computers and human beings are physical objects. Setting aside worries about quantum indeterminacy, the behavior of both chess machines and humans can in principle be predicted by treating them as vast assemblages of elementary physical particles, and applying the laws of physics to those particles. Predicting the behavior of a system in this fashion is called 'taking the physical stance'. For all but the simplest systems, the physical stance is unworkable: the number of particles and the complexity of their arrangements makes practical prediction impossible.

2. *The design stance*. Sometimes it is possible to predict the behavior of a complex system by thinking about what it is *supposed to do*. For example, the people who designed my laptop and the software it's running intended it to follow the rule 'When the *p* key is pressed display the letter 'p' on the screen'. Knowing that that's how my laptop is supposed to work, I can predict what will happen when I press the *p* key.

Making predictions about a system's behavior by thinking about what the system is supposed to do is called 'taking the design stance'. Of course, the design stance doesn't always work. If my software has a bug in it, or if I've forgotten to recharge the battery, pressing the *p* key might not result in the letter 'p' appearing on the screen. (I once dropped a cup of coffee on the keyboard of my computer. Thereafter the only key which worked was the *z* key, and it worked whether I pressed it or not!) When the design stance fails to yield accurate predictions we usually retreat to the physical stance. That is, we stop thinking about what the system is supposed to do, and treat it as a physical object which obeys the laws of physics.

Chess-playing computers are artifacts. They are designed by smart people so that they play chess competently. In the case of artifacts it's usually obvious what the system is supposed to do. But what about human beings and other biological systems? What are they 'supposed' to do? At this point Dennett appeals to Darwin's theory of natural selection: biological systems are 'supposed' to do whatever it is that they were selected to do. Eyes, for example, were selected to provide visual information about the organism's environment, so eyes are 'supposed' to see. The inverted commas around 'supposed' are important. If Darwin's right about the evolution of organisms, nobody designed the eye or intended the eye to do anything. Rather, eyes are the outcome of a great many tiny changes to a pre-existing structure. (For a brilliant introduction to the theory of natural selection see Dawkins 1986.) Consequently, if we are being very careful we should say that the design stance predicts what a complex system will do by considering what it was designed *or naturally selected* to do.

3. *The intentional stance*. Sometimes even the design stance is, in practice, unworkable. This happens when the design is too complicated or simply unknown to us. At this point we can adopt the intentional stance. The intentional stance begins with the assumption that the complex system in question is rational—it believes what it should believe and desires what it should desire. For example, the intentional stance assumes that if you are staring at a nearby cow in good light you will come to believe that there is a cow nearby; and that if you need some cash you will desire to go to the bank. (Old joke. Social worker: 'Why do you rob banks?' Criminal: 'Because that's where the money is.')

Now if we assume that the complex system in question is rational, we can predict its behavior. For example, I can predict what you will do when you are driving a car and approach a red light. First, I can assume you believe that the traffic light is red. Second, I can assume you desire to stop at red lights. (By and large, driving through red lights is not a rational form of behavior!) Putting this together, I can predict that you will stop at the red light. And chances are, I'll be right.

In practice attributing mental states to people is indispensable. Applying the physical stance to systems as complex as human beings is very often simply impossible. Moreover, we don't as yet have a complete understanding of what the various neural systems of the human brain were selected for (or 'supposed' to do). Consequently, when it comes to predicting human behavior we usually rely on the attribution of mental states.

How does all this connect with fictionalism? Dennett notes that we can apply the intentional stance to a chess-playing computer, saying things like, 'It wants to save its knight' or, 'It thinks it should get its queen out early'. However, Dennett asserts that if we actually look at the chess-playing program we will find nothing which corresponds to the attributed thoughts. Very roughly, chess-playing computers work by identifying the available moves and assigning each move a number. The number represents the attractiveness of the move, and the computer executes that move which has the highest number. The algorithms which assign the numbers don't contain instructions like, 'Get the queen out early'. Dennett concludes that, whilst attributing beliefs and desires to the computer is very useful—perhaps even unavoidable—it doesn't really have any beliefs and desires. Similarly, whilst attributing beliefs and desires to other people is very useful—perhaps even unavoidable—if you look inside us you quickly realize that there are no such things as beliefs and desires.

Two comments are in order.

1. The argument from the chess-playing computer to fictionalism about mental states in general is too quick. Notice that we're not inclined to take the attribution of mental states to chess-playing computers very seriously. Most of us dismiss talk about what the computer does or does not believe as 'anthropomorphizing'. (To anthropomorphize something is to inappropriately treat it as a human being. Some people anthropomorphize their pet fish.) If we're right not to attribute beliefs and desires to chess-playing computers, then the fact that there's nothing in the program that looks like a belief or a desire isn't surprising. Moreover, it may yet turn out to be the case that the neural correlates of beliefs and desires will be discovered in our heads. At present we simply don't know enough about the brain to rule out finding beliefs and desires inside our skulls.
2. One of the things which Dennett is fond of stressing is that the intentional stance *works*. And surely he's right to this extent: we can very often predict behavior by thinking about the beliefs and desires of the person in question. Now as we saw in Section 5.3, our everyday network of ideas about mental states constitutes a theory—folk psychology. And, as we saw in Section 5.2, other things being equal the predictive success of a theory is good evidence that

the theory is true. It follows that the predictive success of folk psychology is evidence for its truth. In other words, there is a very considerable tension between Dennett's assertion that the intentional stance is so good as to be indispensable, and his claim that mental states are mere fictions. (In this context it's worth recalling Paul Churchland's eliminativist strategy as described in Section 5.3: he didn't praise folk psychology; rather he set out to show that it's a *lousy* theory.)

5.6 Conclusion

We should accept that mental states might not exist—after all, history is full of examples of people believing in things that turned out not to exist. But that's a pretty big 'might'. At present we have little reason to think that mental states don't exist, and consequently we have little reason to endorse either eliminativism or fictionalism.

SUMMARY

(1) Eliminativism is the doctrine that mental states don't exist.

(2) Like eliminativism, fictionalism denies the existence of mental states, but insists that it's very useful to *pretend* that they exist.

(3) Other things being equal, the predictive success of a theory is evidence for its truth.

(4) Taken together, the everyday platitudes about mental states constitute a theory of the mind. That theory is usually called 'folk psychology'.

(5) Eliminativists like Paul Churchland argue that folk psychology is 'radically false' and that consequently we have no reason to accept that there are mental states. However, Churchland's arguments against folk psychology are open to question.

(6) Dennett has identified three 'stances' from which we can predict the behavior of complex systems like chess-playing computers and human beings. Of these, the intentional stance attributes mental states to the system in question on the assumption that the system is rational.

(7) According to Dennett the intentional stance is, in practice, very often the only available means of prediction.

(8) Dennett argues that, whilst we readily attribute mental states to chess-playing computers, there is nothing inside the machine that corresponds to the mental states we have attributed.

(9) Similarly, he holds that whilst attributing mental states to humans is pretty much unavoidable, there are unlikely to be things inside our heads which correspond to mental states.

(10) Dennett's position faces the following difficulty: if mental states are merely fictional, why does attributing them to complex systems work so well?

FURTHER READING

The classic presentation of eliminativism is Paul Churchland's paper 'Eliminativist materialism and the propositional attitudes' (Churchland 1981). This is not merely important and provocative, it's also highly readable. Another important source is Stephen Stich's book, *From Folk Psychology to Cognitive Science* (Stich 1983).

I highly recommend Horgan and Woodward's reply to Churchland, 'Folk psychology is here to stay' (Horgan and Woodward 1985). For a functionalist reply to eliminativism see Jackson and Pettit 1993. Jerry Fodor brilliantly defends folk psychology in his book *Psychosemantics* (Fodor 1987). Chapter 1 is especially recommended.

The idea of a scientific research program is due to Imre Lakatos. See, for example, Lakatos and Zahar 1978. For a good discussion of Lakatos's views see Newton-Smith 1981: Ch. 4.

Dennett's most important papers are 'Intentional Systems' (Dennett 1971) and 'True Believers' (Dennett 1975). Dennett sometimes objects to being labeled a 'fictionalist'; however, you could be forgiven for thinking he is one. He discusses his attitude to realism about mental states in his paper 'Reflections: Real patterns, deeper facts, and empty questions' (Dennett 1987*b*). Fodor briefly raises the issue of why folk psychology works if it's actually false in his 1990*a*. (My guess is that he's not the only one to air this worry.)

Braddon-Mitchell and Jackson 1996: Ch. 13 and Sterelny 1990: Ch. 7 are both excellent secondary sources on eliminativism. Braddon-Mitchell and Jackson 1996: Ch. 9 is also good on the intentional stance and fictionalism.

TUTORIAL QUESTIONS

(1) What is eliminativism?

(2) What is folk psychology?

(3) Sketch Churchland's reasons for thinking that folk psychology is radically false. Do you think that his reasons are good ones?

(4) Discuss the following argument. 'Churchland tells us that there are no such things as beliefs. In other words he *believes* that there are no such things as beliefs. But that's a contradiction. So eliminativism is false.'

(5) Describe Dennett's three stances.

(6) Why does Dennett think that the chess-playing computer does not really have beliefs and desires?

(7) 'The predictive success of folk psychology gives us good reason to reject Dennett's fictionalism.' Discuss.

Part Two

Mind as machine

6

The computational theory of mind

the only game in town

—Jerry Fodor

Science fiction is full of computers and robots that can think. HAL, the computer in Stanley Kubric's *2001: A Space Odyssey*, is perhaps the most famous example, but there are lots of others: K9 in *Doctor Who*; Data in *Startrek TNG*; and—my personal favorite—the Terminator in (you guessed it) the *Terminator*. We have become comfortable, it would seem, with the idea that a machine could have thoughts. The **computational theory of mind** takes this idea one step further. According to **computationalism** the mind is, quite literally, a computer.

In this chapter we will explore the idea that the mind is a computer. In order to understand that idea we need to be clear about what a computer is. That's the task of Section 6.2. However, before we can understand what a computer is, we first need to understand the distinction between **syntax** and **semantics**. That's the task of the next section.

6.1 Syntax and semantics

It will be helpful to have a rough-and-ready distinction between *basic symbols* and *complex symbols*. A basic symbol is one which has no meaningful parts; a complex symbol is one which is made up of two or more basic symbols. I will use English words as examples of basic symbols, and I will use English sentences as examples of complex symbols. Thus, 'Fodor' is a basic symbol whereas 'Fodor wrote *The Modularity of Mind*' is a complex symbol. (It might be argued that English words can't be basic symbols because they contain meaningful parts—the letters out of which they are assembled. For present purposes I will ignore this complication.)

The syntactic properties of a symbol are the properties which can be detected simply by examining the symbol in isolation. Here are some examples. Consider the basic symbol 'Fodor'. Just by examining that symbol you can work out that it consists of five letters in a certain arrangement. (Strictly, it consists of five letter *tokens*. For the distinction between types and tokens see Section 3.1.) You can also work out that the symbol is black on white and that it is less than three centimeters long. These are all syntactic properties of the symbol 'Fodor'. In contrast, you can't work out that the symbol 'Fodor' refers to a famous American philosopher just by examining it. Nor can you tell the name and address of the typesetter who arranged that symbol on the page. So the properties 'refers to a famous American philosopher' and 'was typeset by Bloggs of 44 Carbuncle St London' are *not* syntactic properties.

It's very common for the syntactic properties of a symbol to be called the symbol's 'shape'. That's not surprising as shape is a good example of a syntactic property. In written English it is customary to end a question with a special symbol—the question mark. That symbol has a characteristic shape—?. We can easily recognize the question mark symbol by its shape. Indeed—and this will come up again later—a *machine* can recognize the question mark symbol by its shape. So shape is a syntactic property. If you're having trouble keeping in mind what the syntactic properties are, just think of them as a symbol's shape. You won't be far wrong.

What about the semantic properties of symbols? Roughly speaking, semantic properties are properties connected with the *meaning* of a symbol. For example, the **reference** of a symbol—what it refers to—is a semantic property. To continue with our example, the basic symbol 'Fodor' refers to a famous American philosopher. The **truth value** of a symbol—whether it is true or false—is also a semantic property. Note, though, that not all symbols have a truth value. The symbol 'Fodor', for example, is neither true nor false. Whilst it is true that Fodor wrote *The Modularity of Mind* and false that Fodor wrote *Alice in Wonderland*, 'Fodor' by itself is neither true nor false.

What kinds of symbols have truth values? Some (but not all) complex symbols have truth values. The complex symbol 'Fodor wrote *The Modularity of Mind*' is true; the complex symbol 'Fodor wrote *Alice in Wonderland*' is false. Both of these complex symbols make a claim about the world. The first example claims that the world is one in which Fodor wrote *The Modularity of Mind*; the second claims that the world is one in which Fodor wrote *Alice in Wonderland*. In general, symbols have the semantic properties of truth or falsity if and only if they make a claim about the world. It is now obvious why the symbol 'Fodor' is neither true nor false. By itself, 'Fodor' makes no claim about the world.

Unlike the syntactic properties, the semantic properties *cannot* be detected by examining a symbol in isolation. Think again about the symbol 'Fodor', and assume you have no idea who (or what) Fodor is. You can stare at that symbol for as long as you like and you will never work out what it refers to. In order to know that the reference of 'Fodor' is a famous American philosopher, you have to look beyond the symbol itself. In particular, you have to work out which person is connected in the right way to that symbol. Similarly, examining the complex symbol 'Fodor wrote *Alice in Wonderland*' in isolation will not allow you to determine its truth value. You have to look at the world beyond the symbol in order to determine that 'Fodor wrote *Alice in Wonderland*' is false.

In summary, the syntactic properties of a symbol can be detected just by examining the symbol. Shape is a good example of a syntactic property. Semantic properties are connected with meaning and include properties like reference and truth value. Since you cannot determine a symbol's semantic properties by examining it in isolation, semantic properties are not syntactic properties. With the distinction between syntactic and semantic properties in place, we can turn to the question, 'What's a computer?'.

6.2 What's a computer?

In this section I'm going to describe what a computer is. I'm not going to talk about keyboards and monitors; rather, I'm going to give a very general description of computation which abstracts away from a great many of the details of real computers.

Speaking very generally, a computer has two features.

1. Computers recognize and manipulate symbols *solely on the basis of their syntactic properties*. Here's an example. I can use the 'find' function of my word processing program to locate the 'Fodor' symbols in the document I'm presently typing. My computer recognizes those symbols by their syntactic properties—perhaps my computer recognizes 'Fodor' symbols by their shape. (Electronic computers don't usually recognize symbols by their shape, but let's pretend they do.) What's especially important is that computers don't recognize symbols by their semantic properties. That's not surprising. After all, my computer has no idea at all what the symbol 'Fodor' refers to. Perhaps 'Fodor' refers to a cat; perhaps it refers to the seventh moon of the seventh planet of Alpha Centuri. My computer simply does not know. *All* my computer has to go on are the properties of symbols which can be detected in isolation; that is, *all* my computer has to go on are the syntactic properties of symbols. So computers are 'syntactic engines'—devices which recognize and manipulate symbols on the basis of their syntactic properties.
2. Whilst computers recognize and manipulate symbols solely on the basis of their syntactic properties, they can nevertheless be arranged so that the way the symbols are manipulated respects the semantic properties of those symbols. Thus it is easy to program a computer so that it begins with the following two complex symbols:

   A. All philosophers are funky.

   B. Fodor is a philosopher.

And ends up with the following complex symbol:

C. Fodor is funky.

The computer recognizes and manipulates the various symbols involved by their syntactic properties; it *does not* recognize and manipulate those symbols on the basis of their semantic properties. After all, the computer does not know who Fodor is, does not know what a philosopher is, and does not know what it is to be funky. Nevertheless, the transition from A and B to C is truth preserving: if A and B are true then C is too. So, whilst the computer is sensitive only to syntactic properties, it manages to respect semantic properties like truth value.

Notice that the transition the computer makes from A and B to C is rational in this sense: the first two complex symbols *provide evidence for* the last one. This is an example of the way that computers can be programmed to carry out at least some kinds of rational inference. We noted way back in the Introduction that the causal relations between thoughts often mirror the rational relations between those thoughts. Computers provide us with our first hint of how that might be achieved.

To sum up, a computer is a device which recognizes and manipulates symbols on the basis of their syntactic properties, but still manages to respect semantic properties like truth value.

It's worth briefly mentioning that computational states and processes are multiply realizable. That is, devices which are physically quite different can nevertheless be in the same computational states and realize the same computational processes. It happens to be convenient to realize computational states and processes in electronic circuits, but in principle they can be realized by a wide range of devices. (See Weizenbaum 1976: Ch. 2 for an explanation of how to build a computer out of toilet paper and stones!) Even amongst electronic computers there is considerable diversity. Your PC and my Mac can undertake exactly the same computations even though they are, from an engineering point of view, quite different.

In the next section I will briefly describe an incredibly simple computer. The simplicity of the computer helps make it clear that it's a syntactic engine. However, it is also clear that its symbolic manipulations respect certain semantic properties.

6.3 Turing machines

Turing machines are very simple computers which, nevertheless, are extremely powerful. Strictly speaking, there are no Turing machines in the sense that no one could ever build one. However, thinking about the design and capabilities of

Turing machines has been very important in the development of mathematical logic and the theory of computation. (Turing machines were the brainchild of Alan Turing (1912–54), an extraordinary British mathematician who, besides making important contributions to mathematical logic and the theoretical foundations of computer science, was involved in cracking the German navy's 'Enigma' code during the Second World War. For a fascinating account of his life and achievements see Hodges 1983.)

A Turing machine consists of three parts.

1. A very long tape (for example, a very long strip of paper) divided into squares. (Strictly speaking, the tape should be infinitely long; hence, strictly speaking, Turing machines can't be built.) Symbols can be written in the squares. There is a finite 'alphabet' or list of symbols.
2. A 'head' which can do the following four things:

   (i) read the symbol in a square;
   (ii) erase the symbol in a square and replace it with another symbol from the alphabet;
   (iii) move one square either left or right; and
   (iv) halt (that is, cease all activity).

   What the head will do on any one occasion is determined by the symbol it is reading and the 'state' it's in. (More about states in a moment.)
3. A 'machine table' which specifies for each symbol in the alphabet and each state of the head what the head should do. The machine table will specify whether the head should leave the symbol as it is or replace it; whether the head should move left or right; and what state the head should be in next. (Alternatively, the machine table might simply order the head to halt.)

Let's look at a simple example: a Turing machine for adding together pairs of numbers (strictly, for adding together pairs of positive integers). The alphabet consists of two symbols: '—' and 'X'. (The '—' symbol simply indicates that the square is blank.) If we want the machine to add together 2 and 3, we set up the tape as shown in Figure 6.1.

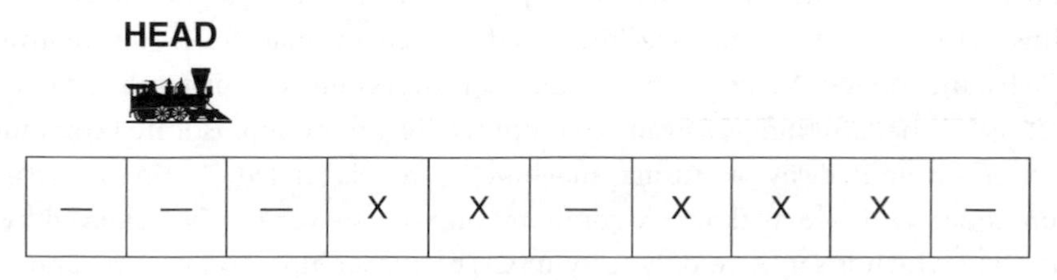

Figure 6.1 The head and tape of a Turing machine about to add 2 and 3

Table 6.1 The Turing machine table for adding two numbers.

	Input: X	**Input: –**
State: 1	no change/R/2	no change/R/1
State: 2	no change/R/2	X/L/3
State: 3	no change/L/3	no change/R/4
State: 4	—/halt	

The left sequence of Xs represents the number 2; the right sequence represents the number 3. The head is initially located to the left of the left sequence of Xs and is in state 1.

The machine table (Table 6.1) instructs the machine to write down the sum of two numbers. You read the machine table as follows. Take for example the top left square. It tells the head what to do when it is in state 1 and is reading a square which contains an X. The instruction in that square is 'no change/R/2', which means 'don't change the symbol, move one square to the right, and move into state 2. The instruction 'X/L/3' means 'replace the present symbol with an X, move one square left, and move into state 3'.

The basic idea behind the machine table is as follows. The head moves right until it reaches the left sequence of Xs. It then keeps going until it reaches the blank (i.e. —) that separates the two sequences of Xs. It replaces the blank with an X and heads left. When it reaches the next blank (i.e. after it has passed all the Xs) it moves one step right and replaces the leftmost X with a blank. The result (in our example) is a series of 5 Xs; that is, the machine has calculated that the sum of 2 and 3 is 5. Obviously, the same process works for any two sequences of Xs separated by a blank; in other words, the machine table will suffice for the addition of any two positive integers. You might like to play around with the machine table and satisfy yourself that it actually works.

So far we have examined in some detail Turing machines and their machine tables. For our purposes, what's significant about Turing machines is that they are 'syntactic engines'; that is, the head of the Turing machine is sensitive only to the syntactic properties of the symbols on the tape. Nevertheless, given the right machine table, a Turing machine will respect the semantic properties of its inputs. Thus, in the case of the Turing machine just described, the machine is quite unaware of what the series of Xs means; nevertheless, it successfully completes the addition.

It seems that anything that can be computed by a more sophisticated computer can be computed by a Turing machine. (This is called 'Turing's thesis'.) Consequently, it seems that any computation whatsoever can be achieved by a machine which is sensitive only to syntax. The recognition and manipulation of symbols solely in virtue of their syntactic properties is thus surprisingly powerful.

6.4 The computational theory of mind

According to the computational theory of mind (hereafter CTM), thoughts are complex symbols which have both syntactic and semantic properties. We have seen that complex *linguistic* symbols like 'Fodor is funky' are made up of basic symbols like 'Fodor'. Similarly, according to CTM the *thought* that Fodor is funky is a complex symbol made up of basic symbols. However, we cannot assume that the mental symbol which refers to Fodor (the philosopher) is the English word 'Fodor'. It may be that the mind has a language or code of its own. We will return to this idea in Section 6.5. For the moment we will just accept that the mental symbol which refers to Fodor is the English word 'Fodor'.

So far we have seen that, according to CTM, thoughts are complex symbols with syntactic and semantic properties. What about thinking? According to CTM, thinking involves the recognition and manipulation of thoughts purely on the basis of their syntactic properties. However, whilst thoughts are manipulated solely on the basis of their syntactic properties, those manipulations respect the semantic properties of the thoughts involved. Thus, say that I believe that

D. All philosophers are funky,

and:

E. Fodor is a philosopher.

These thoughts lead me to believe that

F. Fodor is funky.

According to CTM, the mental processor which achieves the transition from D and E to F is sensitive only to the syntactic properties of the thoughts involved. Nevertheless, the transition is truth preserving; that is, if D and E are true, so is F. Moreover, the transition is rational in the sense that the thoughts D and E provide evidence for the thought F.

Putting all this together we can say that, according to CTM, thoughts are complex symbols with syntactic and semantic properties. Thinking—the manipulation of thoughts—is achieved by processors which, whilst sensitive only to the syntactic properties of the thoughts involved, nevertheless respect their semantic properties. In other words, thinking is computation.

This is, to put it mildly, a beautiful idea. Indeed, it might even be true! We have already seen that CTM offers an account of the rationality of thought; I will now briefly sketch three further virtues of CTM.

1. We have seen that, according to CTM, thinking is **computation**. And we know that computation is possible because computers—the one on your desk or at

the library—*do exactly that*. The existence of computers therefore gives modest support to CTM since it shows that at least some physical structures are capable of performing computations. (I say *modest* support because the existence of computers does not establish that the *mind* is a computer; it only shows that computation is physically possible.)

2. We saw in Chapters 3 and 4 that mental states can be multiply realized. If mental states are computational states, then computational states must be multiply realizable. In Section 6.2 we noted that computational states and processes can indeed be multiply realized. In other words, CTM accounts for the multiple realizability of mental states.

3. CTM requires that thoughts are complex symbols. We saw in Section 6.1 that a complex symbol is built up from basic symbols. (Recall the way that the complex symbol 'Fodor wrote *The Modularity of Mind*' contains the basic symbol 'Fodor'.) More precisely, complex symbols have a *structure*. That is, they consist of basic symbols *organized in a certain way*. Even though the complex symbols 'Lassie bit Bloggs' and 'Bloggs bit Lassie' are made up of *exactly the same basic symbols*, they are quite distinct. What makes them distinct is the way the basic symbols are organized. In other words, they are distinct because they have different structures. In Section 6.5 we will examine a powerful argument which aims to establish that thoughts must have a structure. Demonstrating that thoughts are structured is not enough to establish that CTM is true: perhaps thoughts are structured but thinking is not computation. Nevertheless, establishing that thoughts are structured would considerably advance the claim that the mind is a computer.

So far in this section we have garnered a certain amount of support for CTM; however, problems abound. Here I will briefly mention four difficulties which we will later take up in detail.

1. We have seen that computational processes respect the semantic properties of the symbols involved. This raises an important issue: how do the symbols get their semantic properties? The symbols in a conventional computer get their semantic properties from *us*. The 'Fodor' symbols in this document refer to a certain American philosopher *because I say they do*. It is because *I* am thinking about a certain American philosopher that my 'Fodor' symbols refer to the author of *The Modularity of Mind*. I could, if I wanted to, write a document about Russian literature in which my 'Fodor' symbols refer to the Russian novelist Fodor Dostoyevsky. It's my intention to use 'Fodor' to stand for the American philosopher rather than the Russian novelist which determines that my 'Fodor' symbols refer to the author of *The Modularity of Mind* rather than the author of *Brothers Karamazov*.

So far we have seen that the symbols of conventional computers get their semantic properties from the intentions of the humans using the computer. But where do human mental symbols get *their* semantic properties from? There seem to be, broadly speaking, two possibilities. Either mental symbols somehow get their semantic properties from each other, or they get their semantic properties by being related in some special way to things in the world beyond the mind. Neither possibility is without its difficulties. We will return to these issues in Chapter 9.

2. If thinking is computation, then anything which performs the right sort of computations is a thinker. In Section 6.6 we will consider an apparent counterexample to CTM: a set-up in which all the right computations appear to have been performed and yet no (relevant) thinking has gone on.
3. A further difficulty for CTM takes the form of a rival account of mental processes. Called '**connectionism**', the rival account is the topic of the next chapter.
4. Finally, it's not at all clear that CTM has the resources to account for consciousness. Many people have the intuition that a computer could carry out all the right computations and yet not be conscious. I will say a little bit more about computationalism and consciousness in Section 6.6.

6.5 The language of thought

We have seen that, according to CTM, thoughts are complex symbols which are made up of basic symbols arranged in certain ways. In other words, thoughts are structured. In this section we will consider an important argument which concludes that thoughts are indeed structured entities.

Let's begin by thinking about public languages like English. Consider the sentence, 'Lassie bit Bloggs'. If that sentence is meaningful then so is the one obtained by transposing the two proper names: 'Bloggs bit Lassie'. Similarly, if the sentence 'Smith is smarter than Jones' is meaningful, then so is 'Jones is smarter than Smith'. More generally, if 'X did Y to Z' is meaningful then so is 'Z did Y to X'.

The property of languages just described is called 'systematicity'. **Systematicity** is only guaranteed if the sentences in the language possess a structure. For imagine a language L in which sentences have no structure. Let's assume that in L the basic symbol 'S' means that Lassie bit Bloggs. Notice that there is no guarantee that L has another basic symbol which means that Bloggs bit Lassie: maybe there is; maybe there isn't. On the other hand, if the sentences in the language are structured as they are in English, with word order indicating who did what to whom, it will always be possible to transform one meaningful sentence of the form 'X bit Y' into another meaningful sentence of the form 'Y bit X'.

So the systematicity of language entails that sentences have structure. Let's turn now to a particularly striking feature of public languages—**productivity**. Languages are productive in that we can build new meaningful sentences out of old sentences or parts of old sentences. For example, from 'Bloggs is short' and 'Bloggs is silly' we can obtain the new sentence 'Bloggs is short and Bloggs is silly'. And from 'Bloggs is short and Bloggs is silly' and 'Bloggs is slimy' we can obtain 'Bloggs is short and Bloggs is silly and Bloggs is slimy'. You're not going to get an A+ in your English test for the last sentence, but it is grammatical. This process can be extended indefinitely, making longer and longer sentences until you die of boredom.

The example of productivity just given generates longer and longer sentences, but it doesn't make them more complex. However, it's possible to make sentences which are not only longer but of greater complexity (not to mention interest). For example:

The girl is on the swing.

The girl in the blue blouse is on the swing.

The girl in the blue blouse designed in Paris is on the swing.

The girl in the blue blouse designed in Paris last season is on the swing.

The girl in the blue blouse designed in Paris last season by a beer-swilling Australian cricket fan is on the swing.

You get the idea.

Like systematicity, productivity is only possible because sentences are structured. Old sentences and phrases can be recycled as parts of new, longer, and/or more complex sentences. Once again, imagine that there is a language which lacks structure. The language may have a basic symbol which means 'Bloggs is short' and another one which means 'Bloggs is silly', but there is no guarantee that it will have a symbol which means 'Bloggs is short and Bloggs is silly'.

So far we've been talking about public languages like English. Parallel considerations apply to thought which seems to be both systematic and productive. Let's do systematicity first: if you can think that Lassie bit Bloggs then you can think that Bloggs bit Lassie. Now productivity: if you can think that Bloggs is short and you can think that Bloggs is silly, then you can think that Bloggs is short and Bloggs is silly. We noted in the language case that systematicity and productivity require that language is structured. A similar conclusion arises in the case of thought: thoughts have structure. That is, thoughts are made up of basic symbols assembled into more complex structures.

The conclusion we have just reached amounts to saying that thoughts are, in important respects, language-like; in other words, we think in a language.

This idea is often called the 'language of thought' hypothesis (Fodor 1975). Fodor argues that the language we think in is not the public language we talk in. He holds his position because neither small children nor nonhuman mammals can *talk*, but it seems preposterous to claim that they can't *think*. The special language in which we are said to think is sometimes called 'mentalese' to distinguish it from public languages like English. Other philosophers have argued against this view, arguing that we do indeed think in a public language. In their view, we begin life with a rudimentary version of mentalese, but once we learn to speak a public language we abandon mentalese and think in (say) English.

I won't enter into the mentalese versus public language debate here. For our purposes what's important about the systematicity and productivity of thought is that they make it plausible that thoughts are complex, structured symbols. And that's exactly what CTM requires. Of course, CTM requires more than structured symbols: it requires processes that recognize and manipulate those symbols on the basis of their syntactic properties and in ways which respect their semantic properties. Nevertheless, the plausibility of the language of thought hypothesis lends considerable support to CTM.

6.6 The Chinese room

We saw in Section 6.4 that CTM is compatible with the multiple realization of mental states and processes because computational states and processes can be multiply realized. It follows that if CTM is true mental states and processes could in principle be realized by a digital computer. That is, a digital computer could have (or be) a mind. This idea underpins a research program called *strong artificial intelligence* (or 'strong AI'). The aim of strong AI is to develop programs such that the digital computers running those programs would—quite literally—have minds.

Many practical difficulties lie in the way of actually building an intelligent computer. However, setting aside the practical difficulties we can note that CTM entails that a digital computer could think. So if CTM is true then strong AI is possible. Conversely, if strong AI is *impossible*, CTM is false. The contemporary American philosopher John Searle has constructed a thought experiment which seems to show that strong AI is impossible and, consequently, that CTM is false. For reasons that will be clear in a moment, Searle's thought experiment is called the 'Chinese room'.

Strong AI researchers have attempted to program digital computers to understand simple stories (see Schank and Abelson 1977). For example, the computer might be expected to understand a simple story about eating in a restaurant. The computer is given three kinds of input:

1. The story.
2. Some general information about restaurants and the kinds of things that typically occur there. For example: people eat in restaurants; people order their food from waiters; people are usually required to pay for what they have ordered; and so on. Researchers in strong AI call this information a 'script'.
3. Some questions about the story.

If the scientists have managed to program the computer properly then, according to strong AI, the computer will not merely answer the questions correctly, it will literally understand the story.

Now for Searle's ingenious counterargument. As it happens Searle speaks English but doesn't understand a word of Chinese. Searle imagines that he is sitting in a room (the 'Chinese room') and receives three sets of Chinese characters and a set of instructions in English. The instructions tell him how to manipulate the three sets of Chinese characters to obtain yet another set of Chinese characters. Following the instructions proves to be very difficult. As he doesn't read Chinese, Searle has to laboriously identify the Chinese characters purely by their shape. After a lot of effort he finally manages to obtain a fourth set of Chinese characters which he hands to the people waiting outside the room.

It turns out that the three sets of Chinese characters are, respectively, a simple story (in Chinese), some general information about the setting of the story (in Chinese), and a set of questions about the story (in Chinese). The instructions in English are the equivalent of a computer program, and Searle is the computer. In laboriously following the instructions he has carried out the computer program, and the set of Chinese characters he has produced are sensible answers to the questions about the story.

It seems overwhelmingly obvious that Searle does not understand the Chinese story. (Compare the situation in the Chinese room with a situation in which Searle is asked to read a story in English. Searle understands the English story; he doesn't understand the Chinese one.) But it follows that strong AI is in deep trouble. For, according to strong AI, a suitably programmed computer *could* understand a simple story. What Searle has apparently shown is that following a computer program is insufficient for understanding. After all, Searle follows the program to perfection, but he hasn't got a clue what the story is about. And if that's right, CTM is in deep trouble for, as we have seen, if strong AI is impossible then CTM is false.

So far we have seen that the Chinese room example prompts the intuition that strong AI is impossible. Searle follows up the Chinese room thought experiment with the following argument:

1. Programs are formal (syntactical).

2. Minds have contents (semantic contents).

3. Syntax is not identical [with] nor sufficient by itself for semantics.

Therefore,

4. Programs are not sufficient for nor identical with minds; i.e. strong AI is false.

(Searle 1991: 526)

Searle's point is that understanding a story involves knowing what the various symbols (i.e. the words) *mean*. That is, understanding a story involves grasping the semantic properties of the symbols in the story. Clearly, when he is in the Chinese room, Searle has no grasp of the semantic properties of the symbols involved. He is only aware of the shapes of the symbols; that is, he is only aware of their syntactic properties. Searle concludes that, since any computer system is sensitive only to syntactic properties, no computer system is aware of the relevant semantic properties, and so no computer is able to understand a story.

The Chinese room argument has generated an enormous amount of discussion. Let's begin with a reply to the Chinese room offered by Fodor (Fodor 1980*b*). Fodor agrees with Searle about the importance of semantics. However, unlike Searle, Fodor thinks that the symbols of a computer *can* have semantic properties and, in other publications, he has indicated the theory of semantics he thinks will do the trick (see, for example, Fodor 1990*d*). We will look at Fodor's theory in Chapter 9. For the moment let's return to the Chinese room and see how Fodor's suggestion fares.

According to Fodor, the symbol 'Mt Everest' refers to a certain mountain on the border of Nepal and Tibet because there is an appropriate connection between the mountain and the symbol. Similarly, the Chinese symbol 'XYZ' refers to Mt Everest because there is an appropriate connection between the mountain and the Chinese symbol. In Chapter 9 we will see how Fodor spells out 'appropriate connection'. Notice, though, that the presence or absence of that connection won't be obvious to Searle when he is in the Chinese room. All Searle is aware of is the shape of the symbols in front of him. Say that he comes across the symbol 'XYZ' and that that symbol is appropriately connected to Mt Everest. Searle won't know that the symbol is appropriately connected to Mt Everest, nor will he know that 'XYZ' means Mt Everest. Consequently, Searle will not understand the story. In other words, *even if the symbols have a semantics*, Searle will not understand the story.

It's time to pause and consider what's involved in understanding a story. To understand a story is—amongst other things—to be in a certain conscious state.

We sometimes describe this state by saying that we are *aware* of what the story means. Thus it is very natural to say that when Searle reads a story written in English he is aware of its meaning, but when he 'processes' a Chinese story in the Chinese room he is not aware of its meaning. This suggests that a crucial difference between Searle when he processes a Chinese story and Searle when he reads an English story is a difference of consciousness: only in the latter situation is Searle conscious of the content of the story. It follows that the Chinese room set-up is insufficient for conscious awareness of the meanings of stories.

Something important follows from that conclusion. The activities Searle undertakes in the Chinese room are purely computational activities. Consequently, if the Chinese room set-up is insufficient for conscious awareness of the meanings of stories, then *computation* is insufficient for conscious awareness of the meanings of stories. And this result would seem to generalize: computation is insufficient for consciousness.

The moral we have drawn from the Chinese room thought experiment is that computation is insufficient for consciousness. We cannot draw the quite distinct moral that computation is insufficient for *intelligence*. Searle's argument leaves untouched the claim of strong AI that a suitably programmed computer can respond with intelligence to a story. That Searle lacks conscious awareness of the meaning of the story does not show that *intelligent but unconscious* processing of the story is occurring.

It's hardly surprising that consciousness turns out to be a problem for CTM. As we saw over and over again in Part 1, consciousness is a problem. Period. We'll get to consciousness in Part 4.

6.7 Conclusion

CTM is a powerful idea. It offers an account of rational thought, and it is supported by the existence of computers, by the multiple realization of mental states, and by the structure-dependent properties of thought. However, it's not all blue skies and beer. As the Chinese room suggests, CTM has a problem with consciousness. Moreover, a quite extraordinary alternative conception of the mind exists. That's the topic of the next chapter.

SUMMARY

(1) Symbols have both syntactic and semantic properties. Syntactic properties are those which can be recognized by examining the symbol in isolation. Shape is an example. Semantic properties are concerned with meaning. They include

reference and truth value and cannot be recognized by examining the symbol in isolation.

(2) Very generally, computers are devices which manipulate symbols solely in virtue of their syntactic properties but which nevertheless manage to respect their semantic properties.

(3) Turing machines are very simple computers which are extremely powerful. It's obvious that Turing machines are just 'syntactic engines'.

(4) According to CTM, thoughts are complex symbols and thinking is computation.

(5) At first glance the Chinese room appears to show that computation is insufficient for intelligence. I argue that it shows something quite different: that computation is insufficient for at least some kinds of conscious awareness.

FURTHER READING

For a good introduction to the idea of computation, see John Haugeland's *Artificial Intelligence: The Very Idea* (1985), Chs 2 and 3. Haugeland 1985 also contains an excellent discussion of Turing machines (see pp. 133–40).

The great champion of CTM is Jerry Fodor; see in particular his *The Language of Thought* (1975). Fodor 1980*a* is an important presentation of his ideas, but it isn't easy. For a good, sympathetic discussion of the language of thought hypothesis see Sterelny 1990: Section 2.2. For a less sympathetic discussion see Braddon-Mitchell and Jackson 1996: Ch. 10. (It's always a good idea to read the less sympathetic authors!)

Michael Devitt and Kim Sterelny defend the view that whilst we begin life with mentalese, we gradually come to think in a public language. See Devitt and Sterelny 1987: Section 7.3. Peter Carruthers adopts a similar view. His *Language, Thought and Consciousness* (1996) is rather hard, but you might like to take a peek at Section 2.7.

It's worth noting that Fodor himself thinks that computation can't be the whole story about the mind. He expresses his doubts in *The Mind Doesn't Work that Way* (Fodor 2000, especially Chs 2 and 3). The book is in part a reply to Steven Pinker's *The Way the Mind Works* (Pinker 1997): hence the title.

The Chinese room was first discussed by John Searle in his 'Minds, Brains and Programs' (Searle 1980). The volume of *Behavioral and Brain Sciences* in which it appeared also contains a number of important commentaries. Fodor's reply (Fodor 1980*b*) is especially recommended. A more accessible version of the Chinese room argument is Searle 1990. For good textbook-style discussions of the Chinese room see Braddon-Mitchell and Jackson 1996: 107–11 and Sterelny 1990: Section 10.2.

TUTORIAL QUESTIONS

Easy ones

(1) Is CTM compatible with physicalism?

(2) Write a list of syntactic properties; write a list of semantic properties.

(3) Describe the Turing machine. Why is it impossible to build a real Turing machine?

(4) Fill in the blanks to complete the following sentences:

According to CTM, thoughts are . . .
According to CTM, thinking is . . .

A hard one

(5) Compare and contrast CTM and functionalism.

Finally, one for general discussion

(6) Could a computer be conscious?

7

Connectionism

A revolution in the making?

—William Bechtel and Adele Abrahamsen

In the previous chapter we examined the computational theory of mind in some detail. For more than a decade CTM was, as Jerry Fodor famously remarked, 'the only game in town'. However, in the mid-1980s a rival conception of the mind emerged—**connectionism**. According to connectionism, the mind is a connectionist network (or an assemblage of such networks). Exactly what a connectionist network is will become clear in a moment.

Connectionism is, in my view, a very important development. After describing connectionist networks in Sections 7.1 and 7.2, I go on to discuss the claim that the mind is, in significant ways, a connectionist network. Where appropriate I emphasize the ways in which connectionism and CTM differ. This will allow us to assess, to some degree, the status of the debate between connectionism and CTM.

A brief terminological note. Sometimes connectionist networks are referred to as 'neural networks' or 'neural nets', and sometimes they are referred to as 'parallel distributed processors'. The last expression is often abbreviated to 'PDP'. I will stick to 'connectionist network', occasionally abbreviating it to 'network'.

7.1 What connectionist networks are like

A connectionist network is made up of a large number of *units organized into layers*. In a typical connectionist network there are three layers—an *input* layer, a *hidden* layer, and an *output* layer. Each unit in the input layer is connected to every unit in the hidden layer, and each unit in the hidden layer is connected to every unit in the output layer. Figure 7.1 gives the basic idea. Note that, whilst the network depicted in Figure 7.1 has three input units, four hidden units, and two output units, networks may have any number of units in any given layer. Many networks have considerably more units than the one shown in Figure 7.1.

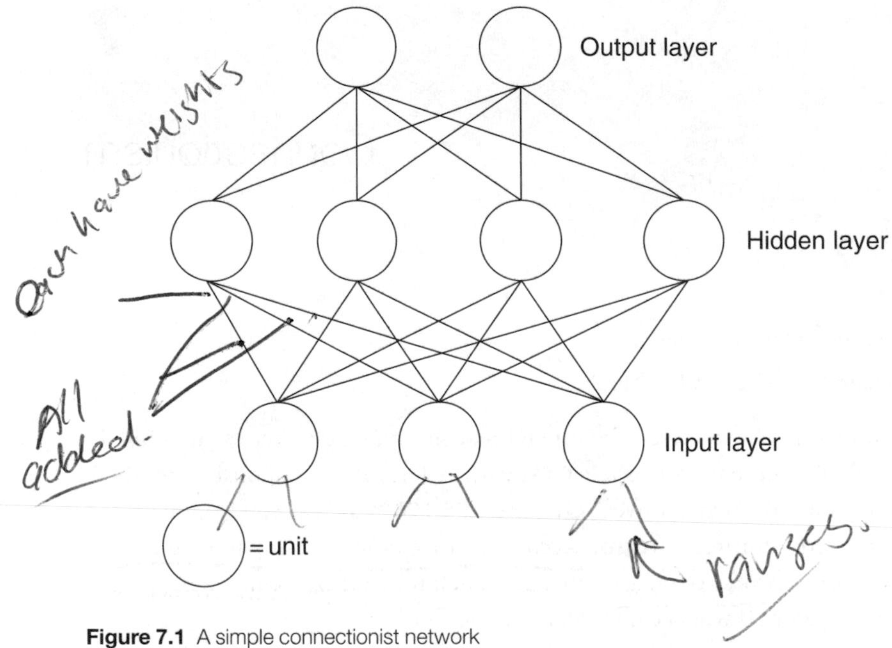

Figure 7.1 A simple connectionist network

The easiest way to grasp how a connectionist network actually works is by looking at an example. I have borrowed the following example from Paul Churchland (1988: 157–62), who in turn got it from Gorman and Sejnowski 1988.

Submarines find their way around using sonar. Sonar relies on the fact that sounds echo back from most kinds of objects. The submarine emits a powerful pulse of sound and then 'listens' for any echoes. The echoes are then analyzed to determine the size, shape, and location of the objects which reflected the sound. The trouble is, just as quite different kinds of objects sometimes look alike, quite different kinds of objects sometimes 'sound' alike. That is, the echoes generated by quite different kinds of objects can be very similar. Now submariners are especially keen to detect mines. However, it's very hard to distinguish between an echo from a mine and an echo from a rock of similar shape and size. (No doubt the people who design mines make them that way.) Consequently, there is considerable interest in military circles in developing the technology to accurately distinguish mines from rocks. This is where connectionism comes in. Connectionist networks have been developed which can fairly reliably distinguish mine echoes from rock echoes. I will now describe a simplified version of such a network.

The input to the mine-detecting network is, in a sense, an echo. However, the echo must be 'encoded' in a form which the network can process. Here's how it's done. Sounds come in different *frequencies*. (A high-frequency sound has a high pitch; a low-frequency sound a low pitch.) The first step is to analyze how powerful (i.e. loud) the echo is at a range of frequencies. Our simplified network has only three frequency ranges—low, medium, and high. An echo can now be encoded as a *triple* of three numbers, one for each frequency range. For example, the echo from a particular rock might be encoded by the triple <9, 1, 3>, which means that the volume of the echo in the low-frequency range was 9; the volume of the echo in the medium range was 1; and the volume of the echo in the high-frequency range was 3.

The encoded echo is now used as the input into the connectionist network in Figure 7.1. Each unit in the input layer is assigned one frequency range. For example, the left input unit is assigned the low-frequency range; the middle input unit the medium-frequency range; and the right input unit the high-frequency range. Each input unit is then activated, the degree of activation being determined by the volume in the relevant frequency range. So, if a particular echo is encoded by the triple <9, 1, 3>, the left input unit receives an activation of 9; the middle input unit an activation of 1; and the right input unit an activation of 3.

We noted earlier that each input unit is connected to each hidden unit, and that each hidden unit is connected to each output unit. The way the activation of the input units spreads down these connections is affected by the *weights* of the connections. The simplest connection weights are numbers in the range -1.0 to $+1.0$. The amount of activation passed along the connection from unit A to unit B is determined by multiplying the activation of A by the weight of the connection. In our example the activation of the left input unit is 9. If the weight of the connection from the left input unit to the leftmost hidden unit is 0.5, then the leftmost hidden unit receives an input of 4.5 from the left input unit ($0.5 \times 9 = 4.5$).

Notice that the connection weight can be less than zero. Say that the weight of the connection between the left input unit and the leftmost hidden unit is -0.3. In that case the leftmost hidden unit would receive an input of -2.7 ($-0.3 \times 9 = -2.7$) from the left input unit. When a unit receives a negative input it becomes *inhibited*; that is, it becomes less inclined to be activated.

Since each unit in the input layer is connected to every unit in the hidden layer, the leftmost hidden unit is connected to all three input units. The total input that the leftmost hidden unit receives is the total of the input it receives from the input units. The same goes for the other three hidden units.

How the hidden units respond to the input they receive depends on their *activation function*. The activation function is a mathematical formula which calculates the degree of activation of a unit from the total of its inputs. (If you feed the value of the total inputs of a unit into the formula, it will give back to you the degree of activation of that unit.) Quite often the activation function is such that, if the total input to a unit is below a certain 'threshold', the unit is not activated at all. We won't bother about the mathematical details here. If you're interested see Bechtel and Abrahamsen 1991: 39–47.

So far we have talked about the way that the activation of the input units spreads to the hidden units. The spread of activation from the hidden units to the output units occurs in the same way; that is, the degree of activation of the output units is determined by (i) the degree of activation of the hidden units; (ii) the weights of the connections between the hidden units and the output units; and (iii) the activation function. Overall, the degree of activation of the output units is determined by the degree of activation of the input units, the various connection weights, and the activation function.

Let me try to sum up what's been said so far. Connectionist networks consist of lots of units arranged in layers. When the input units are activated the activation spreads through the network, first to the units in the hidden layer, and from there to the units in the output layer. Each unit in one layer is connected to every unit in the next layer. The connections are 'weighted'—some transmit a lot of activation; some very little. A connection may even transmit what we might call 'deactivation'; that is, they inhibit the recipient unit. A unit in the hidden layer or the output layer sums (i.e. adds together) all of its inputs. How the unit responds to the total input it receives depends on the activation function.

So far we have only described the 'architecture' or general structure of a typical connectionist network. We turn now to the important issue of *training* a network to perform the required task.

Digital computers have to be programmed. A program is a list of instructions which tells the computer what to do. In contrast, connectionist networks are not programmed; rather, they are trained. The training process involves presenting the network with a sample input and then adjusting the connection weights in such a way that the network's response to the input is improved. This is repeated over and over, with more samples presented and more adjustments made. Eventually the network responds to the vast majority of inputs correctly.

In the sonar case, training begins with a large selection of encoded echoes, some from mines and some from rocks. The set of encoded echoes is called the *training set*. A randomly selected encoded echo is presented to the network. Let's assume that that encoded echo is from a mine. Initially the network's connection weights are set at random—each connection is simply assigned a random number between −1.0 and +1.0. The activation from the input units spreads to the hidden units and then to the output units. One output unit is declared to be the 'mine' unit; the other the 'rock' unit. Say that the rock output unit is activated quite strongly but the mine output unit isn't activated at all. In that case the network has made a mistake since it has given the output 'rock' when in fact the encoded echo is from a mine. No matter. Small adjustments are made to the connection weights so that the rock output unit is less active and the mine output unit is more active. A second encoded echo from the training set is now selected at random—this time it might be from a rock. The new encoded echo is presented to the network, and once again the activation

back propagation

spreads through the network to the output units. At this early stage of the training process it is unlikely that the network will be able to identify the rock echo correctly, so further small adjustments are made to the connection weights. This process is repeated over and over until the network can identify rock echoes and mine echoes with considerable accuracy. The network has now been trained.

I said that small adjustments are made to the connection weights. Which connection weights are adjusted, and by how much? The most popular technique for adjusting connection weights is called 'back propagation' (or 'backprop'). As the name suggests, in back propagation errors are traced from the output units *backwards* towards the input units. The weights of those connections which activated the correct output unit are increased; those which inhibited the correct output unit are decreased. Conversely, the weights of those connections which activated the incorrect output unit are decreased; those which inhibited the incorrect output unit are increased. (For the mathematical details see Bechtel and Abrahamsen 1991: 85–97.)

The training process can be very slow—typically a very large training set is required. The slowness of training is due to the very large number of connections in a workable connectionist network. (NETtalk, a connectionist network trained to pronounce written words, had 18,829 weighted connections.) As training typically involves multiple adjustments to every connection weight, training takes a long time. However, the large number of connections has a great advantage in terms of processing speed. Once a connectionist network has been trained, it can process inputs very quickly. This is because many units work simultaneously, with each unit performing just one small aspect of the overall task. (We return to this point in the next section.)

The connectionist network described in this section is an example of a *feedforward* network because the flow of activation is always forwards, from the input units to the output units. Not all connectionist networks are feedforward. In *recurrent* networks there are connections leading *backwards* from either the hidden units or the output units. Whilst these kinds of networks are very important when it comes to modeling dynamic processes, I will not discuss them here. (For an excellent introduction see Churchland 1995: Ch. 5.)

7.2 Some important properties of connectionist networks

In this section I want to draw attention to a number of important properties of connectionist networks.

1. *Connectionist networks can learn.* In the previous section we saw that a connectionist network can be trained to carry out certain tasks (e.g. mine detection).

Nobody programs the network or tells the network how to achieve its task. Rather, the connectionist network is presented with a large number of examples and any errors it makes are corrected. In other words, the network learns by a process of trial and error.

The capacity of connectionist networks to learn is very striking. Lots of physical devices can *store information*, but connectionist networks are doing more than that. In the sonar case, the network is identifying the subtle features which distinguish rock echoes from mine echoes. The training process allows the network to extract these features from the training set. Another way to express this point is to say that the network has learnt a *rule* for distinguishing rock echoes from mine echoes. This brings us to a very important point: *a properly trained network can accurately handle new cases which were not included in the training set*. For example, the mine-detecting network can determine with considerable accuracy whether a new echo is from a rock or a mine. In other words, the network can *generalize* from old cases to new ones.

2. *Connectionist networks process in parallel.* Two processors are said to be in *parallel* if they work simultaneously; they are said to be in *series* if they work one after the other. (Figure 7.2 provides an analogy.) In a connectionist network, many units are activated simultaneously; that is, the connectionist architecture is highly parallel. In contrast, the architecture of most conventional computers is serial: there is a single processor (or 'CPU') which carries out one operation at a time.

One considerable advantage of parallel processing is speed. If lots of units tackle different aspects of the overall task simultaneously then, other things being equal, the task will be finished more quickly than if each unit waits its turn to complete its part of the task.

3. *Representations in connectionist networks are 'distributed'*. Information is represented in connectionist networks in two quite distinct ways. On the one hand, information about a particular input is represented in the activation pattern which that input brings about in the network, with different features of the pattern representing different properties of the input. On the other hand, the rule a trained

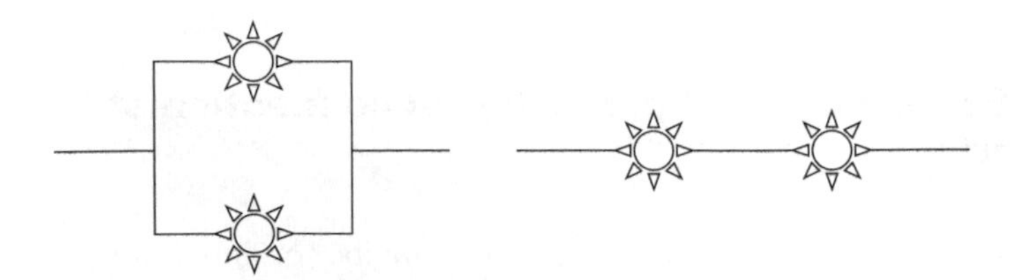

Figure 7.2 Parallel versus serial processing. On the left are two light bulbs wired in parallel; on the right are two light bulbs wired in series

network has extracted from its training set is represented in the network's connection weights. (Remember: training a network involves a large number of minute adjustments to its *connections*.)

Both of these ways of representing information are *distributed*, in that a large number of units or connections are typically involved in each representation. For example, in the sonar case it's unlikely that the activation of any single unit will represent the overall shape of the object; rather, different units will represent different aspects of the shape, with the overall shape represented by all those units taken together.

4. *Processing in connectionist networks is 'local'*. How a hidden unit behaves depends on two things: (i) its activation function; (ii) the activation it receives from the input units. These factors are said to be 'local' in that they are either properties of the unit in question, or properties of its inputs. Importantly, there is no central command system which controls the hidden units. The same remarks apply to the output units: their behavior is also determined by entirely local properties. In contrast, processing in a conventional digital computer is non-local, with each processing step directed by a highly centralized control system.

The humble traffic roundabout provides a good analogy for local processing. In Australia we drive on the left and give way to the right. When a driver approaches a roundabout she only has to consider the traffic on her right: if it's clear on her right she can go. In this situation control of the traffic is highly localized. Each driver makes her own decision based solely on the presence or absence of vehicles on her right. Now consider an intersection controlled by traffic lights. How each driver behaves is dictated by the device which makes the lights change. The device makes all the 'decisions' about traffic flow. In this situation control of the traffic is entirely nonlocal.

5. *Connectionist networks tolerate poor-quality input*. Imagine that the submarine's 'listening' device is faulty. Perhaps it can no longer register the volume of an echo across the whole range of frequencies. Consequently, the input to the network will be substandard. Amazingly, connectionist networks are fairly tolerant of poor-quality input. In the sonar case, the network will still accurately categorize an echo as 'rock' or 'mine' even though the input from the listening device is degraded. Of course, the network can't tolerate unlimited amounts of input degradation. As the input gets worse and worse, the network's accuracy slowly declines.

6. *Connectionist networks 'gracefully degrade'*. Imagine that Bloggs has just finished training a big connectionist network when—whoops!—he drops his coffee cup right onto the network. Quite a few connections are severed and some units are completely wrecked. Surprisingly, the network will probably still work moderately well. Of course, how well it works will depend on how much damage Bloggs did. As the amount of damage increases, the network's accuracy declines.

7.3 Connectionism and the mind

According to connectionism, the mind is a connectionist network (or assemblage of connectionist networks). In this section we survey the evidence in favor of connectionism. In general, arguments in support of connectionism identify properties shared by connectionist networks and either mental states and process or the brain. Obviously, similarities between networks and the mind or brain support connectionism; dissimilarities discredit connectionism.

1. *Good at what we're good at; bad at what we're bad at.* Humans are very good at perceptual recognition. We can recognize a friend's face from a blurry photo; we can recognize a friend's voice on a bad phone line; and we can read a friend's handwriting even if it is messy (or 'artistic'!). As we have seen, connectionist networks are also good at perceptual recognition tasks, even when the input is of poor quality. In contrast to the case of perception, humans are very bad at mental arithmetic (try multiplying 357 by 943 'in your head'), and they are bad at remembering and recalling large amounts of data (try to memorize and recite the first page of the phone book). Connectionist networks are also very poor at these sorts of tasks.

Advocates of connectionism often emphasize that digital computers are poor at perceptual recognition but amazingly good at mathematical tasks and data crunching. In other words, whilst connectionist networks are good at what we are good at and bad at what we are bad at, digital computers are bad at what we are good at and good at what we are bad at! This is taken as evidence *for* connectionism and *against* CTM.

We saw in the previous section that connectionist networks can learn, and that they can generalize from previous cases to new ones. These are perhaps the most impressive features of networks. And of course humans too can learn and generalize to new cases. For example, you can learn how to distinguish a Monet from a Renoir, and you can go on to distinguish Monets and Renoirs that you've never seen before. So, in this very important respect, human cognitive performance is strikingly like that of connectionist networks.

Discussion. Are connectionist networks good at what we are good at; bad at what we are bad at? Amongst the kinds of tasks humans are said to be bad at are mental arithmetic and data crunching. But is this true? Notice that most people who are numerate can do at least modest arithmetical tasks in their head. (What's $6 + 6$? What's 20×5?) Moreover, with practise, most people can become competent at mental arithmetic. At least to some extent we are poor at mental arithmetic because, in a world in which calculators are cheap and reliable, there is usually little need to do it. Consequently, very few people practice their mental arithmetic.

In addition, the methods (or 'algorithms') for doing arithmetic taught at school are generally not very appropriate for mental arithmetic because they place heavy demands on memory. (Every number you write down when you do a pen-and-paper calculation has to be remembered when you do the same calculation in your head.) People who are very good at mental arithmetic typically develop their own methods which place fewer demands on memory. (See Howe 1989: 160–2 for a description of George Parker Bidder, the 'Calculating Boy', who developed his own algorithms for mental arithmetic.) Given these considerations, it's not clear how bad—or good—we are at mental arithmetic. Consequently, the status of the argument from our poor performance at mental arithmetic to the truth of connectionism is uncertain.

Similar remarks apply to remembering and recalling large amounts of data. No human will ever be able to handle large amounts of data as well as today's digital computers can; nevertheless, people can learn to memorize and recall surprisingly large amounts of data. In some societies the education system places great stress on rote learning, and people in those societies can perform prodigious feats of memory. The nineteenth-century English writer and politician Thomas Babbington Macaulay could recite by heart vast amounts of literature, including Milton's *Paradise Lost* which is 10,565 lines long. (See Howe 1989: 163–4.) Given these considerations it's not clear just how good at handling large amounts of data humans are capable of becoming, and so once again the proconnectionist argument is hard to assess.

Notice also that the superior data-crunching capability of modern digital computers relative to humans doesn't say very much either for connectionism or against CTM. The data-handling power of digital computers is essentially a technological feature of such machines. There is nothing in the notion of computation itself (see Section 6.2) which entails that computers are fast and reliable data crunchers.

What about the claim that both humans and connectionist networks are good at perceptual recognition? It's not clear that this observation alone provides much support for connectionism. The observation would strongly support connectionism only if computational systems were incapable of such tasks. For a long time it seemed that they were; however, that's changing. For example, there are commercially available devices for face recognition which are computational in the sense defined in Section 6.2. Consequently, the degree of support provided to connectionism by the ability of connectionist networks to handle perceptual recognition tasks is hard to determine.

2. *Brain-like architecture.* We saw in Sections 7.1 and 7.2 that connectionist networks are highly parallel structures, with each unit in one layer connected to every unit in the next layer. The brain also has a highly parallel structure, with an enormous amount of interconnection between neurons. (Some neurons

connect—or 'synapse'—with 10,000 other neurons.) The parallelism of connectionist networks means that they 'degrade gracefully' (see previous section). Similarly, the human brain degrades gracefully. For example, a small stroke in the area of the brain responsible for language is likely to lead to partial rather than total loss of language. The victim will very probably retain some capacity to use language, with the nature of the deficit closely correlated with the location of the brain damage.

The parallelism of connectionist networks allows them to complete their processing tasks very quickly. Similarly, the human brain is able to undertake basic perceptual recognition tasks very quickly. Brain researchers have divided the time it takes to perform a basic recognition task by the response time of a typical neuron. The result is about 100; that is, between receiving the stimulus and responding to it there is only enough time for 100 neurons to fire one after the other. This is known as the '100 step rule'.

The 100 step rule is often taken as evidence for connectionism and against CTM. A highly parallel architecture can respect the 100 step rule because, in effect, it breaks up the task into a number of small jobs which are performed simultaneously. Each of the smaller jobs requires less than 100 steps (often a lot less). On the other hand, a digital computer would take perhaps millions of computational steps to achieve a basic perceptual recognition task, and thus violates the 100 step rule. We will return to this issue in the next section.

Discussion. We have seen that both the human brain and connectionist networks are highly parallel. There are, however, significant *dissimilarities* between connectionist networks and the human brain. For example, communication between neurons is achieved chemically by molecules called 'neurotransmitters'. So far about 40 neurally active substances have been discovered in the human nervous system, of which 11 are neurotransmitters (Churchland 1986: 79). Connectionist networks entirely gloss over this level of neurological detail. Whether or not that is significant only time—and a lot more research—will tell.

A particularly worrying dissimilarity between connectionist networks and the brain concerns training. We saw in Section 7.1 that connectionist networks are usually trained using a technique called 'back propagation'. However, it's unclear whether anything like back propagation occurs in the brain. Paul Churchland has speculated that the climbing fibers of the cerebellum may be involved in the back propagation of error signals (Churchland 1988: 164–5). However, he candidly admits that it is not yet known whether they are or not.

Finally, networks typically must be presented with many thousands of training examples before they can learn the required process. This is in sharp contrast to humans who can learn at least some things very quickly. For example, according to Steven Pinker, young children learn on average a new word every two hours that they are awake (Pinker 1994: 151). Notice that this problem cannot be overcome by making connectionist networks bigger, with more hidden units. The more hidden units the more connections, and the more connections the longer it takes to train the network.

7.4 Rationality, language, systematicity

There are at least three aspects of human cognition that should worry the advocate of connectionism: rationality, language, and the systematicity of thought. These difficulties are connected in that each seems to require representations which are structured. I will take up the issue of structured representations at the end of this section.

1. *Rationality*. We saw in the Introduction that the causal relationships between mental states sometimes mirror the rational relationships between their contents. For example, there is a *causal* relationship between my thought that Bloggs is dumb and my thought that someone is dumb (the first caused the second), and there is a *rational* relationship between 'Bloggs is dumb' and 'Someone is dumb' (if the first is true then so is the second). As noted in Chapter 6, CTM allows us to understand how this can be so. The question now arises: can connectionism account for the rationality of thought?

Maybe; maybe not. One important aspect of rationality is *validity*. A valid argument is one which, if the premises are true then so is the conclusion. Connectionist networks have been trained to determine if simple arguments are valid or not (Bechtel and Abrahamsen 1991: 163–74). Bechtel and Abrahamsen chose six very simple, valid forms of argument, and six superficially similar, invalid forms of argument. Two examples will suffice to give the flavor of Bechtel and Abrahamsen's experiment. One of the valid forms was:

Premise 1. If A then B.

Premise 2. A.

Conclusion. B.

Logicians call arguments of this form '*modus ponens*'. (A concrete example: if Sally dyes her hair then Neil will laugh. Sally dyes her hair. Conclusion: Neil will laugh.) One of the invalid argument forms was:

Premise 1. If A then B.

Premise 2. Not A.

Conclusion. Not B.

Logicians call this 'denying the antecedent'. The Sally and Neil example will help us see why it's invalid. An invalid argument form is one in which the premises can be true and yet the conclusion false. Let's assume that if Sally dyes her hair then Neil will laugh (Premise 1). And let's also assume that Sally did not dye her hair (Premise 2). It does not follow that Neil will not laugh. True, he won't laugh because Sally dyed her hair. However, he might laugh because Bloggs just told him a really funny joke. So denying the antecedent is not a valid form of argument.

Bechtel and Abrahamsen created a large training set of examples of the six valid argument forms and the six invalid argument forms. The examples were created by systematically replacing the capital letters (A, B, etc.) with small letters (p, q, etc.). All in all, there were 576 examples in the training set. After training the network was able to distinguish valid from invalid arguments with some accuracy. It follows that connectionist networks can model at least some aspects of rational thought.

However, we need to proceed with caution. To begin with, the network needed over half a million training trials to obtain an accuracy of only 76 per cent. Even with a *further two million* training trials the network was still only 84 per cent accurate. This is hardly a triumphant result. Second, the arguments involved were exceedingly simple—much simpler than the kinds of arguments humans can, with practise, assess for validity. Finally, there is a great deal more to reasoning than recognizing that an argument is valid or otherwise. For example, in probabilistic reasoning the issue of validity simply does not arise. It may be that in the future connectionist networks will successfully model many aspects of human reasoning. At present, though, the rationality of thought provides a major challenge to connectionism.

2. *Language*. All human languages exhibit an extraordinarily rich grammatical structure. The following example from Steven Pinker (1994: 40–1) nicely illustrates the way sentences are structured. Consider the formation of questions from declarative sentences (i.e. statements). For example, from the declarative sentence:

A unicorn is in the garden.

we can obtain the question:

Is a unicorn in the garden?

At first glance it might seem that we formed the question by moving the verb 'is' to the front of the sentence. But things are more complex than that, as the following example shows.

A unicorn that is eating flowers is in the garden.

In this case there are two occurrences of 'is'. Which one do we move to the front in order to obtain the corresponding sentence? *Not* the first 'is' we come across, because then we would obtain the following ungrammatical utterance:

Is a unicorn that eating flowers is in the garden?

Rather, we must move the second 'is' to obtain:

Is a unicorn that is eating flowers in the garden?

This example indicates that sentences are not simply lists of words. They have a structure. We can use brackets to indicate the relevant aspect of sentence structure:

[A unicorn] is in the garden.

[A unicorn that is eating flowers] is in the garden.

In each case, the part of the sentence in brackets is the *subject* of the sentence. The subject of the sentence indicates the thing which the sentence is about. We form questions from declarative sentences by moving the 'is' *which follows the subject* to the front of the sentence. Thus:

Is [a unicorn] in the garden?

Is [a unicorn that is eating flowers] in the garden?

(In some sentences we find not 'is' after the subject but 'are'. In that case we move the 'are' from after the subject to the front of the sentence.)

So far we have noted that sentences have structure. This raises the following important question. Does connectionism have the resources to capture that structure? To explore this issue, Jeffrey Elman (1992) trained a connectionist network to complete sentences by supplying a word with the correct grammatical type. He began with a vocabulary of 36,405 words, and used it to generate a corpus of 10,000 sentences. There were, roughly speaking, two kinds of sentence in the corpus. I will call the first kind 'simple'. The following sentences are simple:

Boys hear boys.

Boy chases boy.

I will call the second kind of sentence 'complex'. The following sentences are complex:

Boy chases boy who chases boy.

Boy who boys chase chases boy.

There were four training phases. In the first phase, the network was trained only on simple sentences; in the second phase the network was trained on a mixture of 75 per cent simple sentences and 25 per cent complex sentences; in the third phase it was trained on 50 per cent simple sentences and 50 per cent complex sentences; and in the final phase it was trained on 25 per cent simple sentences and 75 per cent complex sentences. The network was then tested by giving it novel, complex sentences from which the last word was omitted. The network's task was to complete the sentence by providing a grammatically suitable word. It performed its task surprisingly well.

This is a promising result. However, it remains to be seen whether Elman's approach can be 'scaled up' to handle full-blown grammars and large vocabularies. Consequently, more research is required before we can conclude that connectionist networks can model all aspects of human language use.

3. *Systematicity*. In Section 6.5 we noted that thought is systematic. Anyone who can think that Lassie bit Bloggs can think that Bloggs bit Lassie, and anyone who can think that Jones is smarter than Smith can think that Smith is smarter than Jones. It's not obvious, though, that connectionist networks are capable of being systematic in the way thought is. A connectionist network which is trained to process a sentence like 'Lassie bit Bloggs' cannot necessarily process the sentence 'Bloggs bit Lassie'—it will all depend on how the network has been trained.

Moreover, critics of connectionism have offered a general argument to the effect that connectionist networks cannot exhibit genuine systematicity. They begin by arguing that systematicity can only be explained if thoughts have structure. To see this, imagine that my thoughts are marbles rolling around in my head. My thought that Lassie bit Bloggs is (say) a red marble. Now my having a red marble in my head in no way guarantees that I am capable of having another marble—say a blue one—which is the thought that Bloggs bit Lassie. That is, there's nothing about my having a red marble which makes it more (or less) likely that I can have a blue one. In contrast, according to CTM thoughts are built up from concepts in much the same way that sentences are built up from words. (See Section 6.5 for details.) A person who can think that Lassie bit Bloggs has (i) the concepts 'Lassie', 'bit', and 'Bloggs' and (ii) the syntactic know-how to assemble concepts into thoughts. Consequently, anyone who can think that Lassie bit Bloggs can think that Bloggs bit Lassie. That is, the right kind of structure pretty much guarantees that thought is systematic. Of course, this argument only shows that structure is *sufficient* for systematicity; it doesn't show that structure is *necessary* for systematicity. Maybe someone will one day find a way of having systematicity without structure. However, at present positing structure is the only way we have of explaining systematicity.

So far we have seen that the right sort of structure is (as far as anyone can tell) required for systematicity. Connectionism's critics go on to argue that representations in connectionist networks are like marbles in that they don't have the right sort of structure. (See especially Fodor and Pylyshyn 1988 and Fodor and Mclaughlin 1990.) If they're right, connectionism is in big trouble.

In a moment we will take a brief look at the issue of structured representations. However, before doing so it's worth noting that some connectionists don't accept that thought is systematic. It must be conceded that whilst the standard examples of systematicity certainly make it *seem* that thought is systematic, we don't have much by way of an *argument* that it is systematic.

4. *Structured representations*. We have seen that possessing structured representations is (as far as anyone knows) the only way to explain the systematicity of thought. Similar remarks apply to rationality and language. Let's begin with rationality. Recall the example of a valid argument (*modus ponens*) given earlier in this section:

Premise 1. If A then B.

Premise 2. A.

Conclusion. B.

There are very many instances of *modus ponens* which humans can think about. (Previously we saw this one: If Sally dyes her hair then Neil will laugh. Sally dyed her hair. Conclusion: Neil will laugh.) It's entirely implausible that we learn these instance one by one. Rather, it would seem that we learn the general argument form and apply it over and over again. But applying the argument form over and over again requires representing the *structure* of premise 1; it requires seeing that premise 1 has parts, and one of those parts is identical to premise 2. So rational thought requires structured representations.

Now let's turn to language. We noted earlier that we can form questions from declarative sentences. For example, from:

A unicorn is in the garden.

we can obtain:

Is a unicorn in the garden?

By far the most plausible explanation of this capacity is that we represent declarative sentences as having a structure that identifies which part of the sentence is the subject. These representations allow us to form questions by moving the 'is' (or 'are') which immediately follows the subject to the front of the sentence. Consequently, language users must have structured representations.

So rationality, language, and systematicity all point in the same direction: they indicate that the human mind must be capable of deploying structured representations. Consequently, connectionists must be able to show that connectionist networks can deploy structured representations. Connectionists are well aware of this challenge and have made serious attempts to develop structured representations in connectionist networks. I think it's fair to say that they have not yet entirely succeeded. But it's also fair to say that their efforts are promising.

7.5 Conclusion

What conclusions should we draw about connectionism, and about the rivalry between connectionism and CTM? In my view, it's too early to make strong claims about connectionism. It's clear that research on connectionist networks is exciting and important; however, there remain aspects of human cognition which connectionist networks cannot, as yet, successfully model. A great deal of research remains to be done. I hold a similar view about CTM. The computational theory of mind is extremely important; however, many issues remain to be resolved. Moreover, we must not rule out the possibility that they are both right—that in their own way each adequately describes the human mind at some level of abstraction. And we must not rule out the possibility that they are both wrong—maybe the truth lies somewhere else.

SUMMARY

(1) Connectionist networks consist of simple units arranged in three layers—input, hidden, and output.

(2) Connectionist networks can be trained to respond correctly to a class of inputs.

(3) Once trained, networks exhibit some important properties. In particular, they can generalize to new cases not presented during training; they can handle substandard input; and they can degrade gracefully.

(4) According to connectionism, the mind is a connectionist network (or a group of such networks).

(5) In support of connectionism it has been claimed that connectionist networks are good at the kinds of cognitive tasks humans are good at, bad at the kinds of cognitive tasks humans are bad at. However, it's very hard to determine the status of this claim.

(6) In support of connectionism it has been claimed that connectionist networks are brain-like. However, whilst networks are brain-like in some important ways, they're not brain-like in other ways. It's unclear if these dissimilarities are important.

(7) It is at present unclear whether connectionist networks can successfully model rationality, language, or the systematicity of thought. The crucial issue here is whether connectionist networks can deploy structured representations.

(8) In conclusion, connectionism is important and exciting; however, a great deal of research remains to be done before we can form firm judgements about connectionism. Similar remarks apply to CTM.

FURTHER READING

A good, clear introduction to connectionism is provided by Paul Churchland in his *Matter and Consciousness* (1988: 156–65). His *The Engine of Reason, the Seat of the Soul* (1995) provides a more extensive discussion, and covers both feedforward and recurrent networks. Both are highly recommended.

Kim Sterelny provides an outstanding discussion of connectionism in his *The Representational Theory of Mind* (1990: Ch. 8). Andy Clark's *Microcognition* (1989) and *Associative Engines* (1993) discuss many of the philosophical issues in a fairly accessible way. Chapter 4 of his *Mindware* (2001) is also recommended. All of these works are harder than this one.

Chapters 2 and 3 of Bechtel and Abrahamsen 1991 cover the technical details of connectionist architecture and training in considerably more detail than I have done.

Two important collections of papers on connectionism and the philosophy of mind are Ramsey, Stich, and Rumelhart 1991 and MacDonald and MacDonald 1995.

Two important discussions of systematicity and the need for structured representations are Fodor and Pylyshyn 1988 and Fodor and McLaughlin 1990. Unfortunately, neither is easy. For a reply see Horgan and Tienson 1992, which is also very hard.

TUTORIAL QUESTIONS

Easy ones

(1) Briefly describe the basic architecture of a connectionist network.

(2) Briefly describe the mine-detector example.

(3) What does it mean to say that connectionist networks 'compute in parallel'?

(4) Carefully discuss the claim that humans are not good at mental arithmetic. Is it true? What bearing does it have on the debate about connectionism?

(5) In what ways are connectionist networks brain-like? In what ways are they dissimilar from brains?

A hard one

(6) Does systematicity require structured representations?

Part Three

Mind in a physical world

8

Physicalism and supervenience

I'm a material girl living in a material world

—Madonna

In Chapters 2–4 we considered three *physicalist* theories of mental states: behaviorism, the identity theory, and functionalism. Physicalist theories of mental states contrast with the dualist theories we examined in Chapter 1. So far we have just relied on an intuitive understanding of the distinction between physicalist and nonphysicalist theories. In this chapter we will explore an important way of defining physicalism. It's important to stress that our task here is purely *definitional*. We're trying to give a good definition of physicalism; we're not trying to show that physicalism is true.

According to physicalism, mental states *depend on* physical states. Roughly, the idea is that if you fix all the physical properties you automatically fix all the mental properties. To get a grip on this idea, recall the identity theory. According to the identity theory, mental states are identical to physical states of the brain. So, if we fix the physical properties of the brain we automatically fix the mental properties. In contrast, according to substance dualism, mental states are *independent of* physical states: fixing the physical properties of the brain is insufficient to fix the mental properties. The nonphysical mind can change the state that it is in by, for example, doing a bit of reasoning, without there being any change in the brain.

The idea of automatically fixing one set of properties by fixing another set of properties is called **supervenience**. Property A supervenes on property B if fixing property B is sufficient to fix property A. (Alternatively, and equivalently, property A supervenes on property B if there can be no change in property A without a change in property B.) If physicalism is true, the mental properties *supervene* on the physical properties. In this chapter we will explore the idea of supervenience in a little detail. However, before turning to supervenience, we need to get clearer on exactly which properties are the physical properties.

8.1 Physical properties

When I was a boy I was intrigued by a diagram in an old science textbook. The diagram showed the dissected thigh muscle of a recently killed frog. The experimenter was shown stimulating the muscle with an electrode. The stimulated muscle contracted sharply, and the force of the contraction was recorded on a revolving drum.

What kind of properties do we need to think about if we are fully to understand the contraction of the frog's muscle? First of all, there are the properties which are of interest to the physiologist. When explaining the contraction of the muscle, the physiologist will talk about the kinds of cells which make up the frog's thigh muscle, and the arrangement of those cells. She will go on to talk about the way the electrical stimulus brings about the contraction, and the way in which the elasticity of the muscle and its tendon causes the muscle to spring back to its original length.

At some point she will start to discuss the molecules involved in, for example, the way the cells process energy. Very detailed discussions of those molecules will probably be left to an organic chemist. The chemist will introduce other properties into the explanation—properties of molecules and of the atoms out of which the molecules are built. Finally, a physicist will discuss atomic structure and the forces which operate between and within atoms. In doing so she will rely on the strange properties discovered by quantum theory.

We have seen that a thorough explanation of the contraction of the frog's muscle will appeal to physiological properties, chemical properties, and quantum properties. These are the physical properties.

Notice that I have deliberately chosen an example in which psychological properties play no part. Even if we accept that frogs have mental states, it's clear that mental states do not play a part in the contraction of the dissected frog's muscle because the muscle is completely isolated from the frog's brain, and everyone—even dualists—think that a brain is essential if mental states are to impact on muscles. We do not need to talk about psychological properties to understand the contraction of the frog's muscle, and they are not included in the physical properties. So the physical properties *include* the properties discussed by physicists, chemists, and biologists (including neurobiologists) and *exclude* the properties discussed by psychologists.

8.2 Introducing the supervenience approach to physicalism

Imagine that scientists succeed in building a machine which can make a perfect physical copy of any physical object. If you put your favorite coffee cup into the machine, it makes a perfect physical copy of your favorite coffee cup. What's a perfect physical copy? One object is a perfect physical copy of another if and only if they have exactly the same physical properties. Consequently, the duplicate coffee cup will have exactly the same physical properties as the original one. For example, if the original cup is white then the duplicate will be white. And if the original cup has a mass of 175 grams (roughly: weighs 175 grams) then the duplicate will have a mass of 175 grams. And so on for every physical property of the original cup. If the original has some physical property P, then the duplicate will also have property P.

In fact, the previous paragraph contains a small error. We considered making a perfect physical duplicate of a coffee cup, and we said that one object is a perfect duplicate of another if and only if they have exactly the same physical properties. But there will be at least two physical properties which the original cup and the duplicate won't share: age and position. Inevitably, the original cup will be older than the duplicate, and they won't be located in exactly the same place. (Even if they are kept on the same shelf, one will be a little to the right of the other.) For the moment we will ignore this complication and say that the original cup and the duplicate have their physical properties in common.

The idea of perfect physical duplication gives us a way of expressing the doctrine of physicalism about mental states. Imagine putting a person into the machine and making a perfect physical duplicate of them. What will the duplicate be like? According to physicalism, the duplicate will be exactly the same as the original person. In particular, the duplicate and the original will have the same mental states: if the original person is in pain, the duplicate will likewise be in pain. In short, according to physicalism, a perfect physical duplicate of someone will automatically be a perfect mental duplicate of them.

To get this idea quite clear, think for a moment what a substance dualist would say about the perfect physical duplicate. According to substance dualism, a person is a composite of a physical body and a nonphysical mind. The machine will make a perfect copy of the physical body, but won't be able to reproduce the nonphysical mind. Consequently, the duplicate will be mindless—it will have no mental states whatsoever.

If physicalism is true a perfect physical duplicate will be a mental duplicate of the original person; but if substance dualism is true a perfect physical duplicate will not be a mental duplicate of the original person. Philosophers often use the term 'supervenience' to sum up the ideas we have been developing here.

Think again about the original coffee cup. I said that it was white, and that a perfect physical duplicate would also be white. In that case we can say that the color of the cup *supervenes* on the physical properties of the cup. Here's another example. I said that the original cup had a mass of 175 grams and that a perfect physical duplicate would also have a mass of 175 grams. In that case we can say that the mass of the cup *supervenes* on the physical properties of the cup. More generally: if some property P of an object is also a property of a perfect physical duplicate of that object, then P supervenes on the physical properties of the object.

We've seen that, according to physicalism, a perfect physical duplicate of a person would also be a perfect mental duplicate. Using the idea of supervenience we can say that, according to physicalism, the mental properties supervene on the physical properties. Indeed, we'll take this as *definitional* of physicalism: physicalism about mental states is the view that the mental properties supervene on the physical properties. A consequence of this definition is that substance dualism is *not* a form of physicalism since, if substance dualism is true the mental properties do *not* supervene on the physical properties. And surely this is the right result. Substance dualism is not a form of physicalism because it quite explicitly posits the existence of nonphysical objects.

8.3 Refining the supervenience approach to physicalism

Our aim is to get clear on what physicalism about the mental states amounts to. In the previous section we made a lot of progress towards meeting this challenge. We said that, according to physicalism, the mental properties of a person supervene on the physical properties of that person. In this section we refine the idea of supervenience in order to avoid certain difficulties.

We saw in the previous section that the original coffee cup and the duplicate coffee cup will not be exactly the same. For example, the original will be older than the duplicate, and they will be located in different positions. Similarly, the original person and the duplicate person will not be exactly the same. Say that the original person was born in 1983 and entered the copying machine in 2002. Then immediately after the copying process is finished the original person will be 19 years old whereas the duplicate will be brand-new. Moreover, the original person and the duplicate will be in different places. Even if they stand next to each other, one of them will be slightly to the right of the other.

As time goes by, differences between the original person and the copy will accumulate. By 2010, the original might have broken her leg, fallen in love, and acquired a taste for deep pan pizza. In contrast, the copy might have become a doctor, traveled to Africa, and taken up rap dancing. But let's set aside the differences that will emerge by 2010. Far more interesting differences exist at the very moment the duplicate is created. Let me explain.

I have memories of most of the places I have lived in or visited, but I have no memories of Alaska for the simple reason that I have never been there. (I have a variety of *beliefs about* Alaska, but these are not *memories of* Alaska.) Now say that the original person lives in New York and has lots of memories of a trip she took to Australia a couple of years ago. If we ask her whether she remembers going to Australia she will say 'yes'; and if we ask her to recall some of her memories she will remember the famous Opera House and the Sydney Harbor Bridge. Now imagine that we make a perfect physical duplicate of the original person and ask her whether she remembers going to Australia. She will say 'yes'; and if we ask her to recall some of her memories it will seem to her that she remembers the famous Opera House and the Sydney Harbor Bridge. But she won't really have memories of Australia because she has never been there; and she won't really be able to recall the Opera House and the Bridge because she has never seen them.

We have seen that, immediately after duplication, the duplicate won't have any memories and therefore her mental states will not be identical to those of the original person. Some philosophers believe that there will be other mental differences between the original and the duplicate. According to these philosophers, there are important differences between the **content** of the original person's beliefs and those of the duplicate. However, we won't take up that issue here; see Section 9.6 for relevant discussion.

The way to avoid the problem about differences of memory (and also about differences of age and location) is to introduce the idea of a **possible world**. A possible world is a way the world might have been. In one possible world Hitler gave up politics and became a dog trainer. In another, the sun exploded and the Earth was fried. In yet another the universe consists of nothing but a single star, alone in empty space. These are all ways the world—our world, the actual world—might have been.

Philosophers argue about how we should understand the idea of possible worlds. Some philosophers think that they are just a useful way of talking; others think that they are real in exactly the same way that this world is real! Fortunately, we don't need to worry about that issue here. For our purposes, we can just think of possible worlds as ways that our world could have been.

Now think of a possible world which has exactly the same physical properties as our world, and no other properties. All the physical properties of our world are 'copied over' to the duplicate world, but none of the nonphysical properties are copied over. The duplicate world will contain an object which corresponds to the George W. Bush of our world; call him 'duplicate Bush'. If physicalism is true, duplicate Bush will have exactly the same mental states as the George W. Bush at our world. However, if substance dualism is true, duplicate Bush will not have the same mental states as the George W. Bush at our world. For the possible world we are considering is only a physical duplicate; nonphysical properties will not be copied over. Consequently, none of the nonphysical mental properties substance dualism posits will be copied over.

We can use the apparatus of possible worlds to give a new, refined account of supervenience. On this view, property P supervenes on the physical properties if and only if property P exists in that possible world which has exactly the same physical properties as our world, and no other properties. With this view of supervenience in place we can once again define physicalism about mental states as the view that the mental properties supervene on the physical properties.

We can see how this refined supervenience approach to physicalism avoids some of the problems which beset the earlier, cruder approach. When we imagine a possible world which is a physical duplicate of this one, we imagine a structure whose parts are the same age as the corresponding parts in our world. For example, if the George W. Bush in our world is 54, the duplicate Bush in the duplicate world will also be 54. Moreover, there is no problem about position. Say that the George W. Bush in our world is one meter east of the flagpole; then the duplicate Bush in the duplicate world will be one meter east of the duplicate flagpole. Finally, notice that the problem about memory also evaporates. Say that the George Bush in our world remembers visiting Alaska. Then, if physicalism about mental states is true, the duplicate Bush in the duplicate world will have a memory of visiting duplicate Alaska.

8.4 A problem for the supervenience approach to physicalism?

According to physicalism about mental states, duplicate Bush will have the same mental properties as the George W. Bush at our world. According to substance dualism, duplicate Bush will have none of the mental properties George W. Bush has at our world. But what about property dualism? We shall see that property dualism offers a special challenge to the supervenience account of physicalism.

In Chapter 1 we saw that, according to property dualism, mental states are nonphysical properties of the brain. On this view, the complex physical properties of the brain cause the nonphysical mental properties. Imagine for the sake of argument that property dualism is true of our world. In that case, George W. Bush's mental properties are nonphysical properties caused by the physical properties of his brain. Now think of a possible world which has exactly the same physical properties as our world, and no other properties. That world will contain a perfect physical duplicate of George W. Bush's brain. But if property dualism is true, the physical properties of the duplicate brain will cause nonphysical mental properties. Indeed, since the duplicate brain is a perfect physical copy of George W. Bush's brain, it will have the same nonphysical mental properties as George W. Bush's brain. In other words, it seems that if property dualism is true, the mental properties supervene on the physical properties, and so property dualism turns out to be a kind of physicalism!

Fortunately, there is a straightforward way out of this difficulty. I didn't think it up myself—Frank Jackson suggested it to me in conversation.

Science has discovered a great many *laws of nature*. A law of nature is a generalization which links one sort of event with another sort of event. For example, 'Rotten eggs float on water' is a law of nature because it links one event—an egg being rotten—with another event—the egg's floating on water. (Next time you want eggs for breakfast, you can check how fresh they are by putting them in a glass of water and seeing if they float.)

We can say that a *physical* law is one which links one sort of *physical* event with another sort of *physical* event. 'Rotten eggs float on water' is a physical law because it links one physical event (the decomposition of an egg) with another physical event (the egg's floating on water). In contrast, the laws posited by property dualism are not physical laws. For they purport to link one sort of physical event—my brain being in a certain physical state—with a *nonphysical* event—my having a certain (nonphysical) mental state.

Let's return to the idea of a possible world which has exactly the same physical properties as our world, and no other properties. We can now see that we failed to completely specify what that world is like because we said nothing about what *laws of nature* operate at that world. In keeping with the spirit of physicalism, we should consider a possible world which (i) has exactly the same physical properties as our world and no other properties; and (ii) has exactly the same physical laws as our world and no other laws. In that case the duplicate world will not be a world in which the laws posited by property dualism hold. As we have seen, those laws are not physical laws. Consequently, even if property dualism is true of our world, the physical properties of duplicate Bush's brain will *not* give rise to any mental properties. In other words, if property dualism is true mental properties do *not* supervene on the physical properties, and so property dualism is not a form of physicalism.

SUMMARY

(1) Property A supervenes on property B if fixing property B is sufficient to fix property A; that is, property A supervenes on property B if there can be no change in property A without a change in property B.

(2) Roughly speaking, the physical properties are the properties over which theories in physics, chemistry, or biology quantify.

(3) According to the supervenience approach to physicalism, the mental properties supervene on the physical properties.

(4) For our purposes we can take a possible world to be a way this world—the actual world—might have been.

(5) We can refine the supervenience approach to physicalism as follows. Consider a possible world which has exactly the same physical properties as our world and no other properties. Then physicalism is true if and only if that possible world is a mental duplicate of our world.

(6) A further refinement to the supervenience approach to physicalism is required to avoid the unwanted conclusion that property dualism is a form of physicalism: we must consider not merely a possible world which has exactly the same physical properties as our world (and no others); we must consider a possible world which, in addition, has exactly the same physical laws as ours (and no others).

FURTHER READING

Unfortunately, most of the literature in this area is pretty hard. By far the best place to start is Braddon-Mitchell and Jackson 1996: 14–27. A valuable but much less accessible account is Lewis 1983*a*. An important collection of papers on supervenience and the mind is Kim 1993. See also Kim 1998: Ch. 1.

On the issue of which properties are the physical properties, Ravenscroft 1997 is worth a look.

TUTORIAL QUESTIONS

(1) Give some examples of physical properties.

(2) Why is it a bad idea to include the psychological properties amongst the physical properties when defining physicalism?

(3) Convey, in a couple of sentences, the idea of a possible world.

(4) State the supervenience approach to physicalism.

(5) Using the supervenience approach to physicalism, explain why (i) the identity theory is a physicalist theory; and (ii) substance dualism is not a physicalist theory.

(6) What special problem does property dualism raise for the supervenience approach to physicalism? Can it be resolved?

9

Content

Now is the winter of our discontent made glorious summer . . .

—Shakespeare

If only.

—Bloggs

In the Introduction we noted that some mental states are *about* things; that is, they *represent* some thing or things as being a certain way. For example, Bloggs's belief that Mt Everest is 8,848 meters high is about Mt Everest and represents Everest as being a certain height. Desires, too, can be about things: Bloggs's desire to have blond hair is about his hair and represents his hair as blond. Other kinds of mental states can also be about things; for example, you can be *happy* that it's your birthday, or *sad* about the weather. However, in what follows I will focus exclusively on beliefs.

Now, according to physicalism, beliefs are states of people's brains. So if Bloggs's beliefs are about things, it follows that states of his brain are about things. But how does a state of someone's brain get to be about Mt Everest? This is the problem of content, and answers to the question just posed are theories of content.

In this chapter we will examine five theories of content, and also look (in Section 9.6) at some important issues that have been raised about content. Before getting started, though, it will be worth having a quick look at some of the terminology that's used in this field. I will try to keep the terminology as simple as possible; however, you're likely to come across alternative terminology when you read around, so it's worth being aware what some of these terms mean.

We have said that some mental states are *about* things; that is, they *represent* things. Mental states which represent things are often said to be *intentional* states. (Note that this is a technical use of the term 'intentional'. In ordinary usage, when we say that someone did something 'intentionally' we mean they did it deliberately. That usage of 'intentional' is quite different from the one technical one.) What a mental state is about is sometimes called the *content* of that state. The content of Bloggs's belief that Mt Everest is 8,848 meters high is the following state of affairs: Everest is 8,848 meters high. Notice that the state of affairs which is the content of a thought doesn't have to be true. Bloggs could believe that snow is black, in which case the content of his belief is false.

The state of affairs which is the content of a mental state is sometimes called a '**proposition**'. The English philosopher Bertrand Russell (1872–1970) coined the phrase **propositional attitudes** to refer to mental states that have content. His idea was that when we believe X we take the *attitude* of believing to the *proposition* X; when we desire Y we take the *attitude* of desiring to the *proposition* Y; and so on.

English sentences used to attribute **propositional attitudes** often contain a 'that clause' straight after the psychological verb: 'Bloggs believes *that he is cool*'; 'Sally wishes *that Bloggs would go away*'. The 'that clause' describes the content of the mental state: 'that he is cool' and 'that Bloggs would go away', respectively. Find the 'that clause' and you've found the content.

Finally, recall that in Section 6.1 we noted that the semantic properties of a symbol are the properties to do with the symbol's meaning. Sometimes philosophers who are interested in the problem of content say that they are seeking a *semantics* for mental states (or a 'psychosemantics'); they may also say that they are interested in the *meaning* of mental states.

9.1 The resemblance theory

According to the resemblance theory of content, my dog thoughts are about dogs because my dog thoughts *resemble* a typical dog. More generally, my thought about X is about X because it resembles X.

Unfortunately, this is not a very plausible idea. To begin with, we need to specify the *respects* in which a thought resembles the thing it represents. In what respects is my dog thought like a dog? The trouble is that just about everything resembles just about everything else in some respect. For example, my laptop resembles the Eiffel Tower. How so? Well, they're both located in space and time. I've seen them both and I'm rather fond of them both. In addition, they're both products of great genius: the Eiffel Tower was designed by the great French engineer Gustave Eiffel; my laptop owes its design to the work of the brilliant American mathematician John von Neumann. So there we go, my laptop resembles the Eiffel Tower! Similarly, there are no doubt *some* respects in which my dog thoughts resemble cats. So why are my dog thoughts about dogs rather than cats?

In response, it might be suggested that the relevant respect is visual appearance: my dog thought is about dogs because the visual experience I have when I think about dogs is very much like the visual experience I have when I see a dog. (It's something like this which the British empiricists intended.) But this idea, too, is fraught with difficulties. To begin with, we are able to think about things which don't look like anything at all. For example, I can think about inflation, but what does inflation look like? Since inflation doesn't look like anything, my inflation thoughts can't be about inflation in virtue of their visually resembling inflation. This kind of objection applies quite generally to thoughts about abstract objects like the number two. Since abstract objects don't have visual appearances, we cannot have thoughts about abstract objects in virtue of having thoughts which resemble them in visual respects. (By the way, the number two is quite distinct from the *numeral* 2. The numeral 2 certainly does have a visual appearance; it looks like this: 2.)

A related difficulty concerns thoughts about classes of objects. I can think about individual dogs like Lassie, but I can also think about dogs in general—about the *class* of all dogs. What does the class of all dogs look like? How can I have a thought which visually resembles the class of all dogs? There seem to be two options: (i) I could have a thought which visually resembles a *representative* dog or (ii) I could have a thought which visually resembles *all* the dogs that will ever exist. The trouble with (i) is explaining why the thought is about all dogs rather than the particular dog which it visually resembles. The trouble with (ii) is that I don't know how many dogs will exist, and so at best my thought will visually resemble some (pretty arbitrary) number of dogs—say 101. So why is my thought about the class of dogs rather than about a group of 101 dogs?

Let's set aside difficulties generated by abstract objects and classes of objects, and focus on thoughts about concrete individuals like Socrates and Lassie. Even here there are serious problems. I can think about something even though I can't distinguish it visually from a number of other things. For example, I can think about the first person to swim in the Nile but, whilst I can form a mental image of a person and label it 'my image of the first person to swim in the Nile', there is no reason to think that my image resembles the first person to swim in the Nile anymore than it resembles millions of other people. So why is it a representation of the first person to swim in the Nile rather than a representation of one of those other folk?

Taken together, these worries are more than enough to motivate a search for a better theory of content.

9.2 The causal theory

Here's another approach to the problem of content. Perhaps my dog thoughts are about dogs because they're caused by, *and only by*, dogs. More generally, my thought about Xs is about Xs because (i) my thought was caused by an X and (ii) nothing but Xs cause me to have thoughts about Xs.

The causal theory is sometimes called the 'indicator' theory, and sometimes 'information semantics'. To see why the name 'indicator theory' is appropriate, think about the indicator which tells you which floor the lift you are riding has reached. If the indicator is working properly, it tells you that you have reached floor seven when, *and only when*, you have reached floor seven. Similarly, if your dog thoughts are working properly, they indicate that a dog is present when, *and only when*, a dog is present. The other name—'information semantics'—is appropriate because in the formal theory of information developed by the American mathematician Claude Shannon, state A carries information about state B if As are caused by, and only by, Bs. For example, the presence of smoke carries information about the presence of fire if smoke is caused by, and only by, fires. For present purposes I will stick with the name 'causal theory'.

The causal theory of content has, very often, been elaborated in the context of the computational theory of mind (see Chapter 6). According to the computational theory of mind, a thought like 'Jake loves dogs' is made up of mental symbols arranged in an appropriate way. One of those mental symbols is about Jake; another is about dogs. Following a widely adopted convention, I will use words written in capital letters to refer to mental symbols. Thus 'JAKE' is the name of a mental symbol which is about Jake, and 'DOG' is the name of a mental symbol which is about (you guessed it) dogs. Adopting this convention we can say that, according to the causal theory of content, DOGs are about dogs because DOGs are caused by, and only by, dogs.

Straightaway we can see problems with this view. I can think about dogs—that is, have the mental symbol DOG—even though I have had no direct causal contact with dogs. (Perhaps I live in a part of the world which is entirely dogless, but I've heard about dogs and often think how much I'd like to see one.) One way to reply to this objection is by allowing that *indirect* causal links between dogs and DOGs can be sufficient to make DOGs be about dogs. For example, maybe I heard about dogs from Bloggs, who saw one on his travels. Thus my DOG symbol refers to dogs because of the causal chain which stretches from a dog to me via Bloggs.

Another worry is this. I can think about the Easter Bunny even though there is no causal connection—not even an indirect one—between my EASTER BUNNY symbol and the Easter Bunny because there is no such thing as the Easter Bunny. (I hope I'm not upsetting anyone here.) One way to respond to this objection is by saying that my EASTER BUNNY symbol is not simple—it's a complex of other symbols like RABBIT and MAGICAL. That response is not available, however, in the case of abstract objects like the number two. It's generally accepted that the number two has no causal impact on the world—nobody ever had their toe squashed by the number two. Moreover, it seems unlikely that my mental symbol TWO is a complex of other symbols. Nevertheless, many people possess the mental symbol TWO.

A further problem arises because the causal pathway from dogs to DOGs is usually quite long. Consider, for example, what happens when Bloggs sees a dog. Light is reflected from the dog's fur and travels to Bloggs's eyes. His lens focuses the light on his retina where it causes a particular pattern of activation. Information about that pattern is then sent along the optic nerve into the brain where it is processed. Finally, a token of DOG is formed deep in Bloggs's brain. Let's call the pattern of activation on Bloggs's retina the 'd-pattern'. There's a causal connection between the d-pattern and Bloggs's DOG token: the d-pattern caused certain activity in Bloggs's optic nerve which caused some stuff to happen in his brain which caused the formation of a DOG token. Consequently, the causal theory of content is committed to the absurd claim that DOGs are about d-patterns of activation on the retina! (Alternatively, perhaps we should say that DOGs are about dogs-or-d-patterns.) This is sometimes called the 'depth' problem because it demands an answer to the question, 'At what depth in the causal history of a mental representation is content assigned?' (see Sterelny 1990: Ch. 6). We will return to the depth problem in Section 9.4.

A similar problem is the 'width' problem (also called the 'qua' problem). When Bloggs looks at a dog, he doesn't see the whole dog; indeed, he doesn't even see the whole surface of the dog. At best he sees the side of the dog closest to him. So, strictly speaking, what caused Bloggs to form a DOG token was not the dog, nor even the surface of the dog, but rather part of the surface of the dog. For convenience, let's call the part of the surface of the dog which Bloggs saw, 'part X'. Since it was part X which caused Bloggs to form a token of DOG, why isn't the content of DOG 'part X'? (see Sterelny 1990: Ch. 6). (It's said that the English philosopher G. E. Moore (1837–1958) was once asked if the sheep had been shorn. He glanced at the sheep and replied, 'Well, this side of them has.')

Important though the difficulties discussed so far are, most of the attention in the literature has focused on a different problem: the *disjunction problem*. The disjunction problem arises because we occasionally misidentify objects. For example, one foggy evening Bloggs mistook a sheep for a dog. That is, a sheep caused him to have the mental symbol DOG. It follows that Bloggs's DOG symbols are caused by both dogs and sheep. (Strictly, Bloggs's DOG symbols are caused by both dogs and sheep-on-foggy-evenings. For present purposes I'll just say 'sheep'.) See Figure 9.1.

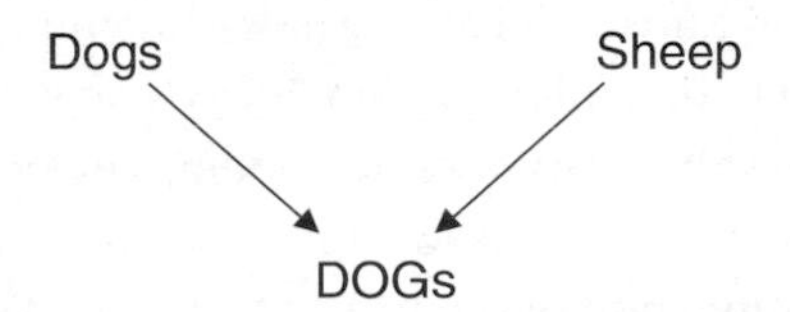

Figure 9.1 The disjunction problem. Bloggs's DOGs are caused by both dogs and sheep

Now according to the causal theory of content, DOGs are about dogs if and only if they are caused by dogs *and nothing else*. But in the case we are considering, a token of DOG was caused by a sheep. Therefore Bloggs's DOG symbols aren't simply about dogs. Rather, since Bloggs's DOG symbols can be caused by either dogs or sheep (and, let us suppose, by nothing else), the content of DOGs is not dogs, but dogs-or-sheep!

Notice that this means that nobody ever misidentifies anything. The natural thing to say about Bloggs's predicament that foggy evening is that he mistook a sheep for a dog. But the causal theory is committed to saying that he *correctly* identified a sheep as a dog-or-sheep.

It's been suggested (see, for example, Dretske 1981) that there is a crucial period in our lives when our DOG symbols get their meaning. Our teachers make sure that, during that period, only dogs get to cause our DOG symbols. That's why DOGs are about dogs, not dogs-or-sheep. However, it seems very unlikely that any such period exists. Whilst I try to avoid saying 'cat' when my toddler is patting a dog, I certainly don't make sure that only dogs cause him to have the symbol DOG. How could I? I don't know enough about the inside of his head to make sure that his DOG symbols are only ever caused in exactly the right way.

The disjunction problems turn out to be a very hard problem indeed. As we will see, it keeps coming back like a bad dream.

9.3 The teleological theory

To understand the teleological theory of content we first need to understand the idea of a **biological function** (sometimes called a 'proper function'). According to the *teleological theory of biological function*, the biological function of an organ is an *effect* of the organ—something the organ *does*. In particular, it is that effect which contributed to the survival and reproduction of the evolutionary ancestors of the contemporary bearers of the organ. Thus the human eye has the biological function of seeing because our ancestors survived and reproduced in part because they had eyes which enabled them to see. You and I have eyes today in part because our ancestors had eyes which, by allowing them to see, increased their chance of surviving and reproducing.

Here's another example. What's the biological function of the heart? We've noted that the biological function of an organ is something that it does. However, the heart does more than one thing. For simplicity's sake, we'll restrict our attention to two of the things the heart does: (i) it pumps blood and (ii) it make those small sounds which the doctor listens to with her stethoscope. Which one of these effects is the biological function of the heart? Is the heart's biological function to pump blood or make little noises?

According to the teleological theory of biological function, the function of the heart is to pump blood rather than make little noises. This is because our evolutionary ancestors survived and reproduced in part because they had hearts that pumped blood; they did not survive and reproduce because their hearts made small sounds. You and I have hearts today in part because our ancestors had hearts which pumped blood, not because they had hearts which made little noises. Consequently, the biological function of our heart is to pump blood rather than make little noises.

We can put the point about biological function quite generally as follows. Say that contemporary members of a species S have an organ O. The biological function, F, of O is that effect of O which contributed to the survival and reproduction of the ancestors of S. In other words, Ss have Os today because the ancestors of S had Os which did F.

Notice that sometimes an organ fails to achieve its biological function. For example, Bloggs's heart may fail to pump blood because his coronary arteries are clogged with cholesterol. Or the chlorophyll in Bloggs's favorite pot plant may fail to trap solar energy because Bloggs forgot to water it. The conditions under which an organ fulfils its biological function are called its *Normal* conditions; the conditions under which it fails to fulfill its biological function are called its *abNormal* conditions. Having a heap of cholesterol in your blood is abNormal for heart function; being dried out is abNormal for chlorophyll function. (Note the capitalized 'N' which serves to distinguish these special uses of 'Normal' and 'abNormal' from other, more familiar uses.)

Discussions of the teleological theory of content almost always turn on the example of a frog which uses its tongue to catch flies. Now the tongue 'snapping' behavior of the frog is under the control of a state of the frog's brain. Let's call that state 'G'. G is caused by the sight of a passing fly and causes the frog's tongue to 'snap'. Presumably, G has the content 'fly zooming by' ('fly' for short).

It turns out that frogs can't distinguish flies from other small black objects. Mean little boys exploit this feature of frogs and amuse themselves by getting frogs to snap at and ingest BBs (the small lead pellets fired by air rifles). When a frog snaps at a BB it's natural to say that the frog misidentified a BB as a fly. But now the disjunction problem arises. Since both flies and BBs cause the frog to have the brain state G, the causal theory of content is committed to saying that the content of G is flies-or-BBs. And in that case the frog doesn't mistake a BB for a fly—it correctly identifies a BB as a fly-or-BB.

The teleological theory of content offers a solution to this difficulty. Plausibly, the biological function of G is to catch flies: it's because the frog's ancestors had a brain state—G—which directed fly-catching behavior that they survived and reproduced. Alas, in contemporary frogs G does not always direct fly-catching behavior: it sometimes directs BB-catching behavior. In other words, mean little boys torturing frogs with BBs constitute abNormal conditions for G.

We can use the claim that the biological function of G is to catch flies to resolve the disjunction problem. Under Normal conditions, G is caused by, and only by, flies; it is only under abNormal conditions that G is caused by BBs. According to the teleological theory of content, the content of a mental symbol is determined by, and only by, whatever causes it *under Normal conditions*. Since BBs don't cause G to occur under Normal conditions, G does not mean flies-or-BBs; it only means flies.

This is a very elegant theory. However, it faces difficulties of its own. Let's return to the idea of a biological function. A couple of paragraphs back we observed that any frog which detected flies would tend to survive and reproduce. However, in the frog's ancestors' environment pretty much any small black object zooming past was a fly, and so any frog which detected small black objects zooming past would tend to survive and reproduce. Consequently, it is **indeterminate** whether the biological function of G is to detect flies or to detect small black objects. It follows that, according to the teleological theory of content, the *content* of G is indeterminate: there is no way of establishing whether the content of G is 'fly' or 'small black thing'. The teleological theory of content, therefore, solves the disjunction problem only by introducing its own kind of indeterminacy. (See Fodor 1987: 104–6; 1990*c*.)

Teleological theorists have responded to this problem, but we won't delve further into the intricacies of the teleological theory. Sterelny 1990: Section 6.6 is a nice example of the kind of response a teleological theory can make to the indetermination problem. See also Millikan 1991.

9.4 Fodor's theory

In this section we will explore a theory of content proposed by the contemporary American philosopher Jerry Fodor (1987: 106–11; 1990*d*). I will begin by giving a loose, intuitive account of Fodor's theory. With that account in hand we can see how Fodor proposes to deal with the disjunction problem. After that, I'll give a more precise account of Fodor's theory, and show how it deals with at least one of the problems which flummoxed the causal theory of content. I'll close this section with a skeptical remark.

Recall the example of the disjunction problem given in Section 9.2. Since both dogs and sheep-on-foggy-evenings cause Bloggs to have DOG tokens, the causal theory of content is committed to the claim that Bloggs's DOG tokens are about dogs-or-sheep-on-foggy evenings ('dogs-or-sheep' for short). Fodor begins to address this problem by observing that the causal connection between sheep and DOGs depends on the causal connection between dogs and DOGS. That is, if there were no sheep, dogs would still cause DOGs; but if there were no dogs, sheep would not cause DOGs.

Fodor then goes on to propose that content is determined only by those causal relations between a thing in the world and a mental representation that are independent of other such causal relations. DOG is about dogs rather than sheep because the causal relationship between dogs and DOGs is independent of that between sheep and DOGs, but not vice versa. And DOG is about dogs rather than dogs-or-sheep because the causal relationship between dogs and DOGs is independent of that between dogs-or-sheep and DOGs, but not vice versa. The problem of disjunction thus appears to have been vanquished.

Recall that in Section 9.2 we noted that the causal theory has a problem with, amongst other things, thoughts about nonexistent entities like the Easter Bunny. Since the Easter Bunny does not exist, it can't be the case that anybody's EASTER BUNNY tokens were caused by, and only by, the Easter Bunny. How does Fodor's theory deal with thoughts about nonexistent objects? This is where we must abandon the loose, intuitive account of Fodor's theory and consider a more precise version.

Fodor articulates his own theory as follows. (Note that I have used capitals for the names of mental representations (e.g. COW) whereas Fodor himself forms the names of mental representations by using inverted commas (e.g. 'cow'). Nothing at all turns on this typographic difference.)

> 'Cow' means *cow* if (i) there is a nomic relation between the property of being a cow and the property of being a cause of 'cow' tokens; and (ii) if there are nomic relations between other properties and the property of being a cause of 'cow' tokens, then the latter nomic relations depend asymmetrically upon the former. (Fodor 1990*d*: 93)

Let's unpack this a bit. First, notice that Fodor uses the expression 'nomic relation'. A nomic relation is a law-like relation; that is, a relation which holds (or would hold) under a very wide range of conditions. Second, note that nomic relations exist between *properties*. That's why Fodor talks about, for example, the property of being a cow rather than about cows. Here's an example of a nomic relation. In the case of water at sea level there's a nomic relation between the property of being at 100°C (212°F) and the property of boiling. This is a nomic relation because it holds (or would hold) under a very wide range of conditions: any sample of water which is located at sea-level will boil at 100°C. Finally, notice that Fodor says that one lot of nomic relations **asymmetrically depend** upon another nomic relation. Here's an example of asymmetric dependence. Say that Joey is the son of Kanga. In that case, whilst Kanga could have existed without Joey existing, Joey could not exist without Kanga existing. There is an asymmetry in their relations of dependence: one depends on the other but not vice versa.

Putting all this together we can say that, according to Fodor, DOGs are about dogs not sheep because: (i) there is a nomic relation between the property of being a dog and the property of being a cause of DOGs; and (ii) whilst there is also a nomic relation between the property of being a sheep and the property of being a cause of DOGs, the second nomic relation asymmetrically depends on the first one. Phew!

Now let's apply Fodor's official version of his theory to the case of Bloggs's EASTER BUNNY tokens. EASTER BUNNYs are about the Easter Bunny if: (i) there is a nomic relation between the property of being the Easter Bunny and the property of being a cause of EASTER BUNNYs; and (ii) if other properties are nomically related to the property of being a cause of EASTER BUNNYs, the latter nomic relations *asymmetrically depend* on the former. Now, on the assumption that the Easter Bunny doesn't exist, there can be no *causal* relations between the Easter Bunny and EASTER BUNNY tokens. However, Fodor insists that there is still a *nomic* relation between the property of being the Easter Bunny and the property of being a cause of EASTER BUNNYs. That is, he insists that *if* the Easter Bunny existed then the Easter Bunny would be a cause of EASTER BUNNYs, and so (other things being equal) EASTER BUNNYs are about the Easter Bunny.

Should Fodor be so insistent? How can he be so sure about the nomic relations of nonexistent properties? Well, we can say at least this much in his defense. Here's an example of a nonexistent property: the property of being Hitler's atom bomb. That's a nonexistent property because the Nazis never got around to building one. (And that, to put it mildly, is a Good Thing.) Nevertheless, there does seem to be a nomic relation between the property of being Hitler's atom bomb and the property of being a cause of London's destruction. After all, it seems quite likely that had Hitler got the bomb he would have dropped it on London. So the idea of nomic relations between nonexistent properties is not unintelligible.

So far we have seen how Fodor can with some plausibility respond to the disjunction problem, and to the problem of nonexistent objects. However, at least one problem that arose for the causal theory also arises for Fodor's theory—the depth problem. In Section 9.2 we noted that, whilst it's true that dogs cause DOGs, dogs also cause patterns of activation on the retina which in turn cause DOGs. We called those patterns 'd-patterns' and asked why, according to the causal theory, the content of DOGs isn't d-patterns or dogs-or-d-patterns. Now let's consider this example from the perspective of Fodor's theory. For ease of expression I'll revert to the loose, intuitive version of the theory. According to Fodor's theory, DOGs will be about dogs rather than d-patterns if the causal link between dogs and DOGs is independent of that between d-patterns and DOGs, but not vice versa. But there is at least one situation in which the causal link between d-patterns and DOGs is independent of that between dogs and DOGs. Imagine that there's a break in the causal chain leading from dogs to Bloggs's d-patterns. (Maybe Bloggs has suddenly developed cataracts.) In that case dogs wouldn't cause DOGs but d-patterns would still cause DOGs. Consequently, it's not the case that the causal relation between d-patterns and DOGs is dependent on that between dogs and DOGs, and so Fodor is committed to saying that the content of Bloggs's DOG tokens is dogs-or-d-patterns. In other words, the depth problem remains a concern. (For a different take on a similar example see Carruthers 2000: 141.)

9.5 Functional role theory

According to functionalism, mental states are the occupants of characteristic causal (or 'functional') roles (see Chapter 4). A thoroughgoing functionalist will insist that all the features of a mental state M are determined by M's causal role. It follows that the *content* of M is determined by its causal role. A functional role theory of content offers an account of how causal role determines content. (Notice that I said that a *thoroughgoing* functionalist will insist that all the features of a mental state are determined by its causal role. In my view, if you're not a thoroughgoing functionalist then you're not a functionalist at all—you're just someone who (sensibly) thinks that causal roles are important. I suspect, though, that the majority of philosophers won't go along with this terminological stricture.)

Here's how functionalist role theories of content usually go. Notice that a person's mental states typically form a causal network. For example, Bloggs's belief that it's Thursday caused him to believe that tomorrow is Friday; his belief that tomorrow is Friday, together with his belief that Friday is payday, caused him to believe that tomorrow's payday; and his belief that tomorrow's payday caused him to believe that tomorrow he will have money to spend.

In addition to the causal network in which mental states are embedded, there is typically an *inferential* network in which the *contents* of those beliefs are embedded. Notice that the contents of Bloggs's beliefs in the example just given take the form of a rational argument from a series of premises to the conclusion 'I (Bloggs) will have money to spend tomorrow'. The argument is represented diagrammatically in Figure 9.2. (Note that some of the premises of this argument have been suppressed, but it'll do for present purposes.)

So far we have simply noted the existence of two networks: a causal one linking mental states and an inferential one linking the contents of mental states. According to functional role theories of content, we assign content to mental states by mapping the inferential network onto the causal one. Figure 9.3 gives the structure of the causal network for the example we are considering.

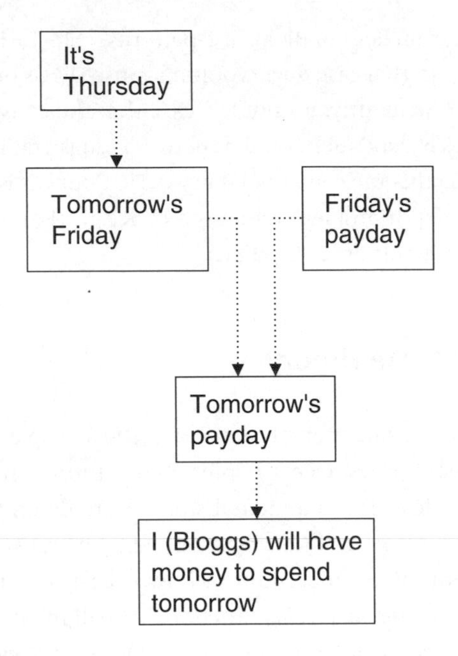

Figure 9.2 An inferential network

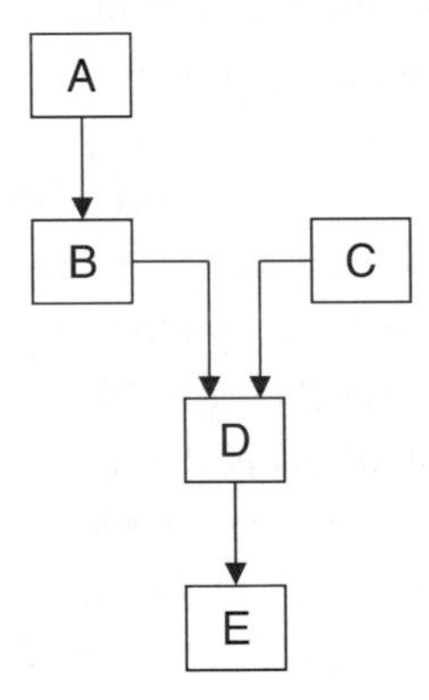

Figure 9.3 A causal network involving five beliefs (A–E)

Notice that I have identified the beliefs in the causal network with letters rather than by content; that is, I have used labels like 'A' rather than 'The belief that it is Thursday'. This is because the whole point of the exercise is to see how functional role semantics attributes contents to mental states. The aim is to figure out the contents of beliefs A–E.

Now it is clear that the network in Figure 9.2 has the same structure as that in Figure 9.3; that is, they are *isomorphic*. So, according to the function role theory of content, we attribute to each mental state in the causal network the contents of the corresponding node in the inferential network:

Content of A → It's Thursday

Content of B → Tomorrow's Friday

Content of C → Friday's payday

Content of D → Tomorrow's payday

Content of E → I (Bloggs) will have money to spend tomorrow

Unfortunately, there are at least four difficulties with this proposal.

First difficulty. There's a problem about uniqueness. Setting aside issues of vagueness and ambiguity, it's plausible that each thought has a unique content. However, the functional role theory of content doesn't guarantee a unique assignment of contents to mental states. To see this, consider the inferential network given in Figure 9.4. (Once again there are a number of suppressed premises.)

The structure of the inferential network given in Figure 9.4 is isomorphic to the causal structure given in Figure 9.3. Therefore the functional role theory of content licences the following attributions of content to mental states A–E:

Content of A → It's Sunday

Content of B → Tomorrow's Monday

Content of C → Monday's mother's washing day

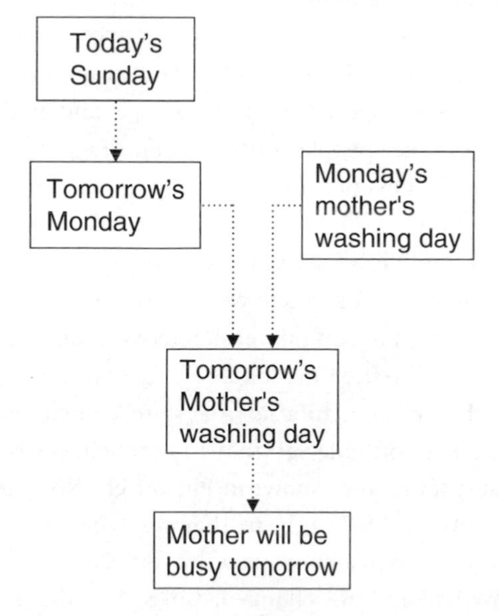

Figure 9.4 Another inferential network that is isomorphic to the causal network given in Figure 9.3

Content of D → Tomorrow's mother's washing day

Content of E → Mother will be busy tomorrow

Consequently, the attributions of content to mental states licenced by functional role semantics are not unique; for example, the theory attributes both the content 'It's Thursday' and the content 'It's Sunday' to mental state A. Moreover, with a little bit of ingenuity we can create an indefinite number of arguments that are isomorphic to the causal structure given in Figure 9.3. Functional role semantics doesn't just licence a little bit of ambiguity: it licences an indefinite amount.

Second difficulty. The content of a mental state is an important determinant of the causal relations of that state. (For more on the issue of content and mental causation see Sections 10.3 and 10.4.) It's because Bloggs has a belief with the content *Sally is cute and cuddly* that he comes to have a belief with the content *Sally is cute*. Had Bloggs begun with a belief with the content *Neil is cute and cuddly* he would not have thereby come to have a belief with the content *Sally is cute*. But if content is an important determinant of the causal relations of mental states, it follows that the causal relations of mental states don't determine their content. In other words, the functional role theory of content has put the cart before the horse: the content of a mental state is not given by that state's causal powers; rather the causal powers of a mental state are given (in part) by its content.

Third difficulty. The functional role approach to content relies on mapping a causal network of mental states onto an inferential network. How, then, do we obtain the inferential network? Well, we develop a network of propositions which are logically or evidentially related to each other. Unfortunately, the mental states of real humans don't always respect the canons of logic and evidence: sometimes we're irrational. For example, people routinely commit the 'gambler's fallacy': they conclude that a random event is more likely to happen just because it hasn't happened for a while. Note, though, that we still attribute contentful states to people who commit the gambler's fallacy. We say, for example, that Bloggs thinks that the six is sure to come up soon. Since we are not always rational, we cannot assign content simply by mapping an inferential network onto the causal one.

Fourth difficulty. According to the functional role theory, the content of a mental state is determined by the causal relations of that state: change the causal relations and you change the state's content. Say that Bloggs believes snow is white but he doesn't realize that it sometimes snows in Pittsburgh. Now imagine that Sally tells him about the snow in Pittsburgh. In that case the causal relations of his belief that snow is white have just changed a tiny bit. Consequently, the content of his belief that snow is white has changed. But surely that's wrong: the content of his belief that snow is white remains the same.

9.6 Wide or narrow?

In recent decades a great deal of attention has been paid to the issue of **wide** versus **narrow content**. The wide/narrow distinction was originally drawn by the contemporary American philosopher Hilary Putnam, although Putnam was primarily concerned with the meaning of linguistic items rather than mental content (see Putnam 1975). In what follows we will focus on the wide/narrow distinction as it applies to mental content.

Here's an example much like that which Putnam used. Bloggs frequently has thoughts about water, and since water is H_2O, when Bloggs has a water thought he's thinking about H_2O. Now, in a distant part of the universe there is a planet that is almost exactly the same as Earth, and living on that planet is a guy who's almost exactly like Bloggs. Let's call that planet **Twin-Earth** and call the guy who's almost exactly like Bloggs 'Twin-Bloggs'.

I said that Twin-Earth is almost exactly like Earth, and that Twin-Bloggs is almost exactly like Bloggs. In fact, with one small exception, Twin-Earth is an atom-for-atom duplicate of Earth, and Twin-Bloggs is an atom-for-atom duplicate of Bloggs. The exception is this: whereas here on Earth the clear liquid which fills lakes, comes out of taps, and is essential for life is H_2O, on Twin-Earth the clear liquid which fills lakes, comes out of taps, and is essential for life is XYZ. (Or, as I will say henceforth, whilst the 'wet stuff' on Earth is H_2O, the 'wet stuff' on Twin-Earth is XYZ.) Moreover, in all superficial respects H_2O is strikingly similar to XYZ—so much so that without a chemical analysis you can't tell them apart.

Now let's consider Twin-Bloggs's thoughts about the wet stuff on Twin-Earth. Bloggs's thoughts about the wet stuff on Earth are about H_2O; it's implausible, though, that Twin-Bloggs is thinking about H_2O. After all, he's never seen, touched, or drunk any H_2O, and he might not even know that it exists. Rather, when Twin-Bloggs thinks about the wet stuff on Twin-Earth he's thinking about XYZ. So the content of Bloggs's thoughts about the wet stuff is distinct from that of Twin-Bloggs's thoughts about the wet stuff. Bloggs's thought is about H_2O; Twin-Bloggs's thought is about XYZ.

What's striking about this case is that, even though Bloggs and Twin-Bloggs's have brains which are in all relevant respects identical, their thoughts about the wet stuff have different contents. It follows that the content of our thought is not entirely determined by our brain states: it's possible for two people to have identical brain states and yet have thoughts with different contents. To use an old slogan: 'Meanings ain't in the head' (Putnam 1975).

With this example before us, we can appreciate the difference between wide and narrow content. Philosophers say that Bloggs's beliefs about wet stuff have different *wide* content to Twin-Bloggs's beliefs about the wet stuff. The contents of their beliefs are wide in that they are **individuated** (or distinguished) by what's going on in the world external to the believers' heads. Bloggs and Twin-Bloggs's thoughts about the wet stuff are distinct, not because their brains are in relevant respects distinct, but because their *environments* are distinct: one's in an H_2O-containing environment, the other an XYZ-containing environment.

Whilst we can recognize a sense in which the content of Bloggs's belief differs from that of Twin-Bloggs's, there's also a sense in which the contents of their beliefs are the *same*. Say that Bloggs believes that he should drink eight glasses of water every day, and that he expresses his belief by saying, 'I should drink eight glasses of water every day'. Then Twin-Bloggs will have a belief which he expresses with the phrase, 'I should drink eight glasses of water every day'. Moreover, note that Bloggs's belief will cause him to behave in certain ways: other things being equal, he'll drink eight glasses of the stuff he calls 'water' every day. Similarly, Twin-Bloggs's belief will cause him to act in certain ways: other things being equal, he'll drink eight glasses of the stuff he calls 'water' every day. Finally, Bloggs and Twin-Bloggs will both feel the same way about the stuff they call 'water'. If Bloggs has a phobia about washing in the stuff he calls 'water', then Twin-Bloggs will have a phobia about washing in the stuff *he* calls water.

So far we have recognized that in many ways Bloggs and Twin-Bloggs would seem to have identical beliefs about the wet stuff. But identity of belief implies identity of content. So if there's a sense in which Bloggs and Twin-Bloggs have the same beliefs about the wet stuff, then there's a sense in which their beliefs about the wet stuff have the same content. The expression *narrow content* is used to pick out the content which Bloggs and Twin-Bloggs share.

The focus of our discussion so far has been Putnam's famous Twin-Earth example. The contemporary American philosopher Tyler Burge (1979) has provided another kind of example of wide content. Say that Bloggs wakes up one morning with a pain in his leg, halfway between his knee and his hip. 'Goodness,' thinks Bloggs, 'I've got arthritis in my thigh.' In fact, arthritis is, by definition, inflammation of a *joint*, so Bloggs can't have arthritis in his thigh. Consequently, Bloggs's belief that he has arthritis in his thigh is false.

Now consider a slightly different situation. Imagine that the medical profession uses 'arthritis' not for inflammation of the joints but for leg pain; that is, imagine that 'arthritis' means 'pain in the leg'. Everything else about the situation remains as before; in particular, Bloggs's brain states are exactly as they were before. But now when Bloggs wakes up in the morning and thinks, 'Goodness, I've got arthritis in my thigh', he has a *true* belief. He really does have arthritis since he has a pain in his thigh and 'arthritis' means 'pain in the leg'.

It's clear that the content of Bloggs's beliefs about arthritis are determined by facts outside Bloggs's head; in particular, they're determined by facts about the way the word 'arthritis' is used in the broader community. So once again we have a case of wide content: meaning ain't in the head.

In everyday life we typically pick out beliefs by their wide content; that is, we identify beliefs in terms of objects external to the believer. (Notice that the examples used by Putnam and Burge appeal to our everyday judgements about content attribution.) However, there's a strong case to be made for arguing that scientific psychology should distinguish beliefs in terms of their *narrow* content. Imagine that Bloggs is transported to Twin-Earth and interpret the content of his desire to drink eight glasses of water per day narrowly. Relying on the principle that, other things being equal, people act so as to satisfy their desires, we can predict that when he is on Twin-Earth Bloggs will drink eight glasses of the wet stuff per day; that is, he will drink eight glasses of XYZ. That sounds like the right prediction to make—after all, he won't be drinking eight glasses of H_2O per day because there's no H_2O for him to drink. Now imagine that Bloggs is transported to Twin-Earth and interpret the content of his desire to drink eight glasses of water per day widely. Understood widely, his desire to drink eight glasses of water per day is the desire to drink eight glasses of H_2O per day. If we now apply the principle that, other things being equal, people act so as to satisfy their desires, we end up predicting that on Twin-Earth Bloggs will drink eight glasses of H_2O per day. And that's got to be wrong since, as we have noted, there's no H_2O for him to drink. Since scientific psychology is in the business of predicting behavior, it seems that scientific psychology should individuate beliefs by their narrow content.

The conclusion I have just drawn is the standard one. However, it's worth noting that not everyone is ready to abandon wide content for predictive purposes. For more on this topic see Further Reading, below.

SUMMARY

(1) Some mental states have content; that is, they are *about* things.

(2) Theories of content attempt to explain how mental states get to be about things.

(3) According to the resemblance theory of content, mental states are about what they resemble. This theory faces severe difficulties.

(4) According to the causal theory of content, dog thoughts are about dogs because they are caused by, and only by, dogs.

(5) The most widely discussed difficulty for the causal theory is the disjunction problem which arises because, in cases of misidentification, dog thoughts are caused by non-dogs—for example, by sheep. In that case the causal theory is committed to the claim that dog thoughts are about dogs-or-sheep.

(6) According to the teleological theory, the content of a thought is determined under Normal conditions. Normal conditions are those under which the relevant organisms evolved.

(7) Fodor appeals to asymmetric dependencies to solve the disjunction problem. Dog thoughts are about dogs rather than sheep because, whilst dogs would cause dog thoughts even if sheep didn't cause dog thoughts, sheep would not cause dog thoughts if dogs didn't cause dog thoughts.

(8) Functional role theories assign content by mapping the causal (or 'functional') relations of mental states onto a network of inferential relations.

(9) The content of a thought is said to be *wide* if it depends on the environment of the thinker; content is said to be *narrow* if it is independent of the thinker's environment.

(10) There are reasons for thinking that scientific psychology should focus on mental states individuated by their narrow content.

FURTHER READING

Good textbook-style introductions to the problem of content are found in Sterelny 1990: Ch. 6; Braddon-Mitchell and Jackson 1996: Part 3; and Kim 1996: Ch. 8. Of these Kim is the easiest; Sterelny focuses on causal and covariance theories.

A nice book-length introduction to the issue of content is Cummins 1989.

The most detailed account of functional role semantics is probably Brian Loar's *Mind and Meaning* (1981). That book is considerably more difficult than this one.

'Fodor's guide to mental representation' (Fodor 1990*b*) is both a classic and surprisingly readable. An early version of the causal theory is Fred Dretske's *Knowledge and the Flow of Information* (1981), and an early version of the teleological theory is Ruth Millikan's *Language, Thought and Other Biological Categories* (1984). The former is hard; the latter very dense. Millikan offers a much more user-friendly version of her views in Millikan 1986. Fodor 1990*c* contains a brilliant discussion of both the causal and teleological theories. See also Fodor 1987: Ch. 4. He presents his covariance theory in Fodor 1987: 106–11; 1990*c*.

The issues surrounding wide and narrow content are introduced in Sterelny 1990: Ch. 5; Braddon-Mitchell and Jackson 1996: Ch. 12; and Kim 1996: 193–207. The classic papers in this area are Putnam 1975 and Burge 1979; 1986. The Burge papers in particular are not easy.

An important—and highly skeptical—discussion of mental representation is Stephen Stich's classic, *From Folk Psychology to Cognitive Science* (Stich 1983). It contains important material on narrow content. See especially Ch. 4. It's not easy, but it's worth the effort.

TUTORIAL QUESTIONS

(1) Describe, and discuss one difficulty with, the resemblance theory of content.

(2) Describe the causal theory of content.

(3) What's the depth problem?

(4) What's the disjunction problem?

(5) 'The ancestors of the modern frog survived because they snapped at flies, not because they snapped at little black things.' Discuss.

(6) Give an example of an asymmetric dependency.

(7) Describe Fodor's response to the disjunction problem.

(8) What did Putnam mean when he said that 'Cut the pie anyway you like, "meanings" just ain't in the head' (Putnam 1975)?

10

Mental causation

> if it isn't literally true that my wanting is causally responsible for my reaching, and my itching is causally responsible for my scratching, and my believing is causally responsible for my saying . . . then practically everything I believe about anything is false and it's the end of the world.
>
> —Jerry Fodor

In the Introduction I gave a list of properties which any theory of mental states must either explain or explain away. Three items on that list were concerned with the causal relations in which mental states are typically involved:

1. Some mental states are caused by states of the world.
2. Some mental states cause actions.
3. Some mental states cause other mental states.

The task of explaining how mental states can have these kinds of properties is often called the *problem of mental causation*. Other things being equal, a theory of mental states which makes sense of mental causation is preferable to one which doesn't. For example, we saw in Section 1.3 that Descartes had difficulty explaining how the nonphysical mind he postulated interacts with the physical body. Descartes made two central claims: (i) that mind and body are radically different kinds of substances and (ii) that mind and body causally interact. As Princess Elizabeth of Bohemia pointed out, these two claims are in tension: how can two radically distinct kinds of substance causally interact?

When it comes to mental causation it might seem that physicalist theories have the upper hand: if mental states are physical states, then surely there can be no problem accounting for mental causation. If only it were that simple. In the 1980s philosophers began to realize that physicalism has its own problem of mental causation. Indeed, the contemporary American philosopher Jaegwon Kim has pointed out that physicalism faces *several* problems of mental causation (Kim 1998: Ch. 2). In this chapter we will consider two problems: (i) what Kim has called the *problem of causal exclusion* and (ii) a problem about the causal efficacy of content.

Before getting under way, a brief clarificatory remark is in order. In what follows I will talk about both mental states and brain states. When philosophers talk about states they are usually talking about *types*. (The type/token distinction is introduced in Section 3.4.) For example, when they say, 'Other things being equal, fear causes screaming', they are making a claim about the type fear; they are only indirectly making a claim about particular tokens of fear. In what follows I will use expressions like 'fear' and 'brain state B' to refer to types, and I will use expressions like 'Bloggs's token of fear' and 'the token of state B in Bloggs's brain' when I want to talk about tokens. I admit that these are pretty ugly expressions; however, in what follows it will be important to keep track of tokens and types.

10.1 The problem of causal exclusion

Bloggs goes to see a horror movie, gets really frightened, and screams. Now, according to physicalism, mental states supervene on physical states; in particular, they supervene on brain states. Let's say that, in Bloggs's case, his fear is realized by a token of brain state B. See Figure 10.1.

Now it's very likely that it is his being in brain state B that causes Bloggs to scream; that is, if we trace the causal pathway backwards from Bloggs's screaming we will, in due course, arrive at brain state B. See Figure 10.2.

But now we have a serious problem. According to Figure 10.2, what makes Bloggs scream is his being in state B; Bloggs's fear does nothing. But that's deeply counterintuitive: surely Bloggs screamed *because* he was afraid. Moreover, we posit

Figure 10.1 Fear is realized by brain state B. The dotted arrow indicates the realization relation

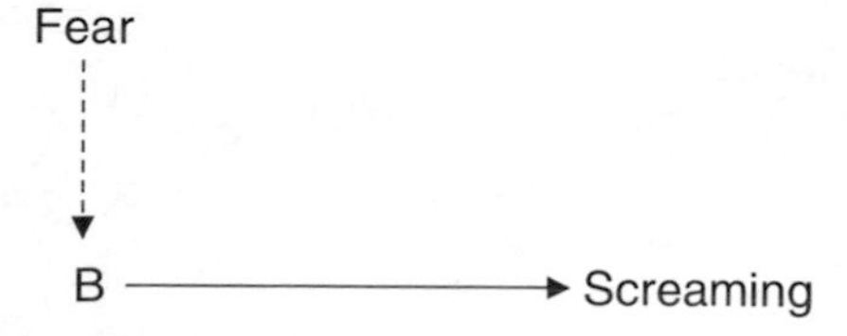

Figure 10.2 Fear is realized by brain state B, and brain state B causes screaming. The solid arrow represents the causal relation

mental states like fear in order to explain behavior. We attribute fear to Bloggs because, under the circumstances, attributing fear to him provides a good explanation of why he screamed. But if Bloggs's fear did not make him scream, then we no longer seem to have much reason for saying that he is afraid. If mental states don't do any causal work, there's little point in positing them.

This is the problem of causal exclusion. Once we allow that mental states are realized by physical states, there no longer seems to be anything for the mental states to do: they are 'excluded' from the causal story.

One way to respond to the problem of causal exclusion is by allowing that Bloggs's fear *and* his being in state B caused him to scream. See Figure 10.3. The situation represented by Figure 10.3 is an example of what philosophers call *overdetermination*. Here's another case. Imagine that Sally tells Bloggs a joke and, simultaneously, Bloggs sees Neil slip on a banana skin. Both of these events cause Bloggs to laugh. Moreover, the events are independent of each other in this sense: if Bloggs had only heard the joke he would have laughed; and if he had only seen Neil slip he would have laughed. In that case Bloggs's laughing is overdetermined: it is independently caused by both the joke and the slipping.

Whilst there are no doubt real cases of overdetermination, it's very hard to believe that every human action is overdetermined. It's simply incredible that everything I do is caused twice over: once by my mental state tokens and once by my brain state tokens. Consequently, Figure 10.3 does not represent a satisfactory response to the problem of causal exclusion.

An alternative response would be to insist on the causal efficacy of Bloggs's fear whilst denying the causal efficacy of state B. (We can think of this as the causal exclusion of brain state B.) See Figure 10.4. But this, too, is unattractive. For whilst

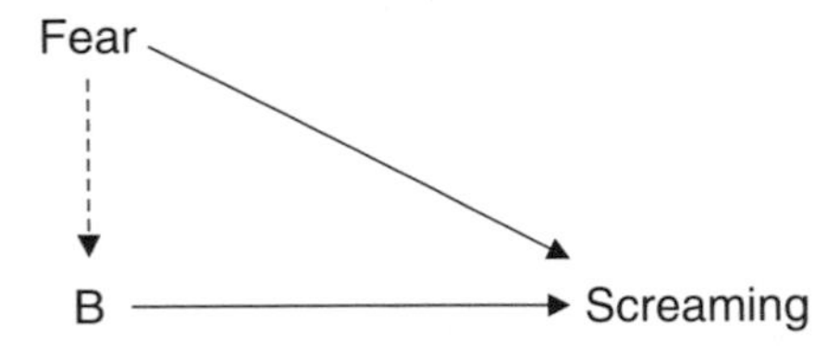

Figure 10.3 A case of overdetermination. Screaming is caused by both fear and brain state B

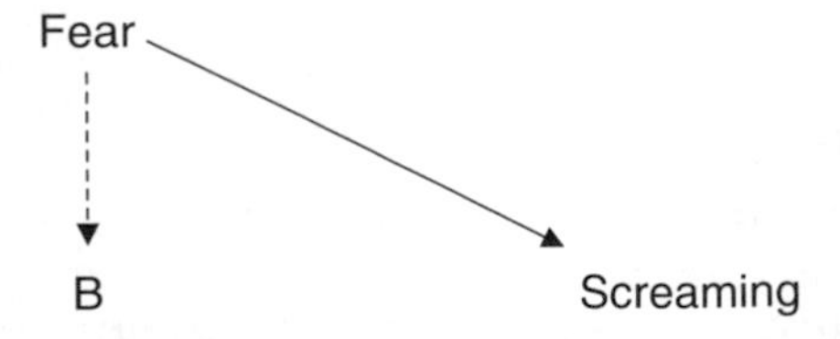

Figure 10.4 Fear causes screaming, but brain state B does not

Figure 10.5 If fear were type identical to brain state B, overdetermination would no longer be a problem

it preserves the intuition that Bloggs screamed because he was afraid, it denies the overwhelmingly plausible claim that a state of Bloggs's brain is causally responsible for his screaming.

Notice that, if the identity theory is true, the problem of causal exclusion does not arise. For say that fear is type identical to brain state B. As it is one and the same state, there is no longer a threat of overdetermination. See Figure 10.5. However, once we allow that fear is multiply realized, this solution is not available to us: it simply won't be the case that fear is type identical to a single physical type. Consequently, since most contemporary physicalists endorse the claim that mental states are multiply realizable, most contemporary physicalists are faced with the problem of causal exclusion.

An ideal solution to the problem of causal exclusion would somehow maintain the causal significance of both mental states and the physical states which realize them, without falling prey to overdetermination. Can we have our cake and eat it too?

10.2 Responding to the problem of causal exclusion

A number of different responses to the problem of causal exclusion have been made. Broadly speaking, they fall into two categories. Those in the first category stress that analogous problems arise in cases in which there can be no serious doubt about the causal efficacy of the states involved. (See, for example, Baker 1993; Burge 1993.) Those in the second category pay careful attention to the identification of tokens of mental states with tokens of brain states. (See, for example, Jackson and Pettit 1990; Kim 1998.)

1. *Me, worry?* Whatever you think about the claim that mental states are multiply realized, it's apparent that a great many properties which we encounter in the actual world are multiply realized. The property of being a stove, for example, is realized by a variety of physical states, as is the property of being a thermostat.

The prevalence of properties which are multiply realized means that the problem of mental causation threatens to generalize. Here's an example. The term 'analgesic' is used to refer to those drugs which reduce pain. There are many different kinds of analgesic, including aspirin, paracetamol, and morphine.

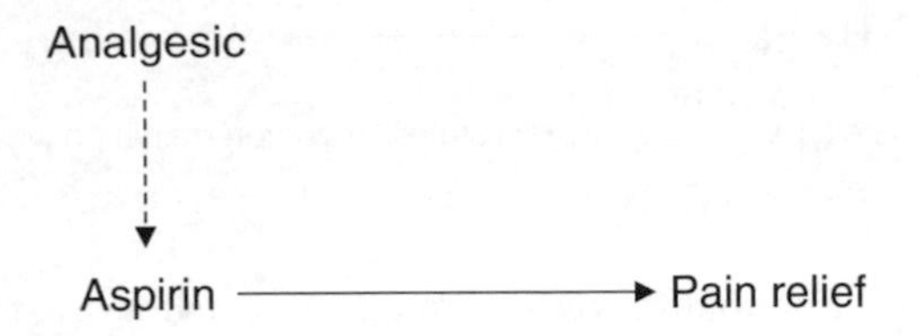

Figure 10.6 The property of being an analgesic is realized by the property of being an aspirin. The property of being an aspirin causes pain relief

These substances differ in their chemical properties, and in the way they affect the nervous system. In other words, the property of being an analgesic is multiply realized. Now imagine that Bloggs has a headache and decides to take an analgesic. Twenty minutes later his headache is gone. As a matter of fact he took two aspirins, and aspirin causes certain changes in the brain which reduce pain. So we have a familiar picture—see Figure 10.6. It seems that all the causal work is being done by the aspirin; the property of being an analgesic is causally inefficacious. It is therefore not only mental causation which is in trouble; by parity of reasoning, *any* property which is multiply realized is causally inefficacious. But this is absurd. It's a deep feature of our explanatory practices that we attribute causal powers to states and properties which are multiply realized. Rather than abandon those practices, we should stop worrying about the metaphysical problems to which they give rise. There must be *something* wrong with the arguments which generated the problems. This is the 'Me, worry?' response to the causal exclusion problem.

I agree that there must be something wrong with the problem of causal exclusion. It's very implausible that analgesics have nothing to do with pain relief, that stoves have nothing to do with saucepans boiling over, and that thermostats have nothing to do with shutting down furnaces. And it's also very implausible that my wanting a coffee has nothing to do with my going to the kitchen. It would be ridiculous to abandon causal explanations couched in terms of multiply realized properties. Nevertheless, following Jaegwon Kim (1998: 61–2), I reject the 'Me, worry?' response. Philosophers want to know how the world 'hangs together' in the most general sense; they want to know how the different parts or aspects of the world relate to one another. The problem of causal exclusion is a classic philosophical problem because it suggests that our understanding of the world is inadequate. We all accept that my desire for a coffee caused me to go into the kitchen; and we all have good reason to accept the account of 'kitchen-directed behavior' offered by the physiologist. But these two claims are in tension, and as philosophers we want to know why. Consequently I don't accept—and I urge you not to accept—the 'Me, worry?' response. I *am* worried, and so should you be.

Figure 10.7 Token identity resolves the issue of the causal efficacy of tokens

2. *Causal efficacy versus causal relevance.* The token identity theorist accepts that Bloggs's fear token is identical to a token of property B in Bloggs's brain. Now physiology has revealed that, other things being equal, tokens of property B cause tokens of screaming. So we have the situation depicted in Figure 10.7. Since the token of fear is identical to—*is one and the same thing as*—the token of B, neither the issue of overdetermination nor the issue of causal exclusion arises.

So is everything fixed? Is it as simple as that? Unfortunately not. So far we have only resolved the issue of the causal efficacy of *tokens* of mental states; we've said nothing about the issue of mental states understood to be *types*. We saw in Section 10.1 that if mental states are type identical to brain states, then the problem of the causal exclusion of mental states doesn't arise. However, according to the token identity theory, fear is not type identical to brain state B; consequently, the problem of causal exclusion—pitched as a problem about types—remains. I will close this section by briefly sketching a reply to this problem due to Frank Jackson and Philip Pettit (1990). Following Jackson and Pettit I will talk about mental *properties* rather than mental *states*. Nothing of substance depends on this shift of focus.

We can distinguish between causal *efficacy* and causal *relevance*. A property is causally efficacious if it is the cause of some effect—if it actually does something. Here's an example: the fire started because the temperature exceeded 300°C. In that case the temperature was causally efficacious—it caused the fire. Now consider another example: the girls stared at Antonio Banderas because he's gorgeous. Gorgeousness is multiply realizable—there are lots of ways to be gorgeous. Indeed, there are lots of ways for a *guy* to be gorgeous (compare and contrast the aforementioned Antonio with Brad Pitt). Consequently, for the reasons discussed in Section 10.1, the causal efficacy of gorgeousness is in doubt. Following Jackson and Pettit, though, we can say that gorgeousness, whilst not causally efficacious, is causally *relevant*. As we have observed, there are lots of ways of being gorgeous: Banderas is gorgeous in virtue of instantiating some property G1; Pitt in virtue of instantiating some property G2; and so on. Banderas's gorgeousness is causally relevant to the staring because, being gorgeous, he instantiates one of the properties which realizes gorgeousness, and that property is causally efficacious of staring. To use Jackson and Pettit's own expression, gorgeousness 'programs for' one of a range of properties any of which is causally efficacious of staring.

Now let's return to the case of fear. Fear—the state of fear—is not causally efficacious: it does not cause screaming. However, fear is causally relevant because it 'programs for' the kind of physical state which *is* causally efficacious in bringing about screaming. Putting this point another way: whilst fear is not, strictly speaking, causally efficacious, it does play a role in the causal explanation of Bloggs's screaming by programming for a property which *is* causally efficacious of screaming.

I will close this section by briefly drawing attention to two difficulties with the Jackson–Pettit position. First, notice that Jackson and Pettit in effect concede that mental states (i.e. types) are causally excluded. Fear turns out not to be causally efficacious after all. Can we live with that? Well, there is still a strong sense in which mental states are causally relevant, and it's still literally true that tokens of mental states are causally efficacious. Nevertheless, even a hint of causal inefficacy is enough to make the stoutest philosopher nervous.

Second, we have been assuming all along that state B is itself causally efficacious. But it is at least possible that B is multiply realizable. Perhaps B is the state of having such-and-such a concentration of a monoamine neurotransmitter in a certain part of the brain. As there are several kinds of monoamine neurotransmitters, B would be multiply realizable. But now the worry about causal exclusion re-emerges. Say that in Bloggs's case B is realized by having a certain concentration of dopamine in the relevant part of his brain. In that case it's the dopamine concentration, not the monoamine concentration, that's causally efficacious. State B merely 'programs for' the dopamine concentration. It seems, then, that Jackson and Pettit are committed to the view that only fairly basic physical and chemical properties are actually causally efficacious; all other properties are at best causally relevant. Jackson and Pettit are aware of this consequence of their views, and maybe they are right not to be overly concerned about it. However, I must admit to being just a little bit worried: it's hard to accept that all properties other than those found in fundamental physics and chemistry are in fact causally inefficacious.

10.3 The causal efficacy of content

According to physicalism, Bloggs's thought that Mt Everest is 8,848 meters high is realized by a token brain state. Let's call that brain state token 'N'. Now, in normal circumstances, N will cause other brain state tokens to come into existence. For example, N might cause brain state token M to come into existence. See Figure 10.8. Since N realizes Bloggs's thought that Mt Everest is 8,848 meters

N ⟶ M

Figure 10.8 Brain state token N causes brain state token M

high, N must be about Mt Everest; that is, N represents Mt Everest as being 8,848 meters high. However, a neuroscientist can explain how N caused M without mentioning that N has the property of being about Mt Everest. She will talk about the pattern of connections between N and other brain states, the fact that N is part of the brain's cholinergic system, and so on. She won't mention that it has the property of representing Mt Everest as 8,848 meters high. So it seems that the content of a thought plays no immediate role in its causal powers. Here's an analogy. A photo of Bloggs will have certain effects on my scanner; for example, it will cause a particular series of 1s and 0s to be sent to my hard drive. The immediate cause of those effects is the way the ink is distributed on the surface of the photo; they are not caused—at least, not immediately caused—by the fact that the photo is a photo of Bloggs. If we asked a computer scientist to describe what's going on when Bloggs's photo is scanned, he would not mention the fact that the photo is a photo of Bloggs—he will talk exclusively about optical resolution, USB ports, and so on.

The upshot of these considerations is that the properties of N in virtue of which it causes M are neurological properties like 'part of the cholinergic system', not representational properties like 'about Mt Everest'. All the causal work is being done by the neurological properties; the representational properties are causally irrelevant. Consequently, the content of a mental state seems to be causally inefficacious. And that's unsettling because it's natural to think that the content of a mental state *is* relevant to its causal powers. Say that Bloggs's belief that Mt Everest is 8,848 meters high causes him to believe that it sometimes snows on top of Mt Everest. It seems that the content of the former belief is essential to its causing the latter belief. If Bloggs's belief had been about Mt Cook rather than about Mt Everest, he would not have thereby come to believe that it sometimes snows on top of Mt Everest.

The problem of the causal efficacy of content is particularly perspicuous in the case of the computational theory of mind. In Section 6.4 we saw that, according to computationalism, thoughts are complex symbols which have both **syntactic** and **semantic properties**. On this view, thinking is the manipulation of complex symbols solely in virtue of their syntactic properties. As we saw in Section 6.1, the syntactic properties are those properties of a symbol which can be identified by examining the symbol in isolation. Semantic properties are not syntactic properties. No amount of staring at the symbol 'Fodor' will reveal that 'Fodor' refers to—is about—a certain American philosopher. It follows that, on the computational view, semantic properties are causally inefficacious: if all the causal work is done by the syntactic properties, and the semantic properties are not syntactic properties, then the semantic properties aren't doing anything.

One way to reply to the problem of the causal efficacy of content within a broadly computational paradigm is by embracing the *syntactic theory of mind* (see especially Stich 1983: Ch. 8). According to this doctrine, psychology should abandon talk of content altogether. Since it is the syntactic properties which do the causal work, psychological theories should refer only to the syntactic properties of mental states. I will briefly return to this idea in the next section.

10.4 Responding to the problem of the causal efficacy of content

When describing the photo case, I remarked that the photo's effects are not *immediately* caused by the fact that the photo is about Bloggs. Nevertheless, there is a less immediate causal connection between Bloggs and the photo's effects on the scanner. The photo is about Bloggs in virtue of the fact that light reflecting off Bloggs was recorded on the film. So Bloggs caused the photo to be as it is, which in turn caused the scanner to do what it did. See Figure 10.9. Since the causal relation is **transitive**, there *is* a causal connection between Bloggs and the scanner's activities. Similarly, if Bloggs's thought about Mt Everest was a thought about Mt Everest because it was caused by Mt Everest, there *would be* a causal connection between the content of N and M. See Figure 10.10. It follows that, if the causal theory of content is true (see Section 9.2), the problem of the causal efficacy of content is resolved. For, if the causal theory of content is true, N is about Everest because Everest caused N (in a suitable way). Since N in turn caused M, it follows by the transitivity of causation that the content of N—Mt Everest—played a causal role in bringing about M.

Since many philosophers reject the causal theory of content (see Section 9.2), the solution to the problem of the causal efficacy of content just sketched won't have universal appeal. Is there something else which can be said about the problem?

Recall the distinction between causal efficacy and causal relevance sketched in Section 10.2. A property is causally efficacious if it actually causes some effect; a property is causally relevant if, whilst not causally efficacious, it 'programs for'

Bloggs ⟶ Photo ⟶ Effects on scanner

Figure 10.9 Bloggs causally impacts upon the photo which in turn causally impacts upon the scanner

Mt Everest ⟶ N ⟶ M

Figure 10.10 Mt Everest causes brain state N which in turn causes brain state M

a property which *is* causally efficacious. We can wield this distinction in the case of content. The relevant causally efficacious properties of brain state N are neurological properties like *is part of the brain's cholinergic system*. N's being about Mt Everest is not causally efficacious. However, the content of Bloggs's belief about Mt Everest is causally relevant because it *programs for* the right causally efficacious properties in the realizer state. So N has the right causally efficacious property *is part of the brain's cholinergic system* in virtue of the fact that it realizes Bloggs's belief about Mt Everest. If Bloggs's belief were about, say, Mt Cook, then it would be realized by a brain state with different causally efficacious properties.

This solution to the problem of the causal efficacy of content is satisfactory only if we are prepared to accept that content is, strictly speaking, causally inefficacious. My guess is that that proposal would make most philosophers feel a bit uncomfortable.

A second response to the problem of the causal efficaciousness of content is due to Fodor. Tucked away in a footnote is a remark to the effect that we can distinguish between the computational story about how mental states interact, and the generalizations which describe the relations between mental states (Fodor 1987: 166, fn. 3). The computational story about how mental states interact is a purely syntactic one. However, the best generalizations about the relations between mental states are intentional ones; that is, they appeal to the contents of mental states. So the representational properties of mental states are of great significance to psychology since it is only by appealing to them that good psychological generalizations can be located; nevertheless, it remains true that the mechanisms which actually manipulate mental states are sensitive only to their syntactic properties. (You might have noticed that I haven't explained *why* Fodor thinks that good psychological generalizations will be intentional. That would take us too far afield; however, you might like to look at Fodor 1987: Ch. 1.)

Finally, notice that Fodor has provided us with a reason to reject the syntactic theory of mind (see Section 10.3). According to the syntactic theory of mind, psychology should stick to generalizations given in syntactic terms because only the syntactic properties are causally efficacious. However, as Fodor points out, it may be true both that only syntactic properties are causally efficacious *and* that good intentional generalizations are available to psychology. Stich is aware of this challenge and has responded (see Stich 1983: Section 8.4). However, we can't take the issue further here.

SUMMARY

(1) As we noted in the Introduction, mental states are involved in various kinds of causal relations. However, understanding these relations—even within a physicalist framework—is not easy.

(2) There is more than one problem of mental causation. This chapter focuses on the problem of causal exclusion and the problem of the causal efficacy of content.

(3) The problem of causal efficacy arises because if, for example, fear is realized by brain state B, and B causes screaming, then fear has been 'excluded' from the causal story about screaming.

(4) Jackson and Pettit distinguish between causal efficacy and causal relevance. A property is causally efficacious if it actually does something; it's causally relevant if it 'programs for' a causally efficacious property.

(5) Jackson and Pettit go on to suggest that whilst mental tokens are causally efficacious, mental types are only causally relevant.

(6) The problem of the causal efficacy of content arises because it seems that all the causal work is being done by the neurological properties of the brain state; the semantic properties of the brain state don't seem to do anything.

(7) One response to the problem of the causal efficacy of content is to argue that, whilst not causally efficacious, content is causally relevant.

FURTHER READING

The literature in this area is not easy. A good place to start is Chapter 6 of Jaegwon Kim's *Philosophy of Mind* (1996). His *Mind in a Physical World* (1998) is a masterful discussion of mental causation and related issues. Whilst written for a professional audience, it's surprisingly readable. Frank Jackson surveys the field and sketches some of his own views in his 'Mental Causation' (1996). This paper is quite hard, but worth a look.

Jackson and Philip Pettit give an account of their ideas about program explanation in their 'Program explanation: A general perspective' (1990). For a critical discussion of Jackson and Pettit see Kim 1998: 72–7.

The classic presentation of the syntactic theory of mind is Stephen Stich's *From Folk Psychology to Cognitive Science* (1983: Ch. 8).

An important collection of papers on mental causation is Heil and Mele 1993. Again, these papers are not easy.

TUTORIAL QUESTIONS

(1) Sketch the problem of causal exclusion.

(2) Give an example of overdetermination.

(3) Distinguish between causal relevance and causal efficacy.

(4) Explain how the distinction between causal efficacy and causal relevance can be applied to the problem of causal exclusion.

(5) Are you satisfied with the claim that fear (that is, the type) isn't causally efficacious?

(6) Sketch the problem of the causal efficacy of content.

(7) State the syntactic theory of mind.

(8) Explain how the distinction between causal efficacy and causal relevance can be applied to the problem of the causal efficacy of content.

Part Four
Consciousness

11

Varieties of consciousness

a mongrel concept

—Ned Block

In this chapter we begin our exploration of consciousness by teasing apart four different *kinds* of consciousness. One kind of consciousness—**phenomenal consciousness**—is so important that it will have a chapter of its own (Chapter 12). A second sort of consciousness—access consciousness—is also of considerable importance, not least because it's sometimes conflated with phenomenal consciousness.

Conflation causes confusion, and confusion is, by and large, a Bad Thing. Indeed, avoiding confusion is the main aim of this chapter. By setting out as clearly as possible the different sorts of consciousness, we can avoid mistaking explanations of one sort of consciousness for explanations of another. Unfortunately, these kinds of muddles are not uncommon. In particular, some writers have set out to explain *phenomenal* consciousness but, apparently without realizing it, have ended up offering explanations of *access* consciousness instead.

This chapter is very much based on the work of the contemporary American philosopher Ned Block. The crucial distinctions and arguments are his, as is the worry about conflation mentioned in the previous paragraph. References to Block's work can be found in the Further Reading section at the end of the chapter.

11.1 Phenomenal consciousness

Sally is blessed with normal color vision. Alas, Bloggs is completely colorblind. When Sally and Bloggs enjoy a romantic moment looking at a gorgeous sunset, their visual experiences are quite different: Sally is having what we might call a 'color' visual experience; Bloggs is having what we might call a 'black and white' visual experience. This is a difference of phenomenal consciousness.

Here's another example. Sally needs to have a tooth drilled for a filling. The dentist offers her a local anesthetic, and she accepts. Bloggs also needs to have a tooth drilled. Being rather foolish, he declines the dentist's offer of an anesthetic. Subsequently, there is a marked difference between Sally's experience and Bloggs's: Sally has a painless drill-and-fill experience; Bloggs has a painful drill-and-fill experience. Once again, there is a difference of phenomenal consciousness.

The contemporary American philosopher Thomas Nagel has introduced a useful expression into discussions of phenomenal consciousness (Nagel 1974). For any phenomenally conscious experience E there is *something that it is like* to have E. Thus we can say that what it is like for Sally to look at the sunset is different from what it is like for Bloggs to look at the sunset; and what it is like for Sally to have her tooth drilled is different from what it is like for Bloggs to have his tooth drilled. More generally, the phenomenally conscious aspects of your mental life are those aspects which it is like something to have.

We have noted that phenomenally conscious experiences arise when people with good color vision look at a red sunset, and when silly people like Bloggs say no to an anesthetic. There are a great many other sorts of phenomenally conscious experiences. There is something that it is like to be tickled, to be hungry, and to be thirsty. There is something that it is like to feel a smooth window and something that it is like to feel sandpaper. There is something that it is like to be too hot, and something that it is like to be too cold. And there is something that it is like to crave chocolate. Some philosophers—for example Ned Block (1994: 514)—think that there is something that it is like to believe that it is Monday or desire that it is Friday. Others—for example David Braddon-Mitchell and Frank Jackson (1996: 123)—are inclined to doubt that there is something that it is like to believe that p or desire that q. They do not, of course, deny that all sorts of feelings can be *associated* with beliefs and desires; however, they think that those feelings come about because the beliefs and desires frequently co-occur with sensations and/or emotions. For example, say that I believe that there is a gunman on the loose and consequently feel afraid. According to Braddon-Mitchell and Jackson, I am not phenomenally conscious of the belief itself; rather, I am phenomenally conscious of the associated emotion of fear.

So far I have given some examples of phenomenally conscious mental states, and I have introduced a useful piece of terminology for picking out phenomenally conscious experiences. But I have not offered a *definition* of phenomenal consciousness in that nothing that I have said would help someone who lacked phenomenal consciousness understand what they are missing. I have not offered such a definition because I don't have one. Indeed, not only do I not have one, I don't have any idea how to go about getting one. It seems to be a deep fact about phenomenal consciousness that we cannot define phenomenal consciousness, and that we cannot describe phenomenally conscious experiences except by appealing to other phenomenally conscious experiences. Thus, I cannot tell you what it is like to taste the yeast extract Vegemite except by saying that it's a bit salty and a bit yeasty. In other words, if you haven't tried Vegemite yourself, all I can do is draw your attention to other, similar experiences.

If you attend to your phenomenally conscious experiences you will notice that they have certain properties. (What's a property? See Section 1.4.) Thus, Sally's experience when she is looking at the sunset has the property of *redness*. Redness is a property of some visual experiences; it should not be confused with *red*, which is a property of some surfaces. In general, if a person with normal color vision looks at a red surface in good light they will have an experience of redness. Similarly, Bloggs's experience at the dentist has the property of *painfulness*. Again, it's important not to confuse painfulness with *pain*. Pain is a neurological state which has the property of painfulness. (Some would say that pain *necessarily* has the property of painfulness—that if it isn't painful, it isn't pain. We won't pursue that issue here.)

The term *qualia* is often used to name properties like redness and painfulness. '**Qualia**' is the plural form of 'quale'. Thus philosophers say that Sally's experience of the sunset had the quale of redness, and that Bloggs' experience at the dentist had the quale of painfulness. This is a useful bit of terminology which I shall often use in this chapter and the next.

Phenomenal consciousness raises a very difficult problem. It seems undeniable that we have experiences with properties like redness and painfulness. That is, it seems undeniable that qualia exist. But what are qualia? Are they physical properties of the brain, and if so what sort of physical properties are they? Alternatively, perhaps qualia are nonphysical properties. They may be epiphenomenal properties—nonphysical properties which are caused by the brain but which do not themselves cause anything. (See Section 1.4 for a discussion of epiphenomenalism.) It turns out that all of these possibilities are in their own ways problematic. We will return to phenomenal consciousness and the difficulties it generates in Chapter 12.

I will close this section by introducing two more bits of terminology. Sometimes philosophers replace the term 'qualia' with 'subjective feels' (or even just 'feels'). For example, they might say that Sally's experience when she looks at the sunset has the subjective feel of redness. Personally I prefer 'qualia' to ' subjective feels' because in ordinary English the usage of 'feel' is restricted to emotions ('I feel happy'), sensations ('I feel hungry'), and textures ('It feels smooth'). It sounds a bit odd to talk about the 'feel' of redness.

You may also come across the term 'phenomenology'. This term has been used by philosophers in all sorts of ways. Of relevance here is its use in expressions like 'the phenomenology of such-and-such experience'. When philosophers talk like this, they are drawing attention to the phenomenally conscious aspects of the experience; that is, to any qualia associated with the experience. So we can say that the phenomenology of Bloggs's experience at the dentist was quite different to Sally's.

11.2 Access consciousness

I believe that the Thylacine (Tasmanian tiger) is extinct. That belief is *accessible* in three ways. (i) It's available for the rational control of speech. For example, if you ask me to name a recently extinct marsupial I'll probably say, 'Thylacine'. (ii) It's available for the rational control of action. For example, if you ask me to show you a Thylacine, I'll take you to the museum, not the zoo. (iii) It's inferentially promiscuous which means that it's available as a premise in all sorts of bits of reasoning. A mental state which, like my Thylacine belief, satisfies (i) to (iii) is said to be **access conscious**.

Contrast my belief that Thylacines are extinct with the information states posited by the contemporary American linguist Noam Chomsky. According to Chomsky, we use a body of information about English grammar when we understand or produce grammatical sentences of English (see, for example, Chomsky 1972: 26–7). For example, buried somewhere in the brains of all English-speakers is the information that declarative sentences in English have a subject–predicate structure; that is, the subject precedes the predicate. Consider the declarative sentence, 'Bloggs is silly'. In this case the subject is 'Bloggs', the predicate is 'is silly', and 'Bloggs' comes before 'is silly'. (Notice that, in principle, it could be the other way around; that is, there could be a language in which the idea that Bloggs is silly is conveyed by saying 'Is silly: Bloggs'.)

So far we have seen that, buried in the heads of English-speakers, is the information that English declarative sentences are subject–predicate. Notice how *deeply* that information is buried. Most speakers of English will not say 'English' in response to a request to name a subject–predicate language. Nor will they hit the buzzer in a game show when asked if English is a subject–predicate language. Nor will they use the information that English is a subject–predicate language in all sorts of bits of reasoning (although they will use it in one very special sort of reasoning: the reasoning that goes on when English-speakers understand and produce English sentences). In short, the information states posited by Chomsky are not access conscious.

Now accessibility comes in degrees. Here's an analogy. The money I have in the bank is fairly accessible to me. I can, if I want, withdraw it. However, my bank puts a limit on how much cash can be withdrawn from a cash machine in any 24-hour period. So whilst my money is pretty accessible, it's not completely accessible: I cannot immediately access large amounts of money via a cash machine. (There is, unfortunately, another reason why I can't access large amounts of money via a cash machine!)

Mental states are also accessible to different degrees. The sorts of states proposed by Chomsky are not accessible. On the other hand, my belief that Thylacines are extinct is highly accessible. In between lie a variety of states which are less accessible than my belief about Thylacines but more accessible than the states Chomsky is interested in. For example, someone may not be able to answer the question, 'What is the capital of Portugal?', but nevertheless be able to answer the question, 'Is Lisbon the capital of Portugal?' If you ask them the first question they're stumped; if you ask them the second question they say (correctly) 'yes'. This example underscores the distinction between the information we can *recall* and the information we can only *recognize as true*. In a case like this, the information about the capital of Portugal is accessible, but only after explicit prompting.

Say that Bloggs can recognize as true, but not actually recall, that Lisbon is the capital of Portugal. Should we say that Bloggs is access conscious of that information? Ned Block, who developed the distinction between access and phenomenal consciousness, would say not. According to Block, a mental state is access conscious only if it is *poised* for the rational control of speech and action, and for use in a wide variety of inferences (Block 1995: 231). Bloggs's information state about Lisbon is certainly not poised to do those things—it has to be prompted very explicitly before it can become involved in the rational control of speech and action, or be used in a wide variety of inferences. Consequently Bloggs is not access conscious of his information state about Lisbon.

It's important to stress that the concept of access consciousness is quite distinct from the concept of phenomenal consciousness. We can, for example, imagine a robot which is access conscious of many things but not phenomenally conscious of them. The robot might believe that it is about to be attacked, and that belief might rationally control its speech, rationally control its actions, and be available as a premise in a variety of inferences. In other words, the robot might be access conscious of being under attack. Nevertheless, there may be nothing that it is like to be that robot—it may be phenomenally unconscious.

The robot I have just described is, of course, imaginary. As far as we know there are no robots which are access conscious to a sophisticated degree; consequently, as far as we know there are no robots which are access conscious to a sophisticated degree but not phenomenally conscious. The point of the example is to make an observation about the *concepts* of access consciousness and phenomenal consciousness. They are distinct concepts because we can readily imagine a robot to which the former concept applies but the latter does not.

11.3 Is access a function of phenomenal consciousness?

What is phenomenal consciousness *for?* What role does it play in our mental economy? A number of authors have suggested that the function of phenomenal consciousness is to make certain mental states access conscious. In other words, what phenomenal consciousness does is 'bring to the surface' mental states which are then available for the rational control of speech and action, and for use in a wide variety of inferences. The strange phenomenon of *blindsight* has been taken to support the claim that the function of phenomenal consciousness is access consciousness.

It's not uncommon for victims of brain injury to lose the capacity to see things in part of their visual field. This is sometimes called 'cortical blindness' to indicate that the problem is with the part of the brain which processes vision, not with the patient's eyes. In a small percentage of cortically blind patients something very odd occurs. Whilst they cannot in any ordinary sense see an object placed in the blind part of their visual field, they can in some circumstances accurately *guess* what the object is like. Here's an example. The experimenter places in the blind part of the patient's visual field a piece of paper clearly marked with either vertical or horizontal lines. The patient is then asked which way the lines are orientated. Not surprisingly, the patient responds by saying that they can't see the lines. However, if the experimenter encourages the patient to guess, they will guess correctly more times than not.

Clearly, some information about the object in the blind part of the visual field is being registered in the patient's brain. However, the patient is, as far as we can tell, not phenomenally conscious of that information; that is, there is nothing that it is like for the patient to see the horizontal or vertical lines. Moreover, it seems that the information is not access conscious. The experiment makes clear that the information is not available for the rational control of speech since the patient cannot volunteer the information that the piece of paper has (say) vertical lines. It is only when the patient gives up trying to answer the question properly and just guesses that the information becomes available. Moreover, there is no evidence that the information about the orientation of the lines is available for the rational control of action, or as a premise in a wide variety of inferences. In sum, blindsight strongly suggests that there can be mental states which are neither access nor phenomenally conscious.

The phenomenon of blindsight has led some researchers to suggest that the function of phenomenal consciousness is access consciousness. After all, the patient has lost phenomenal consciousness of objects in the blind part of their visual field, and access consciousness of those objects has vanished as well. However, whilst access may indeed be the function of phenomenal consciousness, the argument just sketched is not a good one. Notice that what we have in the blindsight case is a *correlation* between loss of phenomenal consciousness and loss of access consciousness. Now that correlation would be explained if phenomenal consciousness caused access consciousness. However, the correlation would also be explained if access consciousness caused phenomenal consciousness, or if both kinds of consciousness were independently caused by a third, presently unknown, factor. (These three possibilities are depicted in Figure 11.1.) So we cannot conclude, on the basis of a simple description of blindsight, that the function of phenomenal consciousness is access consciousness; the most we can say is that it *might* be. (See Block 1995: 242.)

In cases of blindsight both phenomenal consciousness and access consciousness are missing; that is, there is a correlation between the absence of phenomenal consciousness and the absence of access consciousness. Moreover, it seems that there are a great many cases in which both phenomenal consciousness and access consciousness are found; that is, there is a correlation between the presence of phenomenal consciousness and the presence of access consciousness. But is it always like this? Are there real cases—as opposed to merely imaginary ones—in which phenomenal consciousness exists without access consciousness, or access

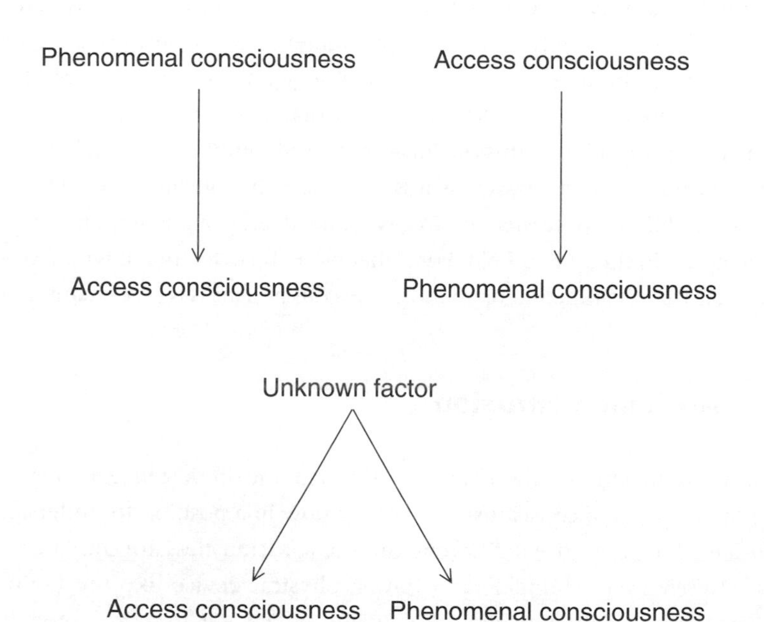

Figure 11.1 Three possible relationships between access consciousness and phenomenal consciousness. The arrow indicates a causal relationship, with the arrowhead located at the effect. Note that all three possibilities are consistent with a simple description of the blindsight phenomenon

consciousness exists without phenomenal consciousness? Block thinks that there is at least one real example of phenomenal consciousness without access consciousness.

The example Block gives concerns an experience familiar to us all. You are deep in conversation with a friend when, at 12 o'clock, you suddenly realize that there has been a loud noise outside for quite some time. It seems that in some sense you were aware of the noise *prior* to 12 o'clock; however, only *after* 12 o'clock did the noise fully impact upon you. According to Block, before 12 o'clock you were phenomenally conscious of the noise but not access conscious of it; after 12 o'clock you were both phenomenally *and* access conscious of it. (See Block 1995: 234.)

Now Block's way of understanding cases like this is not compulsory: we can think of other ways of explaining what is going on. However, if Block is right then there are cases of phenomenal consciousness without access consciousness. And if that's right then the claim that access consciousness is the function of phenomenal consciousness can't be straightforwardly true—at the very least it will have to be qualified to some extent.

I will close this section with a cautionary note. My brief sketch of blindsight is faithful to the way in which blindsight is described in much of the literature. However, it's not entirely clear that phenomenal consciousness *is* completely absent in blindsight; indeed, it's very difficult to get an accurate picture of what is going on in these cases. (Thanks to Gerard O'Brien for drawing my attention to this issue.) The central claim of this section—that blindsight does not establish that the function of phenomenal consciousness is access consciousness—would remain if subjects with blindsight turned out to have some degree of phenomenal consciousness of objects in their blind field. For if that were the case, then it would be highly implausible that the function of phenomenal consciousness is access consciousness.

11.4 Avoiding confusion

In the introduction to this chapter I stressed the importance of being clear about the varieties of consciousness. We are now in a position to understand the confusion which can arise if different kinds of consciousness are conflated.

It's *relatively* easy to understand how a physical device like the brain could implement access consciousness. (Relative to what? We'll see in a moment.) To say that a cognitive system is access conscious is to say something about the flow of information in that system. If Bloggs is access conscious of a pain in his toe then the information that he is in pain is available to the mechanisms which control his speech and behavior, and to the mechanisms which are responsible for reasoning. Now it's certainly not the case that we have a complete understanding of how these mechanisms work. However, we do have a general understanding of the way information is processed in physical devices—Part 2 was devoted to discussing two approaches to that issue—and we are beginning to develop a clear picture of the information pathways in the brain. So whilst we don't yet fully understand how the brain achieves access consciousness, obtaining a full understanding seems to require doing more—perhaps lots more—of the same. That is, it requires doing lots more good science.

The contrast with phenomenal consciousness couldn't be sharper. We have very little understanding of how the brain gives rise to phenomenal consciousness. Whilst we can readily develop hypotheses about how access consciousness is achieved, when it comes to phenomenal consciousness we have very few ideas. In fact, like Block, I would go as far as saying we have *no idea* how the brain generates phenomenal consciousness (Block 1994: 211). The contemporary Australian philosopher David Chalmers has called the challenge of explaining how the brain gives rise to phenomenal consciousness the 'hard problem' (Chalmers 1996: xii), and that must be the understatement of the year.

Now let's suppose that Bloggs really wants to solve the hard problem. Bloggs does a lot of hard work and comes up with a good theory of access consciousness. However, Bloggs has failed to notice the distinction between access and phenomenal consciousness. Consequently, he mistakes his theory of access consciousness for a theory of phenomenal consciousness. It seem to Bloggs that he has solved the hard problem, whereas in fact he has done nothing of the sort.

Let's look at a real case. Bernard Baars begins his book *In the Theater of Consciousness* (1997) by drawing our attention to what he simply calls 'consciousness'. He talks about 'our inner life' and gestures towards 'inner speech and visual imagery . . . bodily feelings like pleasure, pain and excitement; surges of feeling' (Baars 1997: 3). Expressions like these very much suggest that Baars is talking about phenomenal consciousness. There is something that it is like to hear your own voice inside your head or have a visual image; there is something that it is like to experience pleasure, pain, and excitement. He uses the word 'feeling(s)' twice, and we have noted that that is often a way to draw attention to phenomenal consciousness. Moreover, it's hard to see what 'our inner life' refers to if not the stream of phenomenally conscious experience. So it seems very likely that Baars' explanatory target—what he is trying to make sense of—is phenomenal consciousness.

What Baars appears to offer, though, is a theory of access consciousness. His title alludes to the idea that consciousness is like a stage on which some mental states briefly appear. Items on the stage are conscious; items elsewhere in the theater are nonconscious. All the items on the stage (and only the items on the stage) are available as input to a wide range of mental processors, including the processors responsible for behavior and rational thought; moreover, they can be reported in speech. In short, items on the stage are access conscious. (Indeed, the title of Baars' second chapter is 'The theater has limited capacity but creates vast *access*' (Baars 1997: 39; my italics).)

Baars has slipped from talking about phenomenal consciousness to talking about access consciousness. He began by saying that he would offer a theory of the latter, and ended by giving a theory of the former. That he has not offered a theory of phenomenal conscious is apparent if we ask why different items on the stage have different 'feels'. When my pain is on the stage it has the quale of painfulness. When my visual experience of a red sunset is on the stage it has the quale of redness. Why? What makes these two experiences so different? Indeed, what makes these two experiences *like anything at all*? Baars has not even begun to answer these questions.

11.5 Other kinds of consciousness

Block has identified two other sorts of consciousness—**self consciousness** and **monitoring consciousness**. I will briefly discuss these varieties of consciousness in this section.

1. *Self consciousness*. Humans are often said to be self conscious, and it's a matter of dispute whether any other animals are self conscious. What is it to be self conscious? To be self conscious is to have the *concept* of a self and to *apply* that concept to oneself. Saying that much is easy; the hard bit is giving a clear account of the concept of a self. Intriguing though this question is, I will not pursue it here. (Strawson 1958 is an important, although difficult, discussion of some of these issues.) Nor will I pursue the equally intriguing question of whether any of the other higher primates (e.g. chimpanzees and bonobos) are self conscious. (For interesting discussions of the empirical data see Gallup 1982 and Povinelli 1994.)

Notice that it seems possible for an organism to be phenomenally conscious without being self conscious. My guess is that rabbits feel pain; that is, they are phenomenally conscious to at least some extent. However, I think it's very unlikely that their little rabbit brains support the very sophisticated concept of a self; that is, I doubt that they are self conscious. (And cockroaches? I'm pretty confident they don't have *either* phenomenal *or* self consciousness, so don't hesitate to squash 'em!)

2. *Monitoring consciousness*. Imagine a computer which monitors its own activities. For example, it makes a note every time a particular subroutine is called. Humans

are a bit like that. We can monitor and recall at least some of our mental activities. Thus, not only can I feel pain, I can *believe* that I feel pain, and I can *remember* the pain I felt yesterday when I stubbed my toe. 'Monitoring consciousness' is the name given to the capacity to monitor our own mental states.

The contemporary Australian philosopher David Armstrong introduced the idea of monitoring consciousness into the literature (see Armstrong 1968 and 1980). Perhaps the most important development of his idea is the *higher order thought* theory of consciousness (HOT theory). A higher order thought is a thought which is about another mental state. For example, I can *believe* that I *believe* that it is Monday, and I can *believe* that I *wish* that it were Friday. Both of these beliefs are higher order beliefs: the former is about my belief that it is Monday; the latter is about my wish that it is Friday. So, according to HOT theory, a mental state M is conscious just in case there is a second mental state which is about M.

Note that, plausibly, a cognitive system can have higher order thoughts without being phenomenally conscious. For example, some computers have internal states about their own internal states and yet there is little reason to think that they are phenomenally conscious (Rey 1983). Moreover, it's plausible that a cognitive system can be phenomenally conscious without having the relevant higher order states. For example, earlier in this section I remarked that rabbits are very probably phenomenally conscious to some extent. However, it may well turn out that their puny bunny brains are incapable of higher order thoughts. So whilst it seems very likely that rabbits feel pain, it seems a lot less likely that they believe that they are in pain.

SUMMARY

(1) An experience is phenomenally conscious if there is something that it is like to have that experience. There is something that it is like to see a sunset, so we can be phenomenally conscious of a sunset.

(2) Phenomenally conscious experiences have special properties called *qualia*. Redness and painfulness are examples of qualia.

(3) Phenomenal consciousness is deeply puzzling. What are qualia? How do they fit into our growing scientific understanding of the world?

(4) A mental state is access conscious if it is available for the control of speech and behavior, and as a premise in a wide range of inferences.

(5) Some philosophers have argued that the function of phenomenal consciousness is access consciousness. The phenomenon of blindsight is sometimes offered in support of this claim. However, at most blindsight supports the claim that there is a *correlation* between access consciousness and phenomenal consciousness.

(6) Failure to distinguish phenomenal consciousness from other kinds of consciousness can engender much confusion—and has done so.

(7) An organism is *self conscious* when it applies the concept of a self to itself. Self consciousness is distinct from phenomenal consciousness.

(8) 'Monitoring consciousness' is the name given to the capacity to monitor our own mental states. An important development of the idea of monitoring consciousness is higher order thought (HOT) theory. Monitoring consciousness is distinct from phenomenal consciousness.

FURTHER READING

The key work in this area is Ned Block's classic paper, 'On a confusion about a function of consciousness' (1995). The issue of *Behavioral and Brain Science* in which it appeared contains both comments on Block's paper and replies by Block, with further comments and replies appearing in subsequent issues. Block 1995 is reprinted with small changes in Block, Flanagan, and Guzeldere 1997, along with useful discussions by Burge, Chalmers, Churchland, and Dennett. Block 1994 provides a very neat introduction to contemporary work on consciousness, and nicely summarizes his distinctions between the various kinds of consciousness.

A book-length discussion of blindsight is Wieskrantz 1986. See also Bornstein and Pittman 1992.

TUTORIAL QUESTIONS

Easy ones

(1) Briefly describe each of the four sorts of consciousness discussed in this chapter.

(2) Can you explain what it is like to see a clear blue sky to someone who is blind?

(3) Describe the blindsight phenomenon.

Harder ones

(4) Is access consciousness the function of phenomenal consciousness? Discuss with reference to blindsight.

(5) Using Baars' theater analogy as your example, explain how phenomenal might be confused with access consciousness.

12

Phenomenal consciousness

How can technicolor phenomenology arise from soggy grey matter?

—Colin McGinn

Broadly speaking, phenomenal consciousness challenges physicalism in two ways. First, it presents a **metaphysical** challenge: Can qualia be accounted for in purely physical terms? Second, it presents an **epistemological** challenge: even if we accept that qualia are in fact physical, can we understand how the brain generates phenomenally conscious experiences? As far as I know, the first person explicitly to distinguish the metaphysical questions about qualia from the epistemological ones was Joseph Levine (1993). The distinction is, however, implicit in some of Frank Jackson's earlier remarks (1982).

One of the most powerful ways to press the metaphysical challenge to physicalism is Jackson's **knowledge argument** (see especially Jackson 1982; 1986). I present the knowledge argument in Section 12.1, and discuss a series of replies to it in Section 12.2. The epistemological challenge is introduced in Section 12.3. Following standard usage, I call that challenge the *explanatory gap argument*. (The name is slightly misleading as there are in fact a number of arguments at issue.) In Section 12.4 I discuss a variety of replies to the explanatory gap argument, concluding that there really is a serious problem here. In Section 12.5 I briefly discuss functionalism and phenomenal consciousness. Functionalism deserves a section of its own because of the very significant role it has played in recent philosophy of mind. I then sum up my own views in a brief conclusion.

12.1 The knowledge argument

Mary is a super-smart scientist who has been raised from birth in a black and white room. In the room she learns *all* the physical facts of relevance to human color vision—she learns all about the physics of light, the optical properties of the eye, and the anatomy and physiology of the visual system. One day she is released from her black and white prison and sees a ripe tomato in good light. 'Wow!', she says, 'Now I know what red looks like.'

When Mary was in the black and white room she knew all the physical facts of relevance to human color vision. Nevertheless, when she left the room she still learned something—she learned what red *looks like*. That is, she learned about the quale of redness. It follows that the quale of redness can't be a physical property. For if the quale of redness were a physical property, Mary would have known all about it when she was in the room; but she did not know all about the quale of redness when she was in the room, so the quale of redness isn't a physical property. Now physicalism claims that all properties are physical properties. So if the quale of redness isn't a physical property then physicalism is false. This is Frank Jackson's 'knowledge argument' against physicalism (Jackson 1982; 1986). So famous is the knowledge argument that it has even figured in a novel by David Lodge (2001).

I have just presented the knowledge argument in the way it is usually presented. Sometimes, though, Jackson varies the presentation slightly. The variation is important because it allows Jackson to defeat a significant objection which has been raised against the knowledge argument. The variant form of the argument begins the same way, with Mary learning all the physical facts of relevance to human color vision whilst trapped in a black and white room. However, in the variant, when Mary is released she exclaims, 'Gosh! Now I know what *everybody else's* visual experiences are like.' When she was in the room Mary had no idea what the visual experiences of the people outside the room were like. She did not know, for example, what it was like for them to see a ripe tomato in good light. But now that she has left the black and white room and seen a ripe tomato herself, she knows considerably more about the visual experiences of other people. Once again it follows that physicalism is false: there must be nonphysical properties of which Mary had no knowledge when she was in the black and white room. (I am assuming here that the people outside the room all have normal color vision: Mary *did know* what the visual experiences of colorblind people were like before she left the black and white room.)

Given the importance of the variant presentation to defending the knowledge argument, it's worth quoting Jackson's own text:

1. Mary (before her release) knows everything physical there is to know about other people.
2. Mary (before her release) does not know everything there is to know about other people (because she *learns* something about them on her release).

Therefore,

3. There are truths about other people (and herself) which escape the physicalist story.

(Jackson 1986: 293)

Before moving on it is worth briefly dealing with a common worry about the knowledge argument. The worry focuses on the sheer implausibility of the story about Mary. If we really tried to conduct the Mary experiment, we would run into all sorts of practical problems. For example, if Mary cut herself she would immediately see red; if she had brown hair she would (eventually) see brown; if she bruised herself she would see blue. We could, of course, modify the story about Mary in various ways to avoid these problems. (Try this: Mary is forced to wear a special pair of glasses which make everything look black and white. Eventually the glass are removed and she exclaims . . .) However, the crucial point is that Jackson has offered us a *thought experiment*, and one of the great virtues of thought experiments is that they sidestep troublesome details like these.

Thought experiments can be very powerful. Amongst the most skilful users of thought experiments were the physicists Galileo and Einstein. Compared with Einstein's famous tram ride thought experiment, Jackson's Mary case is—well—pedestrian. In Einstein's thought experiment one of the laws of physics is set aside—the tram is pictured as traveling at the speed of light which, by Einstein's own theory, is physically impossible. So we can only condemn Jackson for using a thought experiment if we are also going to charge Galileo and Einstein with the same crime. And before we do *that* we'd better have some pretty convincing arguments against the use of thought experiments up our sleeve. (For a terrific discussion of thought experiments see Sorensen 1992.)

On the basis of the knowledge argument, Jackson decided that physicalism was false. What kind of position did he propose to put in its place? How did he conceive of the relationship between qualia and the brain?

In Section 1.4 we discussed property dualism. According to property dualism, mental states are nonphysical properties of the brain. One special kind of property dualism is *epiphenomenalism* (again see Section 1.4). According to epiphenomenalism, the physical properties of the brain cause a variety of nonphysical mental properties, but not vice versa. Jackson endorsed a special kind of epiphenomenalism. Whilst he rejected the view that *all* mental properties are epiphenomenal, he accepted that *qualia* are epiphenomenal. That is, he accepted the claim that although the physical properties of our brains give rise to nonphysical qualia, the qualia in turn do nothing—they are causally inert.

This is, to put it mildly, a strikingly counterintuitive view. It's natural to think that the hurt I experience when I stub my toe *causes* me to say 'ouch' and rub the damaged part. However, if qualia are indeed epiphenomenal, the hurt I experience when I stub my toe has no causal consequences whatsoever. In particular, I don't rub my toe because it hurts!

How did Jackson arrive at this extraordinary position? Since Jackson accepted the conclusion of the knowledge argument, he became a property dualist about qualia; that is, he accepted that qualia are nonphysical properties of the brain. Notice that if color qualia are indeed nonphysical properties of the brain, then it is no surprise that Mary had no knowledge of them when she was in the black and white room. However, Jackson also accepted what I called in Chapter 1 the *explanatory completeness of physiology* (see Sections 1.3 and 1.4). That is, he accepted that human behavior can be fully explained by appealing to purely physical states such as muscle contractions and nerve impulses. Consequently, whilst he endorsed the claim that qualia are nonphysical, he could not allow them to impact upon behavior because if they did the explanatory completeness of physiology would be violated. So he adopted epiphenomenalism about qualia.

When discussing Jackson's epiphenomenalism about qualia I was careful to use the past tense. I did so because Jackson no longer accepts the conclusion of the knowledge argument, and no longer endorses epiphenomenalism about qualia. He has advanced several considerations against the knowledge argument, one of which we will look at in the next section.

12.2 Responding to the knowledge argument

The knowledge argument has spawned a large literature, and a number of objections to the knowledge argument have been raised. In what follows I will consider four objections. My choice is not (I hope!) idiosyncratic. I have included the 'knowledge-how' reply due to Laurence Nemirow (1980) and David Lewis (1983*b*; 1990) because it's probably the best-known reply; a reply by Paul Churchland (1985; 1989) because it raises an important question; an especially interesting argument by Jackson and his co-author David Braddon-Mitchell (Braddon-Mitchell and Jackson 1996: 134–5); and a reply (better: a series of related replies) which insists that Mary could not have learned all the physical facts in the black and white room (see, for example, Horgan 1984; Loar 1990).

1. *The knowledge-how reply.* Philosophers distinguish two importantly different sorts of knowledge: knowledge-*that* and knowledge-*how*. Here are two examples of knowledge-that:

(i) Bloggs knows that Mt Everest is 8,848 meters high.

(ii) Bloggs knows that Central Park is in New York.

In both cases Bloggs knows a *fact* about the world. In the first case he knows the height of a certain mountain; in the second he knows the location of a certain park. (Notice that the locution 'knows that' appears in both sentences.)

Now consider the following two examples:

(iii) Bloggs knows how to play the trombone.

(iv) Bloggs knows how to swim.

Sentences (iii) and (iv) do not attribute to Bloggs knowledge of some fact or other; rather, they attribute to him a *skill*. Sentence (iii) attributes to Bloggs the skill of trombone playing; sentence (iv) attributes to him the skill of swimming. (Notice that the locution 'knows how' appears in both sentences.)

Let's now apply the knowledge-that/knowledge-how distinction to the knowledge argument.

When I described Mary's predicament I said that when she was in the black and white room she knew all the physical facts of relevance to human color vision. Clearly, this is an example of knowledge-that. Mary is described as knowing all the *facts* about color vision. She knew *that* light is reflected from a range of objects; *that* the reflected light is focused by the lens of the eye onto the retina; *that* information passes from the retina to the brain via the optic nerve; and so on. But what kind of knowledge did Mary acquire when she left the black and white room and saw a red object for the first time?

If we say that Mary acquired knowledge-that then it seems physicalism is indeed false. For Mary is supposed to know all the relevant physical facts when she is inside the room, so if she came to learn more facts when she left the room then those facts must be nonphysical facts. But if there are nonphysical facts for Mary to learn, then physicalism is false.

What about the other option? Perhaps what Mary acquired when she left the black and white room was knowledge-how. On this view, when Mary learned what the quale of redness is like, she learned some new skills. Which skills might they be? Well, Mary learned how to recognize red objects just by glancing at them in good light, and she learned how to imagine red objects.

This is the knowledge-how reply to the knowledge argument. The proponents of the knowledge-how reply insist that Mary did not acquire any new *facts* when she left the room, thereby preserving physicalism. However, they accept that Mary acquired *something* when she left the room: she acquired some new skills. The knowledge-how reply aims to reject Jackson's antiphysicalist conclusion but at the same time to satisfy our strong intuition that Mary gained something when she left the room.

In reply, Jackson (1986) admits that Mary acquired new skills when she left the room, but he doubts that that is all she acquired. It is here that the variant presentation of the knowledge argument becomes important (see previous section). On the variant presentation, Mary learns something about other people when she see a red object for the first time: she learns what their color visual experiences are like. To some extent her new knowledge of other people is knowledge-how; for example, she can now imagine what their color experiences are like. However, Jackson insists that Mary *also* acquired knowledge-that.

Jackson offers the following brilliant argument in favor of his claim that Mary acquired knowledge-that when she left the black and white room

(Jackson 1986: 294). There's an ancient position in philosophy called 'skepticism about other minds'. The skeptic about other minds denies that there are good reasons for thinking that anybody else has a mind. I'm not going to consider the arguments offered for and against this view. Rather, let's suppose that when Mary sees a red object for the first time she initially thinks, 'Now I know what other people's visual experiences are like', but then she starts to have skeptical doubts as to whether those other people have minds at all. After carefully considering the arguments for and against skepticism about other minds, she decides that all those people really do have minds; in particular, she decides that all those people have phenomenally conscious experiences. But what have her careful considerations been about? Surely not her ability to imagine red or recognize red objects in good light. Her concern was whether she was justified in thinking that other people experience the same color qualia as she is now experiencing; that is, she is concerned whether she has got the *facts* about other people's visual experiences right. It follows—provided other people really do have minds!—that Mary acquired at least some knowledge-that when she left the black and white room.

2. *An argument against dualism?* Imagine for a moment that we are all convinced of the truth of property dualism, and that our best theory of the relationship between the physical properties of the brain and the nonphysical mental properties is theory X. Now consider Joseph who has lived since birth in a black and white room. He is incredibly smart and has learned, via black and white textbooks, both theory X and all the physical facts about human color vision. Finally, Joseph is released from the room and sees a ripe tomato in good light. 'Gee,' he says, 'So that's what red looks like.' It seems, then, that Joseph *learned* something when he left the black and white room. But if he learned something when he left the room, theory X plus all the physical facts about color vision can't be the whole story about color vision. Assuming that Joseph has the physical facts right, it follows that theory X must be inadequate in some way. Since 'theory X' is just the name we gave to our best understanding of property dualism, it follows that property dualism is inadequate in some way. This line of reasoning, due to Paul Churchland (1985; 1989), strongly suggests that there is something wrong with the knowledge argument. For it seems that the knowledge argument can be used to 'prove' both the inadequacy of physicalism *and* the inadequacy of property dualism. (Indeed, it seems that the knowledge argument can be used to demonstrate the inadequacy of just about any metaphysical theory of the mind.)

What should we conclude from Churchland's ingenious objection? I think that Churchland's objection invites us to think about exactly what we can expect *any* theory to tell us about qualia. The nature of scientific theories is a controversial issue in the philosophy of science. On one view, a theory consists of a set of sentences (often expressed mathematically) about some aspect of the world. Whilst this conception of scientific theories may not be universally accepted, it's certainly the case that the lessons Mary received in the black and white room consisted of sets of sentences. But if we think of theories in these terms, then it seems highly implausible that possessing a theory of color vision will tell us what it is like to see a ripe tomato in good light. Why would we expect reading and understanding a lot of black and white sentences to give us the *experience* of red? On this view, the knowledge argument tells us something about the limitation of theories, whether they be physicalist theories or theories of some other sort; it doesn't tell us anything about the metaphysics of qualia.

Theories may be limited in the way I have described because of the way our minds are structured. David Lewis has a nice metaphor which we can use to illustrate the present point. (See Lewis 1983*b*. Note that Lewis uses it primarily in support of the knowledge-how reply discussed above.) Imagine a computer which stores a description of any geometric figure with which it is presented. For example, if it is presented with a circle 12 cm in diameter it will store the description:

A circle 12 cm in diameter.

Now imagine a device which stores information about any geometric figure with which it is presented by making and retaining a copy of the figure. If presented with a circle 12 cm in diameter it literally makes and stores a circle 12 cm across. As it happens, both the computer and the copy-and-store machine are built into the same box. However, whilst they share the same box, there are no interesting connections between them. In particular, the copy-and-store machine cannot make (say) a 10-cm square on the basis of a description it received from the computer. As Lewis remarks, 'We might be rather like that' (Lewis 1983*b*: 132). It might be the case that the part of the brain which learns and retains physical theories of color qualia is not connected in relevant ways to the part of the brain which generates color qualia. Indeed, Paul Churchland (1989) has provided evidence that the human brain *is* like that. If this is right, Mary's failure to anticipate what the experience of redness is like is no evidence that physicalism is false. It only shows that the physical theory is not available to the qualia generator.

3. *The 'There must be a reply' reply*. We saw at the end of Section 12.1 that Jackson endorsed epiphenomenalism about qualia. On the basis of the knowledge argument he accepted that qualia are nonphysical properties of the brain; that is, he accepted a restricted version of property dualism. However, he had independent grounds for accepting the explanatory completeness of physiology. Consequently, he concluded that qualia have no causal impact on our behavior; that is, he thought that qualia are epiphenomenal.

We also saw at the end of Section 12.1 that Jackson no longer accepts the conclusion of the knowledge argument. With David Braddon-Mitchell he has advanced what they call the *'There must be a reply' reply*. They begin by noting that epiphenomenalism about qualia is a strikingly implausible doctrine. It entails, for example, that when I stub my toe I do not say 'ouch' and rub the injured part because it hurts, nor do I stop at the traffic lights because they look red. Braddon-Mitchell and Jackson argue that epiphenomenalism about qualia is *so* implausible that any doctrine which entails it must be wrong. (See Braddon-Mitchell and Jackson 1996: 134–5.)

Braddon-Mitchell and Jackson strengthen their case against epiphenomenalism about qualia by pointing out how very odd the Mary story becomes if we accept that qualia are epiphenomenal. According to the Mary story, when she leaves the black and white room and sees a red object for the first time she says, 'Wow! Now I know what red looks like'. It's natural to think that Mary said that because she had just experienced the quale of redness for the first time. That is, it's natural to think that Mary's exclamation was *caused* by her experience of redness. But if qualia are epiphenomenal they could not have caused Mary to say 'Wow!' because, by definition, epiphenomenal qualia don't cause anything.

It gets worse. The Mary story prompts the intuition that Mary learned something about qualia when she left the black and white room and saw her first red object. It's natural to think that she learned something about qualia because of the impact the qualia made on her; in particular, the qualia caused her to have certain beliefs. But if epiphenomenalism about qualia is true that can't be right. Consequently, the advocate of the knowledge argument is in the strange position of claiming that Mary acquires new knowledge of qualia when she leaves the room, but not in virtue of the causal powers of qualia. But if the qualia aren't responsible for Mary's new knowledge, how did it come about and why did she have to leave the black and white room to get it? Mysteries pile upon mysteries.

It's worth thinking about Braddon-Mitchell and Jackson's reply to the knowledge argument in a little more detail. Remember that Jackson came to believe that qualia are epiphenomenal because he believed *both* the conclusion of the knowledge argument *and* that physiology is explanatorily complete. It follows that if, as Braddon-Mitchell and Jackson urge, we reject epiphenomenalism about qualia, then we must reject either the conclusion of the knowledge argument or the explanatory completeness of physiology (or both). Braddon-Mitchell and Jackson are very reluctant to reject the explanatory completeness of physiology; consequently, they reject the conclusion of the knowledge argument.

For present purposes let's simply accept the explanatory completeness of physiology. Braddon-Mitchell and Jackson's argument comes down to this. The knowledge argument entails epiphenomenalism about qualia, but the latter doctrine is crazy so something must be wrong with the knowledge argument. Braddon-Mitchell and Jackson candidly admit that they don't know *what's* wrong with the knowledge argument; their rejection of the knowledge argument is based solely on the fact that it entails epiphenomenalism about qualia. (It should be remembered that Jackson now believes he knows what's wrong with the knowledge argument.)

I find the 'There has to be a reply' reply convincing because, like Braddon-Mitchell and Jackson, I find epiphenomenalism about qualia close to unintelligible. I suspect, though, that antiphysicalists who are impressed by the knowledge argument are not going to be swayed by the 'There has to be a reply' reply. They will insist that they find the knowledge argument so convincing that they are prepared to accept what it entails—epiphenomenalism about qualia. They will insist that the knowledge argument has led us to a surprising discovery about the mind—that qualia are causally inert. There are no clear winners here.

4. *Did Mary know all the physical facts?* We are told that Mary knew all the physical facts when she was in the black and white room. But is that plausible? Might there be physical facts—in particular, facts about what it is like to see red—of which pre-release Mary would inevitably be ignorant? Considerations like this have prompted a variety of interrelated ways of replying to the knowledge argument.

We have already noted the suggestion that the power of theories might be limited so that not even grasping the true theory of the relationship between brain states and qualia would be sufficient to convey what it is like to see a ripe tomato in good light. In that case it may be that qualia are physical and yet Mary may not know, on the basis of her possessing all the relevant physical theories, what qualia are like. A second, related, proposal is that language is limited. On this view there are some physical facts—for example, facts about what it is like to see red—which simply cannot be conveyed in language. In order to know what it is like to see a red object in good light you have to have *seen a red object in good light*. No amount of talk substitutes for the experience itself. A third proposal is that there is something very special about the first person perspective. The facts we learn from the first person perspective are physical facts; nevertheless, we are accessing those facts in a way quite distinct from the third person perspective provided by science. Thus, whilst Mary knew all the relevant facts when she was in the black and white room, she only knew them from the third person, scientific, perspective. After she left the black and white room she became familiar with the same old facts in a new way (see Horgan 1984). And finally it has been proposed that there are certain concepts—*phenomenal concepts*—which can only be grasped by having the experience itself. The states which fall under these concepts are physical states picked out in a wholly new way. On this view, what Mary acquired when she left the black and white room was a new set of concepts which allowed her to think about her (entirely physical) environment in a new way (Loar 1990).

My own view—for what it's worth—is that the correct reply to the knowledge argument lies somewhere in the terrain broadly indicated by the four ideas just sketched. However, filling in the details of these ideas is not easy. Why, for example, is language limited in this way? We seem to be able to express in language a great many facts, so why not facts about qualia? If a convincing reply to the knowledge argument is to be made along these lines we need a detailed account of language (or theories, or the first person perspective, or concepts) which makes it clear why the knowledge argument fails. It's fair to say that, at present, we have no such account.

Moreover, the antiphysicalist about qualia can press the following point. Here's why language is unable to express the facts about qualia—because qualia aren't physical! The asymmetry between the expressive power of language when it expresses facts about (say) ordinary physical objects, and its expressive power when it expresses facts about qualia, testifies to a substantial metaphysical difference between ordinary objects and qualia. A detailed theory of the limits of the expressive power of language may help us reply to the antiphysicalist, but as yet we lack such a detailed theory.

12.3 The explanatory gap

Modern scientists identify lightning with atmospheric electrical discharge. The identification of lightning with atmospheric electrical discharge explains the various features of lightning. For example, it explains how lightning can be harmlessly carried away from a building by a suitably placed copper wire (a lightning rod). Copper is much better at conducting electricity than is the concrete, masonry, and wood from which buildings are typically made. Consequently, the electrical discharge is quickly dissipated through the copper wire, leaving the building unharmed.

Now, according to physicalism, Bloggs's painful experience is identical to some state of his brain. However, unlike the identification of lightning with atmospheric electrical discharge, the identification of Bloggs's painful experience with a state of his brain seems to lack explanatory power. Say that Bloggs's painful experience is identified with the rapid firing of neurons in a certain part of his brain. How does that explain the painfulness? Why does that kind of firing in that part of Bloggs's brain hurt rather than, say, tickle? These questions do not seem to have answers. There is an *explanatory gap* between the firing in that part of the brain and the painfulness.

One of the principal proponents of the explanatory gap argument is the contemporary American philosopher Thomas Nagel. It was Nagel who introduced the phrase 'what it is like' as a way of drawing attention to phenomenally conscious experiences (see Section 11.1). In a famous paper he asked what it is like to be a bat (Nagel 1974). Bats find their way around in complete darkness by a process known as *echo-location*. They emit high-frequency 'squeaks' which echo off nearby objects, and then analyze the echoes in sophisticated ways to yield remarkably accurate representations of their surroundings. (Bat echo-location very closely parallels the sonar deployed by submarines. For a description of sonar, see Section 7.1.) So what is it like to be a bat? What is it like to build up an accurate representation of your surroundings using echoes? We humans have no idea—the experience is simply too far from our own. (Apparently some blind people have a very limited ability to echo-locate; however, there is no reason to assume that the phenomenally conscious experiences they have when they do so are anything like those of a bat.)

Notice that learning all the physical details about bats and how they echo-locate will not help you understand what it is like to be a bat. A lifetime spent studying the neurobiology of echo-location would no doubt reveal many interesting facts, but it would not move you any closer to understanding the phenomenal experiences of bats. There seems to be an unavoidable explanatory gap between studying the bat's brain and understanding its phenomenal life.

The contemporary American philosopher Joseph Levine has assembled two arguments in support of the claim that there is an explanatory gap between brain states and phenomenal experiences. He is not alone in advancing such arguments; however, his arguments are both significant in their own right and indicative of the general thrust of the literature in this area. In the remainder of this section I will briefly sketch Levine's arguments. (See Levine 1983; 1993; 2001. Related arguments have been advanced by Nagel 1974; Kripke 1980: Lecture III; and McGinn 1991; 1999.)

Levine begins by thinking about the case of water and H_2O. According to modern science, water is H_2O; that is, water is type identical to H_2O (for more on type identities see Section 3.1). The identification of water with H_2O is explanatorily satisfying in much the same way that the identification of lightning with atmospheric electrical discharge is explanatorily satisfying: it allows us to understand how water has the properties it in fact has. For example, once we realize that water is H_2O we can understand why water breaks down into hydrogen and oxygen gas in the process called 'electrolysis'.

Levine now shifts to the case of phenomenal consciousness. Let us take pain as our example, and let us assume that pain is identical to a physical property of the brain, P. We have seen that the various properties of water can be explained on the assumption that water is H_2O. Can the same trick be turned in the case of pain and P? In particular, can the identification of pain with P explain the phenomenal property of pain—its painfulness? Levine thinks not. He has two lines of argument.

1. The pain Bloggs undergoes when he stubs his toe is caused by the damage to his toe and causes him to cry out and rub the injured part; that is, pain plays a characteristic role in our mental economy. For convenience I will refer to the characteristic role of pain as the 'pain role'. Now, it's very likely that it is a state of Bloggs's brain which occupies the pain role. Consequently, we have grounds for identifying pain with whichever brain state it is that occupies the pain role. (For a fuller discussion of the idea that mental states occupy certain roles, and for the connections between that proposal and various forms of the identity theory, see Sections 4.1 and 4.2.)

Levine insists, though, that we can readily imagine a person who has a brain state which occupies the pain role, but who is not having a painful experience. In the philosophical literature such a person is called a 'pain-zombie'. When the pain-zombie stubs her toe, she behaves exactly as if she were in pain—she cries out and rubs the injured part—but she has no painful experience. However, argues Levine, if such a pain-zombie is possible then the identification of painfulness with a property of the state which occupies the pain role fails to explain the painfulness of pain. After all, both Bloggs and the pain-zombie have a brain state which occupies the pain role, but only Bloggs has a painful experience. Consequently, there is more to Bloggs's painful experience than having a brain state which occupies the pain role. So we run straight into the explanatory gap: identifying painfulness with a property of the state which occupies the pain role fails to explain the existence of painfulness. (See Levine 1993.)

2. According to Levine, phenomenal properties like painfulness are *simple* in that they have no structure. If you introspect upon a particular painful episode no structure is revealed—there are no details of which you can take note except the contrastive ones of, for example, intense versus mild, or dull versus sharp.

Levine goes on to assert that the lack of structure exhibited by painfulness generates an explanatory gap. For say that episodes of painfulness exhibited plenty of structure, and that different aspects of that structure could be related to the structure of brain property P. In that case the claim that painfulness is identical to P would have some explanatory power, for it would allow us to explain the structure of painfulness in terms of the structure of P. But as our phenomenal properties are pretty much lacking in structure, this kind of explanatory project is largely closed to us. It seems to be a brute fact that painfulness is correlated with P; no explanation appears to be available. (See Levine 1983.)

12.4 Can the explanatory gap be filled?

In this section I will assess Levine's arguments for the existence of an explanatory gap between brain states and phenomenal consciousness (see the previous section). As we have seen, he begins by drawing attention to the possibility of pain-zombies—creatures with a brain state that occupies the pain role but which nevertheless do not experience the quale of painfulness. He then goes on to argue that if pain-zombies are possible, then the fact that the pain role is occupied is insufficient to explain why, in ordinary folk like Bloggs, pain hurts.

I share Levine's intuition about the possibility of pain-zombies. However, I think the argument Levine offers only works against a functionalist account of qualia—it does not work against a type identity approach to qualia. It turns out, though, that an alternative version of the explanatory gap argument creates a problem for the type identity theorist. Let me explain.

According to functionalism, mental properties can be multiply realized. The state which occupies the pain role in Bloggs might be quite different from the state which occupies the pain role in Sally. (See Section 4.1.) Say that the state which occupies the pain role in Bloggs is state P, whereas the state which occupies the pain role in Sally is state Q. Now states P and Q might be very different. In Bloggs the state which occupies the pain role might be c-fiber firing; in Sally it might be a state of a computer chip, or even the pressure in a gas cylinder. It's not obvious why these very different kinds of states should all give rise to the experience of painfulness: some might give rise to the experience of painfulness; others to the experience of joy; and still others to no experience at all. These observations suggest that pain-zombies are indeed possible. Call the state which occupies the pain role in the pain-zombie, 'R'. Whilst R is sufficient for the pain role, it is not sufficient to bring about the experience of painfulness. But if we admit *that,* we have admitted that the presence of a state which occupies the pain role is not, in itself, enough to explain the experience of painfulness. That is, we have admitted the existence of an explanatory gap between having a state which occupies the pain role and having an experience of painfulness.

So far I have argued that if, as functionalism insists, the experience of painfulness is identified with a property of whichever state it is that occupies the pain role, then the explanatory gap looms wide. However, this way of arriving at the explanatory gap does not work in the case of the type identity theory. According to the type identity theory, mental states are type identical with physical states of the brain (see Section 3.2). In particular, experiences of painfulness are type identical with (say) property P. If that's correct, the experience of painfulness is not multiply realized; only organisms that possess property P can have painful experiences. Any organism with a property which occupies the pain role other than P is, on this view, a pain-zombie. Now consider Bloggs who possesses property P and consequently has experiences of painfulness, and a pain-zombie who does not possess P and consequently does not have experiences of painfulness. In virtue of what does Bloggs have experiences of painfulness whilst the pain-zombie does not? The answer is simple. Bloggs has experiences of painfulness because he possesses P!

It's important to notice that the argument given in the previous paragraph does not require the wholesale acceptance of the type identity theory. Rather, the argument requires only the type identification of *phenomenal properties* with certain brain properties. The proponent of this view might still accept that all other mental properties are multiply realized.

Unfortunately, appealing to the type identity of phenomenal properties with brain properties raises another form of the explanatory gap argument. Let's say that painfulness is type identical with brain property P. Then we are still left wondering what it is about P which gives rise to the experience of painfulness. Why do we experience pain rather than (say) itchiness, when our brain is in state P? That question appears to have no answer: it just seems to be a brute fact about P that it is painful. But to accept that it's just a brute fact that P is painful is to accept that there is no explanation of painfulness. The explanatory gap has returned with a vengeance.

Let's now turn to the other consideration offered by Levine. If phenomenal properties exhibited structure, it might be possible to explain that structure in terms of the structure of the underlying brain states. Structure would give us explanatory grip. However, since phenomenal properties are pretty much structureless, this explanatory strategy is unavailable to us. My discussion of this argument is based entirely on considerations offered by C. L. Hardin (1988: see especially 134–42). Hardin focuses not on the quale of painfulness but on the qualia associated with colors—redness, greenness, and the like. It would be interesting to see the extent to which Hardin's response can be generalized to other phenomenal properties, but that's not an issue I can pursue here.

Our color experiences are not entirely without structure; there is, for example, the following striking asymmetry. We can readily have the experience of red, and we can readily have the experience of blue. In addition, we can experience colors in between red and blue—the various shades of purple. However, whilst we can readily experience red and can readily experience green, we cannot experience red-greens. There simply are no color experiences which are to red and green what purple is to red and blue. Why is that? Why isn't there a red-green color experience? Early in the twentieth century the Austrian physiologist Ewald Hering proposed a new theory of color vision which accounts for these facts. Subsequent research both supported and deepened Hering's approach. In the next couple of paragraphs I describe Hering's theory, but be warned: I am leaving out a great many details.

The core of the human color visual system is a pair of 'channels': the red/green (or 'r-g' channel) and the yellow/blue (or 'y-b') channel. Let's begin with the r-g channel and assume that, for some reason, the y-b channel is inactive. When the r-g channel is firing at its 'base' rate the subject has no color experience. When it is firing above the base rate she has a red experience; and when it is firing below that rate she has a green experience. Similar remarks apply to the y-b channel. Assume this time that the r-g channel is inactive. When the y-b channel is firing at its base rate the subject has no color experience. When it is firing above the base rate she has a yellow experience; and when it is firing below that rate she has a blue experience.

Now consider what happens when both channels are active. If both the channels are firing above the base rate the subject has a red-yellow (i.e. orange) experience. If the r-g channel is firing above the base rate and the y-b channel is firing below the base rate, she has a purple experience. Other combinations are, of course, possible. However, no combination yields a red-green experience. To get a red-green experience the r-g channel would have to fire both *above* and *below* the base rate, and that's impossible.

Hering's theory explains why we can have a red-blue experience but not a red-green experience. One aspect of the structure of our color experience has thus been explained by the underlying neural structure. This suggests that Levine might have been too quick when he asserted that there is little chance of mapping the structure of our color experience onto the structure of the brain's color visual system. However, the following worry arises. It's one thing to give neurological explanations of the various relationships between our color experiences; its quite another to explain the color experiences *themselves*. Thus, whilst Hering's theory allows us to see why there can be red-blue color experiences but not red-green ones, it doesn't explain how the experiences of red, blue, yellow, and green occur in the first place. Indeed, it just takes those experiences for granted. The explanatory gap has therefore re-emerged.

12.5 Functionalism and phenomenal consciousness

Functionalism is arguably the most significant position in contemporary philosophy of mind. In this section I will briefly discuss some of the difficulties which phenomenal consciousness presents to functionalism. Many of the issues I will touch upon in this section have already been raised in previous sections. However, it's worth bringing these issues together and relating them directly to functionalism. (See Chapter 4 for an extended introduction to functionalism.)

Two thought experiments are often referred to in discussions of functionalism and phenomenal consciousness. I will discuss these thought experiments under the labels 'absent qualia' and 'inverted qualia'.

1. *Absent qualia*. Can't we imagine a person who has a state inside them which occupies the pain role, but who does not experience painfulness? That is, can't we imagine someone who has a state which occupies the pain role but in whom the quale of pain is 'absent'? We have already explored this possibility using the idea of a pain-zombie (see Sections 12.3 and 12.4). A pain-zombie is precisely a person with a state which occupies the pain role but in whom the quale of pain is absent.

My intuition is that pain-zombies are possible. If I'm right, functionalism is wrong to this extent: the phenomenal properties of mental states are not determined by the functional roles characteristic of those mental states. Given the significance of phenomenal consciousness in our mental lives, that's a pretty big concession.

2. *Inverted qualia*. Can't we imagine two people whose color qualia are systematically inverted? Consider Bloggs and Cloggs who are functionally identical. There's a state inside Bloggs that's caused by seeing blood and causes him to say 'red'; similarly, there's a state inside Cloggs that is caused by seeing blood and causes her to say 'red'. Again, there's a state inside Bloggs that is caused by seeing the sky and causes him to say 'blue'; similarly, there's a state inside Cloggs that is caused by seeing the sky and causes her to say 'blue'. However, whilst the sight of blood brings about in Bloggs the quale of redness, it brings about in Cloggs the quale of blueness; and whilst the sight of the sky brings about in Bloggs the quale of blueness, it brings about in Cloggs the quale of redness. Bloggs and Cloggs are functionally (and behaviorally) identical, but they have different color qualia in response to the same stimulus.

Qualia inversion seems possible, and if it is possible then functionalism is in trouble. For if qualia inversion is possible then there can be variation in phenomenal properties from one person to another without a corresponding variation in functional role. In other words, if qualia inversion is possible then the phenomenal properties of mental states are not determined by the functional roles characteristic of those mental states.

There are reasons, however, to doubt that at least some cases of qualia inversion *are* possible. It turns out that people are inclined to group reds and oranges together, and blues and greens together, and that this tendency is independent of cultural and linguistic differences. In other words, it seems that there is an important phenomenal difference between, on the one hand, reds and oranges and, on the other, blues and greens. Many terms have been used to try to capture these phenomenological differences. Thus reds and oranges are said to be warm, positive, and advancing, whilst blues and greens are said to be cool, negative, and retreating. (For details see Hardin 1988: 128–9.) Now let's return to Bloggs and Cloggs and assume that whilst Cloggs sees blue things as red and red things as blue, all her other color experiences are normal. Plausibly, because blue things bring about in her the quale of redness, she will group the blue shades with the yellow shades as warm, positive, and advancing. However, Bloggs will group the blue shades with the green shades as cool, negative, and retreating. There will therefore be a functional difference between Bloggs and Cloggs.

Notice that this argument only works when the pair of colors which are inverted belong to different sides of the warm/cool divide. Consequently, at best this is a reply to a restricted subset of all the imaginable color inversions. Nevertheless it shows that philosophers were overly hasty when they assumed that all cases of color inversion really are possible. And if they're not, functionalism can resist attack on the grounds that it cannot handle cases of inverted qualia.

12.6 Concluding remarks

Phenomenal consciousness does not, in my view, give us grounds for abandoning physicalism: there is little reason to doubt that episodes of phenomenal consciousness are physical events in the brain. However, I find the arguments offered by Levine in support of the existence of an explanatory gap worrying, and I follow Ned Block in thinking that, at present, nobody has come anywhere near bridging the gap (Block 1994: 211). We have nothing that even remotely looks like an account of how the brain gives rise to phenomenal consciousness, nor do we have many proposals about where we should begin to look for such an account.

SUMMARY

(1) We can distinguish between *metaphysical* and *epistemological* concerns about phenomenal consciousness.

(2) An important argument against physicalism about qualia is Jackson's knowledge argument.

(3) There are a number of important objections to the knowledge argument.

(4) Nagel, Levine, and others have defended the view that there is an unbridgeable explanatory gap between brain and phenomenology. Levine's arguments are especially significant.

(5) One of Levine's arguments—the pain-zombie argument—poses a serious challenge to functionalism about phenomenal consciousness, but not to an identity theory about qualia.

(6) Thought experiments concerning 'absent' and 'inverted' qualia challenge the functionalist approach to qualia. Work in the neuropsychology of vision weakens the inverted qualia challenge to at least some extent.

FURTHER READING

Excellent textbook-style discussions of phenomenal consciousness are Braddon-Mitchell and Jackson 1996: Ch. 8 and Kim 1996: Ch. 7. Ned Block's entries 'Consciousness' and 'Qualia' in Guttenplan 1994 are highly recommended.

Frank Jackson's 'Epiphenomenal qualia' (1982) and 'What Mary didn't know' (1986) are modern classics, as is Thomas Nagel's 'What is it like to be a bat?' (1974). All three are well worth reading (the Nagel is somewhat denser than the two Jackson pieces).

Levine's latest presentation of his views is his *Purple Haze* (2001). In a series of works, Colin McGinn has offered an important defense of the existence of an explanatory gap. See especially his *The Problem of Consciousness* (1991), especially Ch. 1 and his (more accessible) *The Mysterious Flame* (1999), especially Chs 1 and 2. For a response see Brueckner and Beroukhim 2003.

Robert Van Gulick's 'Understanding the phenomenal mind: Are we all just armadillos?' (1993) masterfully discusses many important positions on phenomenal consciousness. Definitely worth a look.

The worry that functionalism cannot account for phenomenal consciousness is as old as functionalism itself. Sydney Shoemaker's 'Functionalism and qualia' (1975) is an important defense of functionalism in this respect.

One of Jackson's more recent papers on phenomenal consciousness is his 'Mind and illusion' (2003). In that paper Jackson advances new considerations against the knowledge argument. Unfortunately, it's rather hard. Three recent discussions of the knowledge argument can be found in Ravenscroft 2005: Part 2. They too are on the difficult side. That volume also contains replies by Jackson.

Three outstanding collections on consciousness are Davies and Humphreys 1993; Block, Flanagan, and Guzeldere 1997; and Smith and Jokic 2003. All three contain important papers on phenomenal consciousness. An important book-length treatment of phenomenal consciousness which denies that the phenomenal supervenes on the physical is David Chalmers, *The Conscious Mind* (1996).

TUTORIAL QUESTIONS

(1) Briefly sketch both versions of the knowledge argument.

(2) Sketch Jackson's argument for epiphenomenalism about qualia.

(3) Outline the knowledge-how reply to the knowledge argument.

(4) What's a pain-zombie?

(5) Sketch the argument from the possibility of pain-zombies to an explanatory gap.

(6) Does type identifying phenomenal properties with brain properties close the explanatory gap?

(7) Describe (i) the absent qualia thought experiment and (ii) the inverted qualia thought experiment. Explain how these thought experiments challenge functionalism.

Appendix: Paper writing tips

If you're an undergraduate taking a course in the philosophy of mind, the chances are you'll be asked to write at least one paper (or 'essay'). Your philosophy instructor will no doubt have their own views on what makes a good philosophy paper, and your first task should be to familiarize yourself with your instructor's requirements. What follows is not intended to override your instructor's ideas—that would be silly. Rather, it's intended to provide some general advice about paper writing. For more on writing a philosophy paper see the Resources section later in this book.

(1) In philosophy we have to have good reasons for the claims we make; that is, we have to *argue* for our claims. So your essay should be an argument, or a series of linked arguments.

(2) Arguments have a logical structure. For example, they have premises and a conclusion. The structure of your essay should reflect the logical structure of your argument.

(3) It's often useful to break your essay into sections, with each section devoted to one part of the argument. Numbering the sections and/or giving them headings is a good idea.

(4) Clarity is very important in a philosophy essay. Try to express your ideas clearly. As a general rule, it's best to use simple, straightforward English. Avoid flowery prose.

(5) An introduction which states what you're going to argue for is helpful, but keep it short and to the point. A brief conclusion is usually warranted, but don't simply repeat what you have already said.

(6) You would be mad not to find out what other philosophers have said about the issue on which you are writing. In other words, you would be mad not to read around. Nevertheless, you should try to think through the issues *for yourself*.

(7) In general, you will be expected to present an argument *in your own words*; you should not rely heavily on quoting from other sources.

(8) If you do quote or paraphrase from another author, you *must* provide references. Philosophy instructors rarely get worked up about which referencing system you use. Choose one which is clear and use it consistently.

(9) Some instructors require that you hand in a computer printout of your paper rather than a handwritten copy. Even if there is no such requirement at your university, try to word-process your paper. There's nothing more demoralizing for the marker than having to struggle with someone's handwriting, and a demoralized marker isn't likely to hand out an 'A+'.

(10) If possible, run your paper through a spellchecker.

(11) Give yourself enough time to work on your paper.

(12) Don't cheat. Don't even think of cheating. (It's usually pretty easy to catch plagiarists.)

(13) Writing philosophy is a *skill*, and the only way to get good at it is to *practice*.

Good luck!

Glossary

asymmetric dependence A asymmetrically depends on B if and only if, whilst A depends on B, B does not depend on A. For example: there being ice on the window asymmetrically depends on the temperature being below 0°C (32°F) since there being ice on the window depends on the temperature being below 0°C, but the temperature being below 0°C doesn't depend on there being ice on the window. (In a very dry climate the temperature may fall below freezing and yet there is no ice on the window.)

behaviorism, methodological The doctrine that psychology should restrict itself to seeking laws which link stimuli to behavior.

behaviorism, philosophical According to philosophical behaviorism, mental states are dispositions to behave in certain ways under certain circumstances.

biological function The biological function of an organ is the effect for which it was selected.

computation A computational process recognizes and manipulates symbols solely on the basis of their syntactic properties (*qv*), but nevertheless respects the semantic properties (*qv*) of the symbols.

computational theory of mind According to this theory, mental states are complex symbols, and mental processes are computational process. In short: the mind is a computer.

connectionism The claim that the mind is a connectionist network (*qv*).

connectionist network A network of highly interconnected basic units which are capable of performing certain cognitive tasks, including simple kinds of learning.

consciousness, access A mental state is access conscious if it is available for the rational control of speech and behavior, and can play a role in reasoning.

consciousness, monitoring The capacity to monitor one's own mental states by, for example, forming beliefs about them.

consciousness, phenomenal A mental state is phenomenally conscious if there is something that it is like to have (or be in) that mental state.

consciousness, self To be self conscious is to have the concept of a self and apply it to one's self.

content The content of a mental state is what the mental state *represents* or is *about*. Whether every mental state has content is a controversial issue.

content, narrow The content (*qv*) of a mental state is narrow if it is solely determined by the internal states of the organism.

content, wide The content (*qv*) of a mental state is wide if it is determined in part by the environment (including the social environment) outside the organism.

disposition See 'property, dispositional'.

dualism, property The claim that mental properties are nonphysical properties caused by the physical (*qv*) properties of the brain. Property dualists disagree over whether the mental properties in turn causally impact upon the brain.

dualism, substance The claim that whilst the body is a physical (*qv*) object, the mind is a nonphysical object.

eliminativism The claim that there are no such things as mental states.

epiphenomenalism A version of property dualism (*qv*) which insists that mental properties do not causally impact upon the brain.

epistemology The philosophical study of knowledge.

explanatory completeness of physiology The claim that all human actions can be explained solely in terms of nerve impulses, muscle contractions, and so forth.

fictionalism The claim that, whilst mental states don't, strictly speaking, exist, it is nevertheless useful to pretend that they do.

folk psychology A theory of human psychology implicit in our everyday talk about mental states and behavior.

functionalism According to functionalism, mental states are the occupants of characteristic causal roles.

identity theory According to the identity theory, mental states are type identical (*qv*) to brain states.

identity, token Token identities occur between tokens. Example: Posh Spice is identical to Victoria Beckham.

identity, type Type identities occur between *types*. Example: water is type identical to H_2O.

indeterminate A property (*qv*) of something is indeterminate if there is no way of precisely specifying that property.

individuate To individuate an X is to distinguish one X from another, or to give a principle whereby one X can be distinguished from others.

knowledge argument Frank Jackson's celebrated argument to the effect that qualia (*qv*) are nonphysical.

Mary The character in the thought experiment which forms the basis of the knowledge argument (*qv*).

metaphysics The branch of philosophy concerned with what exists and how the things that exist relate to one another.

multiple realization A mental state is said to be multiply realized if there is more than one physical state which realizes it. Example (not to be taken too literally): say that pain is realized in humans by c-fiber firing and in squid by d-fiber firing. In that case pain is multiply realized.

necessary A is necessary for B if B would not occur without A.

physicalism The doctrine that the only objects, properties, and events in the world are physical objects, properties, and events.

possible world A way the world might have been. There is a possible world in which Columbus got to India, and one in which Mt Everest is made of cheese. There is, however, no possible world in which triangles have four sides.

productivity A language is productive if we can build new meaningful sentences from old sentences or parts of sentences. For example, from 'Bloggs is happy' and 'Bloggs is hairy' we can obtain 'Bloggs is happy and Bloggs is hairy'.

property A property is a feature of something. Example: Bloggs has the property of weighing 96 kg.

property, dispositional A dispositional property is a tendency to do something, but only under certain circumstances. Example: fragility. Something is fragile if it is likely to break if carelessly handled.

property, semantic The semantic properties of a symbol are those to do with meaning (for example, truth value (*qv*) and content (*qv*)). See also 'semantics'.

property, syntactic The syntactic properties of a symbol are those which can (at least in principle) be discerned by examining the symbol in isolation. A symbol's shape is a good example. See also 'syntax'.

proposition Different philosophers have thought of propositions in different ways. For our purpose a proposition is a state of affairs. If the state of affairs actually obtains the proposition is true; if not, the proposition is false.

propositional attitude A kind of mental state which involves taking an attitude (e.g. of belief or desire) to a proposition (*qv*). Examples: believing that it is Tuesday; wishing that it were Saturday.

qualia The subjective properties exhibited by some mental states. Examples: the hurtfulness of pain; the sweet taste of orange juice.

quantify over A theory quantifies over Xs if it refers (or 'talks about') Xs.

reduction, intertheoretic One theory intertheoretically reduces to another if the former theory can be derived from the latter. The derivation requires bridge laws which identify the terms of the former theory with those of the latter.

reduction, ontological One kind of phenomenon ontologically reduces to another if the two phenomena are type identical. Example: water ontologically reduces to H_2O.

reference The reference of a symbol is the thing it refers to or picks out.

semantics The way the words and sentences of a language get to be meaningful is called the semantics of the language. The term is also used to refer to the study of the semantics of a language. See also 'property, semantic'.

stimuli The 'inputs' to an organism. Anything impinging on an organism to which it is capable of reacting.

substance Roughly: stuff. David Armstrong has defined a substance as anything which could be the only thing in the universe (e.g. your body).

sufficient See 'sufficient condition'.

sufficient condition A is a sufficient condition for B if A is enough for, or guarantees, B. Examples: being in France is a sufficient condition for being in Europe. Being a mammal is a sufficient condition for being an animal.

supervenience Very roughly, 'supervenes' means 'depends'. More precisely: A supervenes on B if and only if there can be no change in A without a change in B.

syntax The syntax of a language is the set of rules which govern the way the words are arranged to form grammatical sentences. See also 'property, syntactic'.

systematicity A language is systematic if interchanging the names in any meaningful sentence yields another meaningful sentence. For example, interchanging the names in the meaningful English sentence, 'Bloggs has a crush on Sally' yields the meaningful English sentence, 'Sally has a crush on Bloggs'.

token An individual. Tokens belong to types (*qv*). For example, Lassie is a token of the type dog.

transitivity of identity The principle that if A = B and B = C, then A = C.

truth value The truth value of a true sentence (or proposition) is *true*; the truth value of a false sentence (or proposition) is *false*.

Twin-Earth An imaginary planet which is a molecule-for-molecule duplicate of Earth except that where we have H_2O, they have a superficially similar compound, XYZ.

type A kind of thing. Examples: all the cats in the world form a type, as do all the mammals.

verificationism According to verificationism, the meaning of a statement is the set of circumstances which, if they held, would make the statement true.

Some useful resources

The following books and websites will help you with your exploration of the philosophy of mind. Some of the books are elementary; others quite hard. Some focus on a single topic or a few topics; others are more general. I have included a few brief notes about each entry.

To find the publication details of the books, go to References.

General books on the philosophy of mind

David Braddon-Mitchell and Frank Jackson, *Philosophy of Mind and Cognition*. A very valuable discussion of the issues in this book, and more besides. Quite a bit harder than this book. Apparently a second edition is in the pipeline.

Keith Campbell, *Mind and Body*. A good introduction to the issues covered in Part 1 of this book (and to a lesser extent Part 4). Easier than this book but somewhat dated.

Paul Churchland, *Matter and Consciousness*. Highly accessible although rather limited. Easier than this book.

Jaegwon Kim, *Philosophy of Mind*. A terrific discussion of many of the issues covered in this book. Quite a bit harder than this book.

Peter Smith and O. Jones, *The Philosophy of Mind*. A good introduction, especially to the more historical material.

Kim Sterelny, *The Representational Theory of Mind*. An excellent discussion of several of the topics covered by this book (especially connectionism, content, and eliminativism). Quite a bit harder than this book.

Books on specific topics

Computational theory of mind

John Haugeland, *Artificial Intelligence: The Very Idea*. A classic. Offers good explanations of the syntax/semantics distinction, the nature of computation, and Turing machines.

Georges Rey, *Contemporary Philosophy of Mind*. The closest thing I know of to a textbook on computational theory of mind, but much harder than this book.

Connectionism

Paul Churchland, *The Engine of Reason, the Seat of the Soul*. An excellent introduction to recent work in connectionism and neuroscience. Admirably succeeds in conveying the excitement of the field.

Andy Clark, *Microcognition*. Discusses a variety of issues in the philosophy of mind from a connectionist perspective.

Consciousness

Peter Carruthers, *Phenomenal Consciousness*. Long and hard but powerfully argued.

David Chalmers, *The Conscious Mind*. Hard, but very rewarding. Defends an antiphysicalist position.

Joseph Levine, *Purple Haze*. A book-length treatment of the explanatory gap problem. Harder than this book.

William Seager, *Theories of Consciousness*. A nice book. Introductory, but somewhat denser than this one.

Content

Robert Cummins, *Meaning and Mental Representation*. A good overview of theories of content.

Jerry Fodor, *Psychosemantics*. A classic. Much harder than this book but worth the effort.

Jerry Fodor, *A Theory of Content and Other Essays*. Another classic.

Stephen Stich, *From Folk Psychology to Cognitive Science*. Very insightful; deeply skeptical in the best sense. Surprisingly readable.

Mental causation

Jaegwon Kim, *Mind in a Physical World*. Harder than this book but surprisingly readable. Very rewarding.

Physicalism

See the entry for Jaegwon Kim's *Mind in a Physical World* under 'Mental causation', above.

Collections—general

Ned Block (ed.), *Readings in Philosophy of Psychology*, vol. 1. A very useful collection which is, unfortunately, out of print. Try your university library or a good secondhand academic bookshop.

William Lycan (ed.), *Mind and Cognition*. There are now two editions of this book, with slightly different contents. Both are excellent.

David Rosenthal (ed.), *The Nature of Mind*. A useful collection of papers which includes some key historical texts. Recommended.

Stephen Stich and Ted Warfield (eds), *The Blackwell Companion to Philosophy of Mind*. A good collection of original papers. Much of it is substantially harder than this book.

Collections—specific topics

Connectionism

William Ramsey, Stephen Stich, and David Rumelhart (eds), *Philosophy and Connectionist Theory*. A goodie.

Cynthia MacDonald and Graham MacDonald (eds), *Connectionism: Debates on Psychological Explanation*. Contains some good papers. Worth a look.

Consciousness

Ned Block, Owen Flanagan, and Guven Guzeldere (eds), *The Nature of Consciousness*. A good collection covering both philosophical and scientific issues.

Martin Davies and Glyn Humphreys (eds), *Consciousness*. Contains a number of valuable papers.

Quentin Smith and Aleksander Jokic (eds), *Consciousness*. Contains a number of important recent papers. Generally a lot harder than this book.

Mental causation

John Heil and Alfred Mele (eds), *Mental Causation*. A good collection. Generally harder than this book.

Reference books and websites

Simon Blackburn, *The Oxford Dictionary of Philosophy*. A remarkable achievement and an indispensable resource.

Samuel Guttenplan (ed.), *A Companion to the Philosophy of Mind*. A terrific collection of mini-essays on a great many topics. Indispensable.

Stanford Encyclopedia of Philosophy. **http://plato.stanford.edu**. A very ambitious attempt to develop the ultimate online philosophy resource. Authors are required to update their article(s) from time to time. It contains plenty of material relevant to the philosophy of mind.

Study guides

Joel Feinberg, *Doing Philosophy*. The subtitle says it all: 'A Guide to the Writing of Philosophy Papers'. This book explains what's important in a philosophy paper—and what's not. It includes information on grammar, referencing, and elementary logic.

Bibliographical database

Philosopher's Index. An electronic database that allows you to search for philosophy books and journal articles by author, keyword, subject, or title. It covers the period from 1940 to the present, and most entries contain an abstract. Friends tell me it's not absolutely complete; they may be right, but it's still an extremely valuable resource. Ask at your university library about accessing it from your campus.

References

ARMSTRONG, D. (1968). *A Materialist Theory of the Mind*. London: Routledge and Kegan Paul.

—— (1980). 'What is consciousness?', in his *The Nature of Mind*. Ithaca, NY: Cornell University Press.

BAARS, B. (1997). *In the Theater of Consciousness*. New York: Oxford University Press.

BAKER, L. (1993). 'Metaphysics and mental causation', in Heil and Mele 1993.

BECHTEL, W., and ABRAHAMSEN, A. (1991). *Connectionism and the Mind*. Oxford: Blackwell.

BLACKBURN, S. (1994). *The Oxford Dictionary of Philosophy*. Oxford: Oxford University Press.

BLOCK, N. (1978). 'Troubles with functionalism', in C. Savage (ed.), *Perception and Cognition, Minnesota Studies in Philosophy of Science*, vol. 9. Minneapolis: University of Minnesota Press, 261–325. Reprinted in Block 1980.

—— (1980). *Readings in Philosophy of Psychology*, vol. 1. Cambridge, MA: Harvard University Press.

—— (1981). 'Psychologism and behaviorism'. *Philosophical Review* 90: 5–43.

—— (1994). 'Consciousness', in Guttenplan 1994.

—— (1995). 'On a confusion about a function of consciousness'. *Behavioral and Brain Science*, 18: 227–47. Reprinted in Block, Flanagan, and Guzeldere 1997.

—— FLANAGAN, O., and GUZELDERE, G. (1997). *The Nature of Consciousness*. Cambridge, MA: MIT Press.

BLOGGS, J. (2002). *My Story*. Melbourne: Antipodean Press.

BOLTON, D., and HILL, J. (1996). *Mind, Meaning and Mental Disorder*. Oxford: Oxford University Press.

BORNSTEIN, R., and PITTMAN, T. (1992). *Perception without Awareness*. New York: Guilford Press.

BRADDON-MITCHELL, D., and JACKSON, F. (1996). *Philosophy of Mind and Cognition*. Oxford: Blackwell.

BRUECKNER, A., and BEROUKHIM, E. (2003). 'McGinn on consciousness and the mind-body problem', in Smith and Jokic 2003.

BURGE, T. (1979). 'Individualism and the mental'. *Midwest Studies in Philosophy* 4: 73–121.

—— (1986). 'Individualism and psychology'. *Philosophical Review* 95: 3–45.

—— (1993). 'Mind-body causation and explanatory practice', in Heil and Mele 1993.

CAMPBELL, K. (1984). *Body and Mind* (2nd edn). Notre Dame, IN: University of Notre Dame Press.

CARNAP, R. (1959). 'Psychology in physical language', in A. Ayer (ed.), *Logical Positivism*. New York: Free Press. Originally published in German in 1932–3.

CARRUTHERS, P. (1996). *Language, Thought and Consciousness*. Cambridge: Cambridge University Press.

—— (2000). *Phenomenal Consciousness*. Cambridge: Cambridge University Press.

CHALMERS, D. (1996). *The Conscious Mind*. New York: Oxford University Press.

CHOMSKY, N. (1959). 'Review of B. F. Skinner's *Verbal Behavior*'. *Language* 35: 26–58. Reprinted in Block 1980.

—— (1972). *Language and Mind* (enlarged edn). San Diego, CA: Harcourt, Brace, Jovanovich.

CHURCHLAND, P. M. (1981). 'Eliminative materialism and the propositional attitudes'. *Journal of Philosophy* 78: 67–90. Reprinted in Lycan 1990 and in Rosenthal 1991.

—— (1985). 'Reduction, qualia, and the direct introspection of brain states'. *Journal of Philosophy* 82: 8–28.

—— (1988). *Matter and Consciousness* (revd edn). Cambridge, MA: MIT Press.

—— (1989). 'Knowing qualia: A reply to Jackson', in his *A Neurocomputational Perspective*. Cambridge, MA: MIT Press.

—— (1995). *The Engine of Reason, the Seat of the Soul*. Cambridge, MA: MIT Press.

CHURCHLAND, P. S. (1986). *Neurophilosophy*. Cambridge, MA: MIT Press.

CLARK, A. (1989). *Microcognition*. Cambridge, MA: MIT Press.

—— (1993). *Associative Engines*. Cambridge, MA: MIT Press.

—— (2001). *Mindware*. New York: Oxford University Press.

COWIE, F. (1999). *What's Within?* Oxford: Oxford University Press.

CUMMINS, R. (1989). *Meaning and Mental Representation*. Cambridge, MA: MIT Press.

DAMASIO, A. (1994). *Descartes' Error*. New York: Putnam.

DAVIES, M., and HUMPHREYS, G. (1993). *Consciousness*. Oxford: Blackwell.

DAWKINS, R. (1986). *The Blind Watchmaker*. Harmondsworth: Penguin.

DENNETT, D. (1971). 'Intentional systems'. *Journal of Philosophy* 68: 87–106.

—— (1975). 'True believers', in A. Heath (ed.), *Scientific Explanations*. Oxford: Oxford University Press. Reprinted in Dennett 1987*a*.

—— (1987*a*). *The Intentional Stance*. Cambridge, MA: MIT Press.

—— (1987*b*). 'Reflections: real patterns, deeper facts, and empty questions', in Dennett 1987*a*.

DESCARTES, R. (1970). *Philosophical Writings* (revd edn). Edited and translated by E. Anscombe and P. Geach. London: Nelson.

DEVITT, M., and STERELNY, K. (1987). *Language and Reality*. Oxford: Blackwell.

DRETSKE, F. (1981). *Knowledge and the Flow of Information*. Cambridge, MA: MIT Press.

ELMAN, J. (1992). 'Grammatical structure and distributed representations', in S. Davis (ed.), *Connectionism: Theory and Practice*. New York: Oxford University Press.

FEINBERG, J. (2002). *Doing Philosophy* (2nd edn). Belmont, CA: Wadsworth.

FODOR, J. (1975). *The Language of Thought*. New York: Thomas Crowell.

—— (1980*a*). 'Methodological solipsism considered as a research strategy in cognitive psychology'. *Behavioral and Brain Sciences* 3: 63–72. Reprinted in Rosenthal 1991.

—— (1980*b*). 'Searle on what only brains can do'. *Behavioral and Brain Sciences* 3: 431–2. Reprinted in Rosenthal 1991.

—— (1983). *The Modularity of Mind*. Cambridge, MA: MIT Press.

—— (1987). *Psychosemantics*. Cambridge, MA: MIT Press.

—— (1990*a*). *A Theory of Content and Other Essays*. Cambridge, MA: MIT Press.

—— (1990*b*). 'Fodor's guide to mental representation', in Fodor 1990*a*.

—— (1990*c*). 'A theory of content, I: The problem', in Fodor 1990*a*.

—— (1990*d*). 'A theory of content, II: The theory', in Fodor 1990*a*.

—— (2000). *The Mind Doesn't Work that Way*. Cambridge, MA: MIT Press.

—— and MCLAUGHLIN, B. (1990). 'Connectionism and the problem of systematicity'. *Cognition* 35: 183–204.

—— and PYLYSHYN, Z. (1988). 'Connectionism and cognitive architecture'. *Cognition* 28: 3–71.

GALLUP, G. (1982). 'Self-awareness and the emergence of mind in primates'. *American Journal of Primatology* 2: 237–48.

GORMAN, R., and SEJNOWSKI, T. (1988). 'Learned classification of sonar targets using a massively parallel network'. *IEEE Transactions: Acoustics, Speech, and Signal Processing*.

GUTTENPLAN, S. (1994). *A Companion to the Philosophy of Mind*. Oxford: Blackwell.

HARDIN, C. (1988). *Color for Philosophers*. Indianapolis, IN: Hackett.

HAUGELAND, J. (1985). *Artificial Intelligence: The Very Idea*. Cambridge, MA: MIT Press.

HEIL, J., and MELE, A. (1993). *Mental Causation*. Oxford: Clarendon Press.

HEMPEL, C. (1949). 'The logical analysis of psychology', in H. Fiegel and W. Sellars (eds), *Readings in Philosophical Analysis*. New York: Appleton-Century-Crofts. Reprinted (with revisions) in Block 1980.

HODGES, A. (1983). *Alan Turing: The Enigma of Intelligence*. London: Hutchinson.

HORGAN, T. (1984). 'Functionalism, qualia, and the inverted spectrum'. *Philosophy and Phenomenological Research* 44: 453–69.

—— and TIENSON, J. (1992). 'Structured representations in connectionist systems?', in S. Davis (ed.), *Connectionism: Theory and Practice*. New York: Oxford University Press.

—— and WOODWARD, J. (1985). 'Folk psychology is here to stay'. *Philosophical Review* 94: 197–226. Reprinted in Lycan 1990.

HOWE, M. (1989). *Fragments of Genius*. London: Routledge.

JACKSON, F. (1982). 'Epiphenomenal qualia'. *Philosophical Quarterly* 32: 127–36. Reprinted in Lycan 1990.

—— (1986). 'What Mary didn't know'. *Journal of Philosophy* 83: 291–5. Reprinted in Rosenthal 1991; Block, Flanagan, and Guzeldere 1997.

—— (1996). 'Mental causation'. *Mind* 105: 377–413.

—— (2003). 'Mind and illusion', in A. O'Hear (ed.), *Minds and Persons. Royal Institute of Philosophy Supplement* 53.

—— and PETTIT, P. (1990). 'Program explanation: A general perspective'. *Analysis* 50: 107–17.

—— —— (1993). 'Folk belief and commonsense belief'. *Mind and Language* 8: 298–305.

KIM, J. (1993). *Supervenience and Mind*. Cambridge: Cambridge University Press.

—— (1996). *Philosophy of Mind*. Boulder, CO: Westview.

—— (1998). *Mind in a Physical World*. Cambridge, MA: MIT Press.

KOSSLYN, S., and KOENIG, O. (1992). *Wet Mind*. New York: Free Press.

KRIPKE, S. (1980). *Naming and Necessity*. Oxford: Blackwell.

LAKATOS, I., and ZAHAR, E. (1978). 'Why Copernicus's programme superseded Ptolemy's', in J. Worral and G. Currie (eds), *The Methodology of Scientific Research Programmes*. Cambridge: Cambridge University Press.

LEVINE, J. (1983). 'Materialism and qualia: The explanatory gap'. *Pacific Philosophical Quarterly* 64: 354–61.

—— (1993). 'On leaving out what it's like', in Davies and Humphreys 1993. Reprinted in Block, Flanagan, and Guzeldere 1997.

—— (2001). *Purple Haze*. Oxford: Oxford University Press.

LEWIS, D. (1966). 'An argument for the identity theory'. *Journal of Philosophy* 63: 17–25.

LEWIS, D. (1972). 'Psychophysical and theoretical identifications'. *Australasian Journal of Philosophy* 50: 249–58. Reprinted in Rosenthal 1991.

—— (1983*a*). 'New work for a theory of universals'. *Australasian Journal of Philosophy* 61: 343–77.

—— (1983*b*). 'Knowing what it's like', in his *Philosophical Papers*, vol. 1. New York: Oxford University Press. Reprinted in Rosenthal 1991.

—— (1990). 'What experience teaches', in Lycan 1990. Reprinted in Block, Flanagan, and Guzeldere 1997.

—— (1994). 'Reduction of mind', in Guttenplan 1994.

LOAR, B. (1981). *Mind and Meaning*. Cambridge: Cambridge University Press.

—— (1990). 'Phenomenal properties', in J. Tomberlin (ed.), *Philosophical Perspectives*, vol. 4. Atascadero, CA: Ridgeview.

LODGE, D. (2001). *Thinks* . . . . London: Secker and Warburg.

LYCAN, W. (1990). *Mind and Cognition*. Oxford: Blackwell.

MACDONALD, C., and MACDONALD, G. (1995). *Connectionism: Debates on Psychological Explanation*. Oxford: Blackwell.

MCGINN, C. (1991). *The Problem of Consciousness*. Oxford: Blackwell.

—— (1999). *The Mysterious Flame*. New York: Basic Books.

MILLIKAN, R. (1984). *Language, Thought and Other Biological Categories*. Cambridge, MA: MIT Press.

—— (1986). 'Thoughts without laws; cognitive science with content'. *Philosophical Review* 95: 47–80.

—— (1991). 'Speaking up for Darwin', in B. Loewer (ed.), *Mind and Meaning*. Cambridge, MA: Blackwell.

NAGEL, T. (1974). 'What is it like to be a bat?'. *Philosophical Review* 83: 435–50. Reprinted in Rosenthal 1991.

NEMIROW, L. (1980). 'Review of Nagel's Mortal Questions'. *Philosophical Review* 89: 475–6.

NEWTON-SMITH, W. (1981). *The Rationality of Science*. London: Routledge.

PENFIELD, W., and RASMUSSEN, T. (1968). *The Cerebral Cortex in Man*. New York: Hafner.

PINKER, S. (1994). *The Language Instinct*. New York: Morrow.

—— (1997). *The Way the Mind Works*. New York: Norton.

PLACE, U. (1956). 'Is consciousness a brain process?'. *British Journal of Psychology* 47: 44–50. Reprinted in Lycan 1990.

POVINELLI, D. (1994). 'What chimpanzees know about the mind', in his *Behavioral Diversity in Chimpanzees*. Cambridge, MA: Harvard University Press.

PUTNAM, H. (1965). 'Brains and behavior', in R. Butler (ed.), *Analytical Philosophy*, vol. 2. Oxford: Blackwell. Reprinted in Block 1980.

—— (1967). 'The nature of mental states', in W. Capitan and D. Merrill (eds), *Art, Mind, and Religion*. Pittsburgh, PA: University of Pittsburgh Press. Reprinted in Block 1980.

—— (1975). 'The meaning of "meaning" ', in K. Gunderson (ed.), *Minnesota Studies in the Philosophy of Science*, vol. 7. Minneapolis, MN: University of Minnesota Press.

RAMSEY, W., STICH, S., and RUMELHART, D. (1991). *Philosophy and Connectionist Theory*. Hillsdale, NJ: Lawrence Erlbaum.

RAVENSCROFT, I. (1997). 'Physical properties'. *Southern Journal of Philosophy* 35: 419–31.

—— (2005). *Minds, Worlds and Conditionals: Themes From the Philosophy of Frank Jackson*. Oxford: Oxford University Press.

REY, G. (1983). 'A reason for doubting the existence of consciousness', in R. Davidson, G. Schwartz, and D. Shapiro (eds), *Consciousness and Self-Regulation*, vol. 3. New York: Plenum.

—— (1996). *Contemporary Philosophy of Mind*. Oxford: Blackwell.

ROSENTHAL, D. (1991). *The Nature of Mind*. New York: Oxford University Press.

RYLE, G. (1949). *The Concept of Mind*. London: Hutchinson.

SCHANK, R., and ABELSON, R. (1977). *Scripts, Plans, Goals and Understanding*. Hillsdale, NJ: Lawrence Erlbaum.

SEAGER, W. (1999). *Theories of Consciousness*. London: Routledge.

SEARLE, J. (1980). 'Minds, brains and programs'. *Behavioral and Brain Sciences* 3: 417–24. Reprinted in Rosenthal 1991.

—— (1990). 'Is the brain's mind a computer program?'. *Scientific American* 262: 20–5.

SHOEMAKER, S. (1975). 'Functionalism and qualia'. *Philosophical Studies* 27: 291–315. Reprinted (with revisions) in Block 1980.

SKINNER, B. (1953). *Science and Human Behavior*. New York: Macmillan.

—— (1957). *Verbal Behavior*. New York: Appleton-Century-Crofts.

—— (1980). 'Selections from *Science and Human Behavior*', in Block 1980.

SMART, J. (1959). 'Sensations and brain processes'. *Philosophical Review* 68: 141–56. Reprinted in Rosenthal 1991.

SMITH, Q., and JOKIC, A. (2003). *Consciousness*. Oxford: Oxford University Press.

SMITH, P., and JONES, O. (1986). *The Philosophy of Mind*. Cambridge: Cambridge University Press.

SORENSEN, R. (1992). *Thought Experiments*. New York: Oxford University Press.

STERELNY, K. (1990). *The Representational Theory of Mind*. Oxford: Blackwell.

STICH, S. (1983). *From Folk Psychology to Cognitive Science*. Cambridge, MA: MIT Press.

—— and WARFIELD, T. (2003). *The Blackwell Companion to Philosophy of Mind*. Malden, MA: Blackwell.

STRAWSON, P. (1958). 'Persons', in H. Feigl, M. Scriven, and G. Maxwell (eds), *Minnesota Studies in the Philosophy of Science*, vol. 2. Minneapolis, MN: University of Minnesota Press. Reprinted in Rosenthal 1991.

VAN GULICK, R. (1993). 'Understanding the phenomenal mind: Are we all just armadillos?', in Davies and Humphreys 1993. Reprinted (in two parts) in Block, Flanagan, and Guzeldere 1997.

WEISKRANTZ, L. (1986). *Blindsight*. Oxford: Oxford University Press.

WEIZENBAUM, J. (1976). *Computer Power and Human Reason*. San Francisco, CA: Freeman.

Index